THEORISING MODERNITY

Reflexivity, Environment and Identity in Giddens' Social Theory

THEORISING MODERNITY

Reflexivity, Environment and Identity in Giddens' Social Theory

edited by
Martin O'Brien, Sue Penna and Colin Hay

Longman
London and New York

Addison Wesley Longman Limited
Edinburgh Gate
Harlow
Essex   CM20 2JE
England
and Associated Companies throughout the world

Published in the United States of America
by Addison Wesley Longman Inc., New York

Visit Addison Wesley Longman on the world wide web at:
http://www.awl-he.com

First published 1999

ISBN 0 582 30743 0

British Library Cataloguing-in-Publication Data

A catalogue record for this book is available from the British Library

Library of Congress Cataloging-in-Publication Data

Theorising modernity : reflexivity, environment, and identity in
    Giddens' social theory / edited by Martin O'Brien, Sue Penna, and
    Colin Hay.
        p.   cm.
    Includes bibliographical references and index.
    ISBN 0-582-30743-0 (ppr)
    1. Giddens, Anthony—Views on modernity.   2. Post-modernism—Social
aspects.   3. Civilization, Modern.   4. Political sociology.
I. O'Brien, Martin, 1957– . II. Penna, Sue, 1949– . III. Hay,
Colin, 1968– .
HM73.T455   1998
303.4—dc21   98–35616
                                                                 CIP

Typeset by 35 in 10/12 pt Palatino
Printed in Malaysia

Contents

The contributors

Floya Anthias is Professor of Sociology and Head of Sociology at the University of Greenwich. She has published extensively in the areas of ethnicity, gender, migration and racism, as well as on Cypriots in Britain. Her latest book, on the Social Divisions of Identity, will be published by Macmillan. She is currently writing a book on young Asians and Cypriots in Britain, and researching into exclusion and citizenship in relation to self-employment practices amongst women and minorities.

Paul Bagguley is Senior Lecturer in Sociology at the University of Leeds. He is currently researching environmental protest movements and New Social Movement theory. He is the author of *From Protest To Acquiescence?* (Macmillan 1991) and co-editor of *Transforming Politics: Power and Resistance* (Macmillan 1999).

Ted Benton is a Professor of Sociology at the University of Essex. He has published extensively in the areas of philosophy and social science, history of biology, and social theory. Recent publications include *Natural Relations* (Verso 1993) and an edited collection, *The Greening of Marxism* (Guiford Press 1996). He is a member of the Red–Green Study Group.

Peter Dickens was trained initially as an architect and is now a Reader in Sociology at the University of Sussex. His areas of research are urban studies, environmental sociology and the links between the natural and the social sciences. He has most recently published *Society and Nature* (Harvester Wheatsheaf 1992) and *Reconstructing Nature: Alienation, Emancipation and the Division of Labour* (Routledge 1996).

Anthony Giddens is one of the leading British sociologists of the post-war period. He has published many books on social theory and the sociology of modern society including, recently, *Beyond Left and Right: The Future of Radical*

Politics (Polity 1994) and *In Defence of Sociology: Essays, Interpretations and Rejoinders* (Polity 1996). He is currently the Director of the London School of Economics.

Jenny Harris is a Principal Lecturer (Research) in the Department of Social Work at the University of Central Lancashire. Her research is in the areas of qualitative methodology and disability studies. She has published widely in these fields, and is the author of *The Cultural Meaning of Deafness* (Avebury Press 1995) and *Deafness and Hearing* (Venture Press 1997).

Colin Hay is a Lecturer in the Department of Political Science and International Studies at the University of Birmingham (UK), a visiting Fellow of the Department of Political Science at Massachussetts Institute of Technology (US), and Research Affiliate of the Center for European Studies at Harvard University (US). He is author of *Re-Stating Social and Political Change* (Open University Press 1996 and winner of the Philip Abrams Memorial Prize), and, forthcoming, *Labouring Under False Pretences?* (Manchester University Press), *Postwar British Politics in Perspective* (co-authored, Polity Press), and *Demystifying Globalization* (co-edited, Macmillan).

Charles Lemert is Professor of Sociology at Wesleyan University, Connecticut, USA. He writes extensively in the areas of social theory, both classic and contemporary, cultural studies and French social thought. He is series editor for the Twentieth-Century Social Theory series published by Blackwell, editor of *Social Theory: the Multicultural and Classic Readings* (Westview Press 1993), co-editor of *The Goffman Reader* (Blackwell 1997) and author of *Sociology After the Crisis* (Westview Press 1995) and *Post-modernism is Not What You Think* (Blackwell 1997).

Nicos Mouzelis is Professor of Sociology at the London School of Economics. His main research interests are in the sociology of development, historical sociology and sociological theory. His main publications include *Politics in the Semi-Periphery: Early Parliamentarism and Late Industrialisation in the Balkans and Latin America* (Macmillan 1986), *Post-Marxist Alternatives: The Construction of Social Orders* (Macmillan 1990), and *Sociological Theory: What Went Wrong? Diagnosis and Remedies* (Routledge 1995).

Martin O'Brien is a Senior Lecturer in Sociology at the University of Surrey. He has published widely on social and cultural theory, social policy and the sociology of environmental change. He is co-editor of *Values and the Environment: A Social Science Perspective* (Wiley 1995) and co-author, with Sue Penna, of *Theorising Welfare: Enlightenment and Modern Society* (Sage 1998).

Sue Penna is a Lecturer in Applied Social Science at the University of Lancaster. Her research interests are in the areas of social inequality, historical and comparative analysis of welfare states and social theory. She has recently published on the application of post-modern perspectives to questions of citizenship, political struggle and social policy and is co-author with Martin O'Brien of *Theorising Welfare: Enlightenment and Modern Society* (Sage 1998).

David Smith is Professor of Social Work and Head of Applied Social Science at the University of Lancaster. His current research is on programmes for juvenile offenders, witness support schemes, and perpetrators of racist violence. He has recently published *Criminology for Social Work* (Macmillan 1995), co-authored *Understanding Offending Behaviour* (Longman 1994) and *Effective Probation Practice* (Macmillan 1994), and co-edited *Ethical Issues in Social Work* (Routledge 1995).

Acknowledgements

The editors would like to thank the contributors to this volume for their participation in this project; it has been a pleasure to edit. In particular we would like to thank Anthony Giddens for his generosity of both spirit and time. Without his co-operation this book would not have been published, but his relentlessly hectic schedule as Director of the LSE meant that the interview had to take place in a gap between his meeting with the Chancellor of Austria and chairing a public lecture by Lord Dahrendorf. This was clearly a less-than-ideal situation, and we are grateful for his kindness and help in making possible the production of this book. Thanks to Guy Masters and Larry Ray for comments on Chapter 6, and to Sara Caro, Lynette Miller and those at Addison Wesley Longman for their help. Jenny Roberts did a wonderful job of copy-editing the manuscript. Finally, we are indebted to Trustees of the Mass-Observation Archive, University of Sussex for permission to reproduce data.

Introduction

Sue Penna, Martin O'Brien and Colin Hay

Are we modern? What is it to be 'modern'? What is 'modernity'? Any non-specialist reader could be forgiven for thinking that the entire discipline of sociology was currently obsessed with these questions. A brief glance through academic publishers' catalogues today would convince the uninitiated that 'the modern' was sociology's *raison d'être*. Were one to count the number of times that the 'modern' or any of its derivatives (modernity, modernisation and modernism) is invoked in academic, political, journalistic or lay discourse, it might reasonably be concluded that no public debate of any kind could be conducted without first establishing just how much, how little, how deeply or, indeed, how superficially the contemporary world is a 'modern' world. Yet, despite the seeming ubiquity of the word, the notion of the modern remains remarkably elusive and not a little illusive. For despite, or perhaps sometimes even because of, the remarkable profusion of references to conceptions of modernity, the answers to some basic questions remain, at best, decidedly blurred. In just what sense might society today be construed as modern? Moreover, supposing that this society is indeed modern, how does this society differ from those past societies, those 'lost worlds' as Lemert (1995) puts it, that were something less than modern? What makes society today a modern society?

In one form or another, these questions are central to the very discipline of sociology itself: of course they are not the only questions that it addresses, but there are important senses in which the answers to these questions (however implicit) undoubtedly influence and shape many of its more substantive and specific concerns. The reason for this preoccupation with the modern and modernity is simply stated. It is, at one and the same time, a question about the implications of social change for each and every individual person and the very trajectory of the societies in which we live; about what possibilities exist or remain, if any, for inducing collective social progress, for controlling what Giddens calls the 'juggernaut' of contemporary global society.

Yet these are not merely contemporary concerns. In important respects, sociology since its inception has been focused on such issues. Indeed, arguably, what sets sociology apart as a distinct intellectual endeavour (with respect to economics, psychology or politics, for example) is precisely this concern with the inevitability of social change. It is this observation, above all others, that has motivated the development of sociological concepts, methods and paradigms and is one of the few axioms that links today's sociology with the visions and hopes of its founding practitioners and definers. The classical sociologies themselves were informed by contrasts between traditional, pre-modern societies and the previously unimaginable complexity of a newly emergent industrial-capitalism. Marx, perhaps the most perceptive classical sociological commentator, recounted how, under the onslaught of capitalism, 'all fixed, fast-frozen relations, with their train of ancient and venerable prejudices and opinions, are swept away, all new-formed ones become antiquated before they can ossify. All that is solid melts into air, all that is holy is profaned, and men at last are forced to face . . . the real conditions of their lives and their relations with their fellow men' (Marx 1848, *The Manifesto of the Communist Party*, cited in Berman 1982: 21). For Durkheim, the societies of late nineteenth century Europe were oscillating between the anomic conditions of liberal individualism and the regimentation of proto-socialist collectivism, having yet to find a means of replacing traditional patterns and modes of social integration. Durkheim considered that the new industrial-capitalist society would resolve the problem of anomie through the development of new forms of solidarity and interdependence, to be found in the division of labour. For Weber, modern societies were defined by their ever-increasing rationalisation, where the pursuit of calculative efficiency (manifest in the inexorable rise of means-end or instrumental rationality) displaced all competing religious or traditional considerations or goals. Seeing in the development of modern societies a 'disenchantment', as individuals were subject to an 'iron cage' of relentless rationalisation, Weber was profoundly pessimistic about the future of the modern world. For all these classical writers, to be modern was an ambiguous and unsettling experience: to lose one's traditional grip on reality, to excise the influence of habit and custom and, in Kant's typically parsimonious formulation, to 'dare to know' the world outside of the dictates and weight of the past.

We draw attention to Marx, Weber and Durkheim, in particular, because however much the discipline of sociology has changed during the twentieth century the questions posed by them remain central to the practice of sociological theorising today. However much each differed from the others in their descriptions of, and prescriptions for, social change, they all developed a sociological focus on the problems and prospects of huge shifts in economic, social and political organisation, on the transformation of tradition and its impact on political power, and on the tensions between individualism and collectivism in industrial societies. The emergence of industrial capitalism from feudal societies – whose power structures were dominated by church and monarchy – led to intense controversies over the possibilities for an eventual liberation from superstition and tyranny, and hence for a rationally ordered collective life. The decline of the power of tradition had disrupted existing institutions and conventions of political governance, whilst the rise of industrial capitalism led to the subordination of social and cultural frameworks of belief and action to the instrumental goals of economic accumulation. In the wake of these large-scale disturbances followed alienation, disenchantment and anomie.

At the same time, shaking off the constraints of tradition, displacing the metaphysical worldviews of the past, seemed to open up the prospect of emancipation and liberation. The present could now be seized in its raw reality, the future determined and directed through the application of positive, enlightened knowledge and action. Progress became not only a possibility but an ambition and a goal: an ideal that might be made real by organising economic, political and social institutions according to rational – rather than theological – principles. The world was conceived as an object that contained an underlying unity, was progressing in a logical way, and was populated by subjects whose access to rational thought would encourage and, in the end, might secure, the best possible means of societal organisation. The underlying mechanisms of historical change were held to be available to discovery by the positive sciences, so that, for many theorists, these knowledges attained a key role in the achievement of social progress. Whether or not the emergent rationalities of Enlightenment philosophy could indeed provide a foundation for political and social progress – and how this might be achieved – formed the substance of considerable dispute and controversy. The ideal of progress through Enlightenment itself depended on a concept of a universal history, moving through different stages of development and culminating in a common destiny. However, the disjuncture between the ideality and the reality of social change in nineteenth-century Europe and beyond exposed the fundamental political and moral dilemmas of an Enlightened culture: neither scientific knowledge nor rational institutional organisation foreclosed on political and moral questions about how the consequences of economic growth and social progress would be experienced or should be addressed.

There are important senses in which the current debate about modernity seeks to revitalise the philosophical and moral foundations of sociology's early formulations of the problem of social change. The modernity debate attempts to reformulate sociology's critical outlook in order to envision the future of human societies, and locates social change at the centre of the discipline's theoretical and analytical agenda. It draws attention, in particular, to the development of new communication technologies, shifts in the world economic order (reflected, especially, in the heightened mobility of capital), altered patterns of political action at local and global levels, and changes in the relationships between work and domestic, public and private behaviours and powers. The consequences, constraints and opportunities generated by these changes are the highly contested building blocks of a debate about the very nature of contemporary societies and where they might be headed.

There are also some significant differences between the past and present constructions of the problems and prospects of social change. In particular, the foundational principles of Enlightenment philosophy – that universal moral codes and values are binding on all rational beings and provide standards for conduct and judgment – have been subject to sustained epistemological, ontological and normative critique. Such principles have been based upon two important assumptions: first, that theory involves a distinction between mind and world, between the subject and object of knowledge; second, that language functions as a neutral medium for the mind to mirror or represent the world (Seidman 1994: 3). Under the impact of post-structuralism and its insistence upon the role of the knowing subject in constructing the object of study, claims to foundational knowledge have been, if not swept away, then severely undermined. If there is no object 'out there', existing independently of the knower, if there is no subject of history, no agent of change, be it the class actor of Marxist theory or the rational actor of liberal theory, if there is no unifying centre or ground of order and coherence, then there is no longer any basis for believing in historical progress, nor of any ultimate resolution to injustice and human misery.

Another important difference is evident in the claim that earlier sociologies, whilst providing important critical tools for understanding social change, generated world-historical theory on the basis of socially and geopolitically specific philosophical conventions. Furthermore, the experiences of change and the dynamics of change described related only to certain groups of people and not to others. In short, it is suggested that, in the revitalisation of classical sociology's moral and analytical concerns, what has come to be theorised as the world's 'modernity' is effectively 'western modernity': an arrangement of social life that is sexualised, racialised and embodied; partial rather than universal, fragmented rather than united. These various dimensions are not understood as simply parallel processes but as inextricably intertwined in mutually constitutive practices and structures in the ongoing reiteration of a project of political and cultural domination. The point, here, is that knowledge of the world's modernity, rather than comprising a representation of the reality of the world which may then form a basis for action in the world, is constitutive of the very world it is said to represent. Such concerns raise the fundamental question of the conditions and foundations of sociological knowledge itself. For, if one accepts such an understanding of modernity as comprising a partial and selective way of knowing the world, as much as a label for an empirical world that is known, then the status of sociology as a specialist knowledge that can be applied to 'real world problems' becomes uncertain. In this regard, debates about sociological knowledge are more than academic nit-picking because they concern the very possibilities for, and conditions of, human intervention in the mediation of social change.

These issues lie at the heart of the theoretical debate concerning the prospects of modernity. On a substantive level, the debate hinges around charting the various changes that western societies have been undergoing in the post-war period. Decolonisation, the collapse of Soviet Communism, the decline of western economies, the disconnection of capital flows from national controls, the declining authority of symbols of cultural and formal political power, new social movement politics, changing lifestyles, changing patterns of employment and consumption, the development of virtual and cyber time/space – all these and more are charted within a context of the 'speeding up' of change under the impact of new electronic and digital technologies. Whether these changes represent a transition to a 'post-modern' era, or an intensification of the dynamics of modernity, is one area of debate. This is, however, overlaid by the theoretical issues of the status of scientific and sociological knowledges, the status of the knowing and acting subject, and the possibilities for a progressive, normative politics. In much the same way as in the early sociologies, the questions now are 'What, if any, might be the nature of the relations between and among social things? And how, if at all, can they be known?' (Lemert 1995: 11, Chapter 9). As in earlier periods, these questions, and the socio-political possibilities implied by different responses to them, have generated ambivalence, pessimism and optimism in roughly equal measure.

Anthony Giddens: social theory and political sociology

Our brief discussion of the revitalisation of classical sociological concerns implies that to engage with questions of progress, social change and the normative grounds of political projects is to engage with the central problematics of sociology. There can be no doubt that the parameters of these debates – what is debated about and in what terms of reference – have been structured significantly by the work of Anthony Giddens. Giddens' approach to social theory remains within the classical sociological tradition and takes as its organising motif the structure–agency problem which he seeks to resolve through his notion of structuration. One of Anthony Giddens' extraordinary achievements has been to encompass the wide-ranging aspects of the various debates we have introduced above and apply these to questions of identity, environment, technological and economic change, new social movement politics, changing family forms, and poverty, for example. As the Director of the London School of Economics and Political Science (LSE) he has accomplished something yet more remarkable (particularly within the British context), becoming a high-profile public intellectual. As such, he has served to place contemporary sociology, and its engagement with the concept of modernity in particular, at the heart of current political debate about what is possible, feasible and desirable in the changing contours of contemporary society. His rare (perhaps unique) combination of prolific and provocative analyses of contemporary social change, and institutional and public influence, has generated immense interest in Giddens' sociology across a range of disciplines and countries, provoking a series of critical engagements with structuration theory and, more recently, with his substantive analysis of modern politics. Given the breadth, sophistication, accessibility and now the influence of his writings, Giddens' work has rightly attracted, as it will continue to attract, much critical scrutiny. It is difficult to be a practising sociologist without engaging at least some aspects of his immense oeuvre.

This collection represents precisely such an engagement. When the editors first approached contributors to this volume, Giddens' book *Beyond Left and Right* was just about to be published and he was still at Cambridge. In the intervening period, he has become Director of the LSE and published numerous pieces about both politics and policy. His ideas have been taken up by the British Prime Minister, Tony Blair, to the extent that, as this introduction is being written, Anthony Giddens is sitting in the White House with Blair and Bill Clinton. This in itself is a quite momentous occasion; that Blair also sees Giddens' ideas as a source for a global reconstitution of the Centre Left is of even greater consequence. It is this turn of events that accounts for the direction this volume has taken, for Giddens' concern with establishing a radical politics, or 'radical centre' that goes beyond the traditional categories of Left and Right has, as might be expected, generated much controversy amongst sociologists.

Giddens proposes that three interconnected processes – social reflexivity, globalisation and detraditionalisation – are changing social life to such an extent that existing social and political institutions are unable to respond adequately to increasing risk, uncertainty and proliferation of lifestyle choices that modernity brings. In such a context, he suggests, the doctrines of the neo-liberal Right and the Fabian and socialist Left cannot provide a satisfactory basis for a revisioning of the political frameworks guiding social life because the combined effects of processes of reflexivity, globalisation and detraditionalisation render the diagnoses and solutions proposed in these doctrines obsolete. In an era of social reflexivity people are demanding access to decision making, challenging traditional modes of authority, and coping with the effects of rapid change and chronic uncertainty. Political projects and programmes that are of relevance to the contemporary world must be founded upon a fundamental transformation in the modes of governance by which the world is organised. This is the basis for Giddens' proposal for a 'generative politics', a politics that is centrally concerned with projects of economic and social reform and with the progressive values that have been at the heart of Left politics. Miliband (1994: 6) argues that generative politics, rather than adopting a predetermined vision of a future society, is 'a politics of a continuing reapplication of a set of values to changing circumstances . . . committed to the creation, development and sustenance of economic opportunities and social commitments in the context of the plural reality in which we live'. Involved in the creation of such a politics is the need for formal political institutions to harness democratising tendencies wrought by processes of reflexivity, globalisation and detraditionalisation.

This analysis, and the prescriptions flowing from it, has provoked controversy and debate, demanding, as it does, a major reorientation of both Fabian and traditional Left thought. The crucial question which arises concerns whether there is any connection between the social theory and the political sociology: whether a consistent account of the politics of the modern can be derived from the theoretical premises that comprise the foundation of the description of the characteristics of the modern. So, whilst this book is concerned with the themes of 'reflexivity', 'environment' and 'identity' in Giddens' social theory, the contributors address them directly in terms of the political consequences and concerns he draws from them and the uses he makes of them. The engagement with Giddens' politicisation of the concepts of reflexivity, environment and identity has served to generate three main strands of concern and criticism. These relate to the relationship between reflexivity and rationality, the relationship between life politics and institutional power, and the relationship between universality and 'difference'.

These three themes are brought together in Martin O'Brien's opening chapter in this volume. O'Brien examines the central components of Giddens' theoretical framework, exploring in particular the theoretical and ontological dimensions of Giddens' social theory. In so doing, he provides a detailed map of the development of structuration theory, from Giddens' critical encounters with the classical traditions of sociology through to his more recent engagements with post-structuralism and social and developmental psychology. He explains how Giddens has reorientated social theory and reveals some of the insights that Giddens' work provides into processes of social change. At the same time, he notes the elusiveness of a resolution to the structure–agency problematic in Giddens' work and questions whether such a resolution is actually required in order to theorise modernity, reflexivity, environment and identity. He uses this theoretical assessment to unpack elements of Giddens' political sociology, proposing that, currently, this sociology lacks an adequate theory of power. As a consequence, the critical agenda of Giddens' social theory is in some tension with the normative agenda of his political sociology.

Ted Benton (Chapter 2) is similarly concerned with the relationship between Giddens' social theory and the political sociology to which it gives rise. He focuses on Giddens' claim that the traditions of the socialist Left and the radical Right are exhausted and mounts a defence of the continuing importance of socialism as both a critical perspective and normative orientation. He begins with a critical appraisal of Giddens' assessment of the relationships between politics and 'modernity' before scrutinizing the exhaustion argument in detail. He argues that, although Left and Right have undergone change, they are by no means exhausted. Pointing to the resurgence of rightist movements – the Christian Right in the USA, the National Front in France, the reformed Fascists in Italy, for example – Benton maintains that such social movements are significant in that they offer diagnoses of current sources of distress and anger, providing normative orientations for political mobilisation. At the same time, social movements concerned with environmental politics, feminism and civil rights, for example, have identified capitalist relations – in particular, unfettered capital accumulation – as the principal cause of escalating inequality, exclusion and environmental destruction. As these movements are concerned with equitable wealth distribution, democratisation and social justice, capital's pursuit of profit at the expense of human needs leads them to an acutely anti-capitalist position. The transnational character of these movements and their substantive concerns means that they can be seen as representing 'New Left' normative orientations, maintaining the core values of socialism as well as a focus on capitalist relations as a key driving force in the structuring of the modern world. This is perhaps Benton's major point of disagreement with Giddens' analysis of modernity. Structuration theory identifies four 'institutional clusters' of modernity – capitalism, industrialism, surveillance and militarism – each generating particular social movements. Yet the political activities of social movements, especially those concerned with environmental issues, inevitably leads them to confront the interrelations *between* these clusters, pointing to the importance of capitalism as a causal mechanism in the direction of modern life. The under-theorisation of capitalist relations in Giddens' recent work obscures its importance in maintaining undemocratic and inequitable structures, and generates an excessively optimistic view of the potential of 'life politics'. The under-theorisation results from an evolutionary model of social change in which 'modernity' comes to replace 'capitalism' as a historical dynamic of global significance but with little persuasive explanatory justification.

Reflexivity and rationality

Reflexivity is important in Giddens' work for several reasons. In theoretical terms, it is a central concept in the theory of structuration, standing for the routinised work of mundanely keeping in touch with the everyday world. In empirical terms, it is a central characteristic of modernity, accounting for the dynamism of modern social systems. In political terms, it is the rational basis of freedom, providing a normative orientation towards personal and social development. The different uses of reflexivity in Giddens' work have given rise to questions about the relationships between reflexivity, rationality and agency. Is it necessary, for example, to theorise a reflexive agent as rational and goal-oriented? To what extent is the everyday world the *sine qua non* of reflexive activity and how does this world produce reflexivity as a normative orientation? Are there alternative approaches to the reflexivity problem that better account for the intersections between its theoretical, empirical and normative dimensions?

These questions are taken up by Paul Bagguley (Chapter 3) and Nicos Mouzelis (Chapter 4). Paul Bagguley's chapter considers how sociologists should analyse social processes of identity formation. Bagguley argues that Giddens' concept of reflexivity is too individualistic and instrumentalist and implies the very separation (and hence dualism) of structure and agency that the theory of structuration seeks to transcend. His discussion centres on two questions: whether life political movements should be understood as a result of modernity's reflexive modernisation, and whether the notion of self-reflexivity can explain identity transformation that occurs in social movement participation. Bagguley argues that the characteristics that Giddens ascribes to life politics (reflected in contemporary social movements) can be found across the nineteenth century, suggesting that 'social reflexivity' is a generic feature of social movements, rather than a unique feature of late modern political movements. If social reflexivity is not historically specific then it is unable to provide a grounding for Giddens' distinction between emancipatory and life politics. This difficulty leads Bagguley to explore the relationship between reflexivity and identity through two case studies – one concerning a group that formed part of the civil rights mobilisation in the USA in the 1960s and one concerning the Greenham Common Women's Peace Camp in the UK in the 1980s.

His analysis of these case studies leads Bagguley to argue that reflexive processes involved in the constitution of identity are both collective and complex because the transformation of an individual's identity is often unintentional, occurring through a gradual unconscious process of acculturation into the mores and practices of a movement. The reasons for joining a movement are varied, sometimes concerned with existential questions, sometimes to gain access to resources, sometimes for instrumental reasons, for example. Once participants become actively engaged, their relationships with others in the movement begin to shift their perceptions and understandings of self and of the social world. These shifting perceptions intensify when participants come into contact with, and particularly into conflict with, an opponent, often the law-enforcement agencies of the state. As participants are confronted with the reality of political power structures, of patriarchal and racist power bases, their understandings of themselves and the society they inhabit undergo further shifts. These various encounters with other movement participants and with conflictual situations induce transformations of self-identity in ways which can be quite unpredictable, and unintended by the individual. It is in this sense that the processes surrounding identity transformation are complex. The transformation of identity is not only of importance for the individual. As the self is transformed in collective action, so is the collective identity transformed. In social movements, the ways that individual identities are transformed are linked inextricably with the development of new collective identities, so collective reflexivity can be distinguished from self-reflexivity. In this sense, such movements can be understood as constituting an expression of collective reflexivity, rather than as an aggregate of self-reflexivities or an arena for them to happen. This analysis leads Bagguley to propose that Giddens' concept of reflexivity is too individualistic and instrumental to form an adequate basis for a sociological understanding of identity transformation in social movements. It also leads him to question why, in structuration theory, feminism is not connected with the institutional clusterings of modernity. As it is a movement of the same order as the civil rights and ecology movements, it might be expected that patriarchy would form an 'institutional clustering' in its own right. This suggests that a certain tendency to intentionalism in Giddens' account of reflexivity is mirrored by a certain residual structuralism in his attempt to 'read off' types of social movement from the four institutional clusterings of modernity.

Nicos Mouzelis, too, is concerned with problematising Giddens' concept of reflexivity. However, whilst Bagguley seeks to supplement the notion of self-reflexivity with a conception of collective reflexivity, Mouzelis concentrates exclusively on the idea of self-reflexivity. He suggests that Giddens' view of reflexivity is rooted in a western cultural tradition that portrays subjects as instrumental, rational actors engaged in means–ends relationships. Thus, although he agrees with Giddens that the extent and nature of reflexivity is qualitatively different under conditions of late modernity, he argues that this is not well captured by the latter's instrumentalist account of reflexivity. Mouzelis counterposes two rather different senses of reflexivity – apophatic and cataphatic – which he suggests are both present simultaneously under conditions of late modernity. Cataphatic reflexivity is broadly synonymous with Giddens' own understanding of reflexivity. Apophatic reflexivity, by contrast, is characterised not by a means–end or instrumental rationality, but by the search for an inner self, a search detached from notions of either tradition or divine revelation. Mouzelis uses this contrast to question the basis on which Giddens claims to overcome the subject–object dualism of sociological theory, noting that 'a perfectly self-reflexive individual . . . would entail the total and impossible rejection of all purposive planning and calculation'. He goes on to suggest that the concept of apophatic reflexivity is, ironically, far more compatible with the idea of the pure relationship than Giddens' own cataphatic conception of reflexivity.

Mouzelis relates his problematisation of the question of reflexivity to the relationship between structure and agency, arguing, like Bagguley, that Giddens' cataphatic understanding of reflexivity relies on a structure–agency dualism at odds with structuration theory. For Giddens, the reflexive subject of late modernity monitors her conduct and in so doing revises her behaviour in the light of an understanding of societal norms, conventions and rules, yet, Mouzelis notes, 'when . . . I distance myself from such rules because I am no longer satisfied with them, when I consider modifying them, then subject–object dualism replaces duality'. Thus, the problematisation of sociological 'dualisms' is itself problematised: subject–object dualism may be both a critical feature of self-reflection and ethical activity and a basic orientation of the self's relation to the other.

Life politics and institutional power

Giddens' analysis of modernity in terms of the reflexive incorporation of self-knowledge into institutional operations and the implications of local–global processes in disembedding social relations, directs attention to the complex relationships between knowledge, action and organisation in modern societies. In proposing that modernity's reflexivity unites individuals, institutions, and geo-political networks together in a single transformative appropriation of subjective, institutional and natural environments, Giddens' argument has raised criticisms that the dynamic of modernity is not sufficiently tied in, analytically, with the institutional clusterings of modernity, and that consequently the possibilities for a generative politics are more limited than Giddens acknowledges. In examining the relationship between structuration theory, life political movements and physical and social environments, Peter Dickens and David Smith explore the relationships between life-politics, life-chances and organised, institutional power.

Peter Dickens (Chapter 5) points out that sociological discussion of the environment is bedevilled by confusion, especially over the concept of 'nature'. Nature is understood in different ways by different people and, more often than not, in different ways within the same discussion. In particular, he suggests (after Soper 1995) that three different senses of nature tend to be conflated: nature as a metaphysical concept relating to the non-human; nature as a realist concept referring to the causal powers and processes of the physical world; and nature as a lay concept referring to a 'pristine' environment uninfluenced and untainted by human intervention. This confusion is compounded by the generally reductionist view of 'nature' held by both social and natural scientists. Arguing for a non-reductionist understanding of nature which recognises that, despite technological intervention into its many facets, it nonetheless maintains an independent reality, Dickens proposes that sociologists need to understand the relations existing between both internal and external natures and their social and political environments.

Focusing on the socio-political environments of the body and the possibilities opened up by new reproductive technologies, Dickens considers how choices about the use of such technologies are structured through complex social and political processes. The social processes involve understandings of, and orientations towards, reproductive technologies, that differ markedly between genders and generations. The political processes involve power relations over knowledge and its application. In this analysis, life politics and

11

the choices entailed therein is rendered problematic by the political uses of abstract knowledges, the patriarchal power of medicine, and the institutional control of technologies impacting on both internal and external nature.

In this context, Dickens challenges the idea that late modernity brings about an extensive qualitative shift in the relationships between social subjects and nature. In particular, he takes issue with Giddens' contention that nature has become infinitely malleable and his related claim that 'manufactured risk' and uncertainty represent defining features of late modernity. Finally, by presenting some data extracts from the Mass-Observation Archive he suggests that new technologies relating to the manipulation and mediation of genetics and 'natural' processes are not regarded as unequivocally (or even equivocally) emancipating or facilitating by women. He concludes by noting that it is, by and large, men who feel most able to detach themselves from these issues and envisage, create, promote, and celebrate such reductionist mass-production processes and the abstract 'freedoms' they supposedly make available for women.

The question of the vantage point from which Giddens conceives, constructs and/or reconstructs late modernity is taken up and developed by David Smith (Chapter 6). Smith's substantive concerns relate to the highly differentiated experience of crime in contemporary societies and the implications for Giddens' conception of a risk society. Smith notes the absence of a sustained engagement with Giddens' recent sociology of modernity in the criminological mainstream. In so doing, he points to his own initial frustration with Giddens' seemingly over-optimistic depiction of late modernity, which tends to play down issues of social division and the uneven distribution of life chances, whilst emphasising the opportunities and challenges thrown up by a brave new world of heightened reflexivity and social dynamism. This, he suggests, accounts at least in part for the seeming unwillingness of more empirically minded criminologists (more sensitive to the uneven distribution of risk and exposure to criminality) to engage directly with Giddens' sociology. Smith draws attention to two problematic claims in Giddens' recent sociology: that late modernity is a world full of clever people making reflexive choices, and that poverty displays a number of creative lifestyle possibilities. Smith assesses these claims in light of research about crime and the circumstances of young offenders. Young offenders are subject to multiple deprivations: family turmoil and breakdown, physical and/or sexual abuse, educational failure and school exclusion, local authority care, unemployment, poverty and illness. Poverty is a brutalising, rather than creative, force. Poverty-stricken areas have the highest crime rates, so that poor people are most likely to be victims of crime: the unequal distribution of victimisation risks parallels the unequal distribution of income, wealth and resources. Lack of access to economic and social resources circumscribes the choices open to disadvantaged people, not only in material terms but also in terms of psychological and emotional orientations to life possibilities.

Though critical of Giddens' optimistic 'Californianism', Smith goes on to propose that there is much in Giddens' recent sociology of late modernity that might usefully be incorporated within a theoretically revived critical criminology. Whilst the picture of poverty, crime and offending highlights the ways in which making choices is not detached from inequitable socio-economic structures, some aspects of Giddens' discussion offer potentially useful theoretical resources for developing alternatives to punitive crime control. Smith, in particular, notes the potential of the concept of fundamentalism to inform an account of the motives underlying racist attacks and other forms of abuse. He also notes the potential affinities between Giddens' concept of 'dialogic democracy' and the notion of 'restorative', 'relational' or 'integrative' justice championed by some criminologists. Smith concludes by noting the potential, as yet largely unrealised, for a fruitful dialogue between Giddens' sociology and a critical criminology that is more sensitive to the socially differentiated and unevenly distributed pathologies of late modernity.

Universalism and 'difference'

The kinds of difficulties that emerge when life politics is explored through questions of organised institutional power point towards issues of universalism in Giddens' work. Empirically, to what extent do forces of social reflexivity, globalisation and detraditionalisation lead to a universal sharing of the experience of modernity? Theoretically, in what ways do these concepts help to ground a subject of social action and understanding that can stand against the decentred 'other' of poststructuralism? In relation to the first point, Giddens argues that globalisation compresses time and space so that, today, people experience phenomena of great diversity, occurring in widely separated time-space locales: late modernity provides a single inhabited world or unitary 'framework of experience' (Hay *et al.* 1994). In relation to the second point, Giddens has described the late modern world as a world in which there are no 'others': a cosmopolitan, experimental world where identities have become unglued from place, tradition and custom. Since there are no basic spatial or social contexts for fixing identities then any identity is a potential vehicle for self-realisation and no identity is 'other' to the self.

Martin O'Brien and Jenny Harris (Chapter 7) assess the claim that late modernity might be understood as providing a unitary framework of experience. They examine Giddens' account of modern interaction and note its dependence on a concept of 'competent' agency that is drawn from ethnomethodological sources. In reviewing this theoretical dependence, they ask whether the 'clever people' of modernity really are as competent at moving across identity-contexts and knowledge-spaces as Giddens suggests. They also ask whether the ethnomethodological notion of competence in structuration theory is used to rehearse normative assumptions about membership of the lived-in world that define partial, not universal, membership status. Instead of posing the multidimensional world of modernity as a collection of open spaces where identities can be realised, O'Brien and Harris propose that there are important senses in which modern everyday and institutional contexts support the submergence, denial or passing of identities. They draw on earlier work by one of the authors (Harris 1995a) and emphasise the interactions between Hearing and Deaf cultures in order to provide an alternative account of modern identity-construction: one that addresses the 'ethnopolitical' as well as the ethnomethodological features of 'competent' agency.

Floya Anthias (Chapter 8) is similarly critical of aspects of Giddens' universalism and, in particular, the reductive use of 'we' in his description of modern experience. Although Giddens is by no means the only subject of her critique, Anthias' analysis nonetheless points to the homogeneous and undifferentiated account of the experience of modernity he presents. She argues that this account might be seen as generalising and extrapolating from the experiences of an identifiable privileged minority who enjoy, as they indulge, the benefits of a late modern world of global communications, travel, new technologies and an attendant proliferation of lifestyle choices. Moreover, Anthias suggests that sociologists should be careful about using the very concept of modernity itself. To the extent that a distinct and qualitatively new 'modernity' can be identified, that modernity is itself both a universalisation of the 'West' and a form of exploitation of the 'subaltern'. Anthias develops this view through a critique of modern and post-modern social theory and argues for a critical sociology that explores both the processes of 'othering' and the relationships between the formation of marginalised identities and struggles over resources. Her analytic framework emphasises hierarchy, inequality and inferiority as key concepts in theorising the heterogeneity of the modern. Whilst acknowledging the philosophical importance of the structure–agency debate she maintains that a social theory of the modern needs to explain the processes that lead to particular outcomes for individuals and groups, at the experiential, intersubjective, organisational and representational levels.

Charles Lemert (Chapter 9) addresses himself explicitly to the question of difference in the context of late modernity. He situates the development of Giddens' work within the context of the Anglo-US sociology of the 1970s, dominated by Parsonian theory. Lemert sees *Beyond Left and Right* as a remarkable summing up and culmination of Giddens' work over the 1980s, and emphasises this period as a time when Giddens established the conceptual basis (in the theory of structuration) for theorising about the social world. Over this time, Giddens has helped to re-invent the vocabulary (and the mode of address) of social theory as well as establishing the 'modern' character of the contemporary world as a major focus of such theory. Lemert, however, questions the extent to which sociologists can be sure about the qualitative novelty of the world we now inhabit and argues that sociological concepts and languages may yet need more revision than even Giddens has attempted. If the world today is in fact radically different from its past, he suggests, then sociological concepts and languages rooted in that past may serve little explanatory or even descriptive purpose. 'What if it is so', he asks, that the world is in a process of change as profound, say, as that occurring from the eighteenth to the nineteenth century? What if this process of change is so fundamental that the world described by modern social theory is little other than a 'virtual order' that relates little, or not at all, to the world as it is inhabited by non-sociologists? 'What if it is so? How will we know?' How can a sociology of the modern account for the possibility of a world that might be post-modern? To ignore these questions, suggests Lemert, is to court a perilous ontology of social existence: one that may fail in its application precisely to the degree that it succeeds in its parsimony. In raising these questions, Lemert returns the book's attention squarely to the ontological, epistemological and normative issues raised in the opening chapter.

Lest readers should determine from the contributors' chapters that all is lost for modern social theory, Chapter 10 concludes the book with an interview with Anthony Giddens in which he takes up some of the issues raised by the contributors. In particular, he responds to some of the critical questions about the natural and the social, reflexivity and rationality and explores some of the connections between the theoretical and political dimensions of his work. He also discusses the potential for a global democratisation of structures of governance in a world of global capitalism, indicating the areas which he sees as causing most concern, and hints at some of the institutional changes through which a more democratic political economy may be brought about. Stating his commitment to a modernist political and theoretical agenda, Giddens explains why the questions raised by much post-modernist work are 'non-issues' for him. The question of 'difference' is, he maintains, best understood through analysing the dynamics of modernity, rather than positing a yet-to-be defined post-modern condition. If such a position makes him 'the last modernist', so be it!

Concluding comments

This volume explores a wide variety of critical issues currently occupying centre stage in contemporary social theory. These include questions about the nature of contemporary societies, the periodisation of social change, the processes of change by which societies are constantly made and remade by reflexive agents, the relationships between the social and the natural and the formation and maintenance of identities, as well as matters of epistemo-logy and methodology. It is a remarkable testament to a far-reaching influence in social science that all of these issues can be explored through the work of a single author. Clearly, any future attempts to fashion answers to these questions are likely to engage with Giddens' sociology of reflexive modernity. Our aim in this volume has been to suggest at least some aspects of a potential agenda for that on-going engagement.

CHAPTER 1

Theorising modernity: Reflexivity, identity and environment in Giddens' social theory

Martin O'Brien

Anthony Giddens' wide-ranging sociological project has been the subject of extensive assessment and evaluation (Held and Thompson 1989, Bryant and Jary 1990, Craib 1992 amongst others) and it is not my intention here to replicate what others have already said. My focus in this chapter is on the relationships between the *theory of structuration* and the *ontology of modern society* in Giddens' opus. The former, comprising a detailed overhaul of sociology's theoretical and methodological outlook, preoccupied Giddens' writings from the early 1970s to the mid-1980s whilst the latter, comprising an attempt to establish the sociological uniqueness of the contemporary world, has occupied centre stage from the mid-1980s to the early 1990s. The publication of *Beyond Left and Right* in 1994 marks a further elaboration of the relationships between these two dimensions of Giddens' sociological project, focusing on the policy consequences of the ontology and an attempt to recapture the normative high ground for an ethical–socialist politics.

The connection between theory and ontology is an important starting point for understanding Giddens' work because he depicts structuration-ism as a theoretical ontology based on the idea that social life consists in its own (re)production through the skilled and knowledgeable enactment of practices by interacting individuals (Giddens, 1990b: 201–4). However, the theoretical and the ontological dimensions of structurationism need to be addressed differently because whilst the standpoint is initially developed as a theoretical ontology of social life as such it later comes to be applied specifically as a theoretical ontology of *modern* social life. The interposition of 'modern' is an important step because it implies that there is something *ontologically* – as well as *theoretically* – unique about 'modernity'. In other words it involves the claim that the (re)production of modern social life is distinct or cut off from the (re)production of non-modern social life such that the theoretical and conceptual resources required to comprehend the modernity of the world needs must differ from those required to compre-hend a world of non-modernity.

The different facets of Giddens' work are closely connected so that the periodisations and distinctions proposed above are more a matter of emphasis than of shifts in standpoint. I do not claim that there has been any sort of epistemological or ontological 'rupture' in Giddens' work but he has been so productive, and has cast his analytical net so widely, that it is necessary to distinguish the different philosophical strands of the structurationist view he proposes in order to have any chance at all of conveying its import. In this chapter I will provide a brief introduction to the development of structuration theory from the 1970s to the 1990s before presenting a critical assessment of some central concepts in Giddens' recent sociological and political writings.

Structuration theory: a brief biography

Structuration theory draws on a wide range of sources, including structural functionalism, hermeneutics, Marxism, psychoanalysis, psychotherapy, ethnomethodology, poststructuralism and social and developmental psychology. It begins in a critical encounter with three sociological traditions (represented by Marx, Weber, and Durkheim) (Giddens 1971), is then clarified theoretically through a reappraisal of hermeneutic sociology (Giddens, 1976, 1979), before being schematised and related to a critical sociology of modern society (Giddens 1995[1981], 1984, 1985) and is still emerging. Giddens' recent application of structurationism to questions of intimacy, identity and political theory has given rise to a series of novel theoretical insights into processes of globalisation, detraditionalisation and democratisation (Giddens 1990a, 1991, 1992, 1994a).

Initially, the contribution of the structurationist perspective to sociology consisted in the elaboration of a new approach to the structure–agency dichotomy in social theory, a dichotomy which underlay the 'two sociologies' problem in post-war social science. On one side of the divide stood the sociology of social structures, which specified the constraints and forces determining people's actions. On the other side stood the phenomenological traditions that specified the mundane creation of an orderly world by interacting individuals. The two sociologies problem itself represented a dualism of structure and agency in the dominant schools of sociological thought: to what extent are human actions, beliefs and wants determined by external, structural forces that are independent of people's will; and to what extent is the structuredness or orderliness of the world a product of people's actions and interactions (see Dawe 1970)? Giddens' response to this division in social theory was to reconfigure the terms of reference of the debate and to propose that structure and agency comprised not a *dualism* but a *duality*. The reconfiguration gave rise to the claim that, rather than being independent and opposed characteristics of social life, structure and agency were two sides of the same social process. Giddens' classic formulation of the duality of structure concept appears in *New Rules of Sociological Method*: 'social structures are both constituted by human agency and yet at the same time are the very medium of this constitution' (1976: 121). The realisation or instantiation of structure in social interaction occurs not because agents consciously intend to reproduce specific properties of social structure but because, tacitly, they share robust mutual knowledges that enable them to achieve orderliness in their everyday encounters. The structure–agency dualism in sociology can be overcome by separating out what agents intend to achieve in their actions (purchase goods, declare their love, earn a living, and so on) from the unintended consequences of those actions (reproduce market relations, realise their gender and sexuality, reproduce class relations, and so on). These unintended consequences arise because agents tacitly share knowledge of *how to* exchange, *how to* court, *how to* labour, for example, in ways that are orderly and structured in their everyday relationships.

Structuration theory, then, originates in Giddens' determination to revise radically English-speaking sociology, a revision initially centred in post-war debates about the significance of sociological classics. In doing so, however, Giddens also wished to retain important frames of reference established by sociology's founding practitioners. *Studies in Social and Political Theory* (1977) – a collection of essays written between 1967 and 1976 – introduces many of the theoretical propositions upon which structuration theory later came to depend, at the same time as situating the emerging theory in relation to classical sociology. It is in these essays that Giddens defines his concern with the role of practical knowledge in social reproduction and with the relationships between social reproduction and social change. Here, also, Giddens situates structuration theory in relation to traditional and, as he acknowledges, familiar sociological problematics, for example, superseding functionalism whilst retaining its core theoretical tasks (1977: 121), debunking the myth of 'the problem of order' by recovering the radicalism of apparently conservative sociological sources (1977: 208–9) and developing a theory of suicide (1977: 297–321).

From the publication of *New Rules of Sociological Method* (1976) and *Central Problems in Social Theory* (1979) onwards, sociology's traditional problems are themselves increasingly problematised. *A Contemporary Critique of Historical Materialism* (1995[1981]), for example, abandons the traditional lines of dispute over social change (evolutionary stages, historical modes of production, functional differentiation, etc.). Instead, Giddens develops a typology of social systems as non-evolutionary time–space relations (and the dissolution of the latter as constraints), and a categorisation of institutional clusters based on logics of signification, domination and legitimation (1981: 23, 29, 47). Whilst *A Contemporary Critique*, together with *The Nation State and Violence* (1985), are explicitly institutional analyses of modern nation states and their interconnections, nonetheless, both make extensive and explicit reference to the dependence of the institutional critique on the notion that social life comprises a set of practices whose reproduction *constitutes* interaction, institutions and structure (1976: 104). *The Constitution of Society* (1984) – which is the formal statement of the theory of structuration and lays the ground for the ontological emphasis that characterises Giddens' recent writings – develops a sophisticated and complex analytical agenda. Here, Giddens attends to the task of outlining a wide range of concepts – rule and resource, regionalisation, routinisation, recursiveness, distanciation, locale and created environment, amongst many others – as well as exploring the relationships between sociology and human geography. The theory of structuration as outlined in *The Constitution of Society* proposes that the concept of 'structure' has no useful descriptive properties of its own since the structuredness of social life arises from the reproduction of routinised practices in interaction. This routinised reproduction of the conditions of action realises the structuring properties of social systems (1984: 25) in concrete terms, since such properties in themselves exist only in a 'virtual' sense unless and until instantiated in interaction.

Across the 1990s, the constitutive role of practice in social reproduction has come to occupy centre-stage in a new way in Giddens' sociology of late modernity. Thus, *The Consequences of Modernity* (1990a) continues the institutional analysis referred to earlier but applied to new questions – in particular, political and moral questions – of trust, risk, environment and life politics. Equally importantly, however, the book also sketches an ontology of the self that forms the basis for the theory of identity developed in *Modernity and Self-Identity* (1991a). Ontologically, self-identity is grounded in relations of trust and security, risk and anxiety. In conditions of modernity, traditional parameters for fixing self-identity – such as kinship, locality or community – break-down: individuals encounter a much wider range of ambiguous social networks and institutions that represent an equally wide range of, often contradictory, personal choices. Individuals must place their trust not in well-tried, familiar kin or communal networks and institutions but in often untried and unfamiliar expert or global networks and institutions. The conditions and parameters of trust and risk spread far beyond the contexts of anyone's personal experience. Amongst other things, the modern world is 'post-traditional' in the sense that individuals are exposed to and actively seek out multiple sources for establishing and maintaining a self-identity. The (late) modern self is an uncertain personal relationship with an indeterminate social world. Theoretically, self-identity comprises a 'reflexive project', one whose coherence must be worked at and striven for across many different social and institutional contexts. As Giddens puts it, the contemporary world is full of 'clever people' (1994a: 7): it is a world populated by skilled and knowledgeable individuals who are experienced and practised at *moving between* social contexts and *using* institutions as resources for sustaining security and stability in their everyday lives. The reflexivity of these individual–social–institutional mediations consists in their openness or susceptibility to continual revision in the light of new knowledge and information (1991a: 20).

Whilst Giddens' work has ranged across many of the major traditions of sociological theory and whilst it has contributed theoretical insights into many different phenomena – from suicide to intimacy – structuration theory itself 'is not intended to be a theory "of" anything in the sense of advancing generalisations about social reality' (1990b: 204). It is, rather, a 'conceptual investigation of the nature of human action, social institutions and the inter-relations between action and institutions' (1990b: 201). Defined in this way, the theory of structuration is said to comprise only one aspect of Giddens' writings rather than the vehicle through which a major overhaul of sociology might be undertaken and a new conception of the contemporary world established. In my view, however, the terms of reference of the theory of structuration remain the only fixed points through which an assessment of Giddens' sociology can be undertaken. For a commentator on Giddens, if not for Giddens himself, there is no way to grasp the significance of any of his work except as the elaboration of the theoretical ontology put forward under the guise of the theory of structuration. Understood in this way, Giddens' theoretical journey from questions of suicide and class to questions of intimacy and identity can be seen as a programme of sociological analysis whose goal is to supersede the dualism of structure and agency across all of the major problematics of contemporary social science. In a programme of such magnitude it is hardly surprising that his work has been the object of widespread commentary and critique. There is now a veritable Giddens industry (of which the present volume may be considered as another of its products) but the industry would never have developed unless the programme had touched questions of fundamental significance to contemporary sociology. In the remainder of this chapter I will examine some of these questions, in particular, of modernity, environment and identity. I will show how Giddens has been able to reorient sociological questions of social change, but I will also note that the two sociologies problem – the dualism of agency and structure – continues to cast a shadow across the structurationist perspective.

Modernity

It might be suggested that the questions to which Giddens' theoretical ontology has been addressed appear to have undergone a radical revision since he first proposed to revise sociological theory. On closer inspection, however, it is clear that Giddens' recent work is a continuing engagement with tasks that he set for structuration theory in his reflections on Marx, Weber and Durkheim. This engagement is, after all, what Giddens set out to do:

> To argue that it must be one of the main tasks of modern sociology to revert to some of the concerns which occupied its founders is not to propose a step which

is wholly regressive: paradoxically, in taking up again the problems with which they were primarily concerned, we may hope ultimately to liberate ourselves from our present heavy dependence on the ideas which they formulated. (Giddens 1971: 247)

In particular, Giddens' theoretical ontology can be understood as a detailed exposition and elaboration of a number of sociological positions introduced in *Capitalism and Modern Social Theory*, two of which are especially significant for my discussion. The first is Giddens' critique of the 'problem of order' (to which I return, below). Here (1971: ix) Giddens proposes that the problem of 'order' as attributed to Durkheim and promulgated by Parsons, in particular, is a sociological myth. In reality, the Durkheimian problem is not order as such but its *changing nature* (see also 1977: 210–12, 251). The second is the rupture or 'discontinuity' between modernity and tradition with which Giddens opens the introduction to the book. Here (1971: xi), Giddens affirms Lord Acton's dictum by claiming that: 'In the modern era, men no longer accept the conditions of life into which they are born as necessarily given for all time, but attempt to impose their will upon reality in order to bend the future into a shape that conforms with their desires.'

In my view, these two connected propositions are the founding sociological statements of structuration theory, namely that: (ontologically) the contemporary world is uniquely modern, and (theoretically) the modern order is inherently transformational: *all* individuals (not only men) attempt to 'bend the future'. I deal with each in turn.

Ontologically, to depict the contemporary world as a world different to its past is, *ipso facto*, to assert its modernity. Modernity, for Giddens, is precisely a historical condition of difference: a displacement of the past and its traditional, natural and metaphysical reference points. That this condition of difference has been accepted in sociological theory can hardly be contested. The contribution of Giddens' structurationist perspective has been to pose the question of this difference as the central problematic of contemporary sociology: in what does the condition of modern difference consist? Or, in other words, what *conditions the difference* of modernity? Giddens responds that the modern world has become thoroughly reflexive: its modernity resides primarily in the internality of its referential systems. I make further comment on the concept of reflexivity below. Here, I note Giddens' argument that whereas the status and power of premodern institutions was grounded in an appeal to 'externally referential systems' – the natural order, the sanctity of tradition or custom, or the dictates of a metaphysical entity – modern institutions orient to the world as a rationalised social relation among subjects and objects. Their status and power are grounded in an appeal to 'internally referential systems': accumulated or scientific expertise, procedural rationality or efficiency and, importantly, trust relations (1990a: 33–8, 79–111, 1991: 185, 147–8, 201). In turn, the rationalisation of the status and power of institutions is produced recursively in social conduct (1979:

65, 69 *et passim*). For Giddens, the modern world is different not primarily in the scale of its social systems, although this is an important feature, but in their malleability and multidimensionality (see below).

Theoretically, Giddens contends that modernity is inherently transformational: change is built into the social systems that make up modern society. The multidimensional modern world is a constant *process* of renewal and reproduction in which the potential for change is immanent to any and every interaction. Giddens' concept of immanent change is derived from his reading of two Durkheimian themes. The first is the emphasis on the *changing nature* of order. The second is the conceptual stretching of Durkheim's notion of 'plasticity'. Giddens exemplifies the first theme by reference to language use: every utterance in ordinary language is the production of a new meaning but that production *reproduces* existing rules of language. The reproduction of the conditions for a meaningful world (as rules of language use) are, from the point of view of any such instance of reproduction, their novel or renewed production (in a new meaning, in new circumstances). The entry of newness into the world – here, the production of novel or transformed meanings – is an orderly phenomenon grounded in the structuring properties of social interaction. There is, for Giddens, no need to counterpose order (as stasis) to change (as chaos) as if they were dichotomous: the changing nature of a world that appears orderly is a consequence of the ways that agents draw upon and reconstitute the structuring properties of social interaction.

Whilst the concept of the duality of structure can be applied to any and all social formations, Giddens uses the theme of the changing nature of order to illuminate the differences between traditional and modern societies. According to Giddens, social reproduction in traditional societies is conditioned by 'place': not only is the individual's day-to-day life largely bound to small spatial territories – in hamlets, villages and towns, for example – but individuals have only very limited access to distant persons and events. Experience and awareness are always spatially situated and institutions are grounded in local customs and habits. The world is 'out there', immutable, distant and intangible. Social reproduction in modern societies, by contrast, makes what was 'out there' immediately accessible to or immediately consequential for everyone: day-to-day awareness, experience and conduct take place in a globalised context where 'place' is only one amongst many points of social reference. Global production, trade and media bring the consequences of human actions to every corner of the world. Individuals are no longer bound by the habits and customs of place and their actions extend beyond any familiar territory they may occupy. Classic examples of these phenomena are the rise of global consumption, and the multi-cultural habits and customs on which it draws, and global environmental change, which I discuss below. The world that used to be 'out there' appears, in modernity, immediately accessible and more or less mutable on a day-to-day basis so that global change and local action become ever more intertwined.

The mutability of the contemporary everyday world – the fact that accepted habits, customs and conduct are endlessly revisable, endlessly transform-able in the light of new information, knowledge and resources – arises from the 'plasticity' of modernity. This, as I have noted, is a concept used by Durkheim to refer to human practices and wants: how humans organise what they desire and do must be 'plastic' since the larger the society the greater the variety of traditions and accepted practices to be found within it, no one of which can claim supremacy over the others:

> thus traditions and practices are able to adapt themselves to a diversity of situ-ations and to changed circumstances. Individual differences, being much less confined, develop more freely and multiply: that is to say, everyone pursues, to a greater degree, his own bent [*son propre sens*]. (Durkheim, cited in Giddens 1977: 240)

For Giddens, not only are traditions and practices plastic but so also are institutions and identities, sexualities and subjectivities. Similarly, 'nature' is no longer a simple condition of life; in modernity, it is dissolved into the social and cultural world and is reconstituted by human practice: the 'hor-izon' of both internal and external nature is destabilised and socialised. The modern world, to paraphrase a popular advertisement, is a 'shapy, bendy' world; its flexible social systems provide media through which individuals order and organise their day-to-day lives. In the plastic world of modernity, social conduct is the bending or 'regrooving' (1979: 128) of practice and tradi-tion, internal and external nature, identity and environment in the recursive reproduction of institutional and everyday life.

This bending and regrooving is a function of the thoroughgoing reflexiv-ity of the contemporary, globalised modern order. The concept of 'reflexiv-ity' has become popular in sociological theory and research in recent times, partly as a result of Giddens' extensive use of the term in describing the structuring properties of social action. Its rapid and widespread uptake across many different fields of work has resulted in a great deal of confu-sion about its theoretical status. At times it is even used to refer to processes of intentional, reflective activity in a way that denies its theoretical value as a means of describing the outcomes of social action without reference to the conscious intentions of acting subjects. Unless some conceptual rigour is introduced into the 'reflexivity' agenda it is likely that it will soon overtake 'lifestyle' (which itself displaced 'community') as the most over-used and ill-defined concept in contemporary sociological theory.

Reflexivity

It is to Giddens' credit that he has expended so much intellectual energy addressing the conceptual status of reflexivity in his revision of modern sociology, although this conceptual status is not without problems. These problems stem from the fact that Giddens defines reflexivity in two distinct senses: in the first, reflexivity refers to action, what Giddens, following ethno-methodology, calls the 'reflexive monitoring of conduct' (1976: 156; 1990a: 36–8); in the second sense, reflexivity refers to knowledge and meaning: 'in the sense that terms introduced to describe social life routinely enter and transform it' (1992: 28–9). Reflexivity in the first sense is, according to Giddens, intrinsic to all human activity (1991a: 20). It is a 'methodology of practical consciousness' (1990a: 98) by which people 'keep in touch' with the phenomenal world (1990a: 36). Reflexivity, here, is the medium of 'sys-temness on the level of social integration' (1979: 77): it is a social activity that reproduces the structures, or structuring properties, of the social world. As Giddens explains: 'Structures exist paradigmatically, as an absent set of differences, temporally "present" only in their instantiation, in the constitut-ing moments of social systems' (1979: 64).

In other words, the reflexive monitoring of action is the moment in which the absent structures of social systems are constituted and instantiated, just as, for Giddens, the instantiation of speech may be said to constitute the absent structures of language. In this sense of reflexivity, the contents of such paradigmatic structures have no bearing on the social processes by which they are constituted. The reflexive monitoring of conduct reproduces tribal societies, feudal societies or dictatorships as efficiently as speech repro-duces French, Urdu, Greek or English, for example. At this theoretical level, then, there is no politics of reflexivity: no account of how the reflexive monitoring of conduct produces one society or social system (or any of its peculiar characteristics) rather than another one. Since the reflexive monitor-ing of conduct is basic to all human life then it is not inherently transform-ative: to be transformative it must make a difference whether something is done or not, how it is done and under what circumstances. The reflexive monitoring of conduct cannot be a transformational activity if it willy-nilly and equally likely forms the basis of any and every conceivable human scen-ario whatsoever. It cannot be conceptualised as transformational because it *cannot be made accountable for what it does*: it cannot tell you whether one thing is the same as another one or is different from it. Interactionally, the reflexive monitoring of conduct may be a wondrous and deeply instructive sociological phenomenon. Politically, it is equivalent to random energy, going everywhere and nowhere at the same time.

The 'difference' of modernity for Giddens – the ontological uniqueness on which I commented above – resides not in the reflexive monitoring of conduct as such, but in a specific post-traditional form of reflexivity, which is the former's 'condition and outcome'. The difference is specifically a fea-ture of the scale of knowledge and information made available in modernity, for in a 'modern' situation:

Decisions have to be taken on the basis of a more or less continuous reflection on the conditions of one's own action. 'Reflexivity' here refers to the use of information about the conditions of activity as a means of regularly ordering and redefining what that activity is. (Giddens 1994: 86)

Note, here, that reflexivity now contains an element of definition: it is about redefining the content of activity rather than systematising its social integration. At base, it refers to whether or not an activity *in fact* instantiates a structure and, if so, *which* structure is instantiated. Maintaining the language analogy introduced earlier, it is a question of what is said and whether it is said in Greek, French or English, and so on. I will return to this question of definition presently. For the moment, I want to note that this second concept of reflexivity cannot form a theoretical basis for the duality of structure. The concept of the duality of structure rests on the ontological claim that mutual knowledge is a robust 'bracketing' of tacit understandings as a medium for achieving systemness at the level of social integration. Reflexivity in the sense of using information is precisely *not* a bracketing of tacit understandings but a formulation and reflective application of understandings that cannot be tacit and practical, discursive and definitional all at the same time.

The two concepts of reflexivity undertake two distinct functions in the structurationist perspective: one concept is used to account for the recursive production of structuring properties, and one concept is used to account for the substance or definition of what is structured. This definitional dualism suggests that the *theoretical* connection between reflexivity and conduct is itself unstable: neither concept of reflexivity alone can form the basis for a sociology of modern society. If the reflexive monitoring of conduct is not unique to modernity but is basic to all human social life, as I have noted, then modern conduct must consist in the reflexive monitoring of a conduct that is uniquely modern. But what is the *theoretical* basis of this uniqueness if not the reflexive monitoring of conduct? Is it that the quantity and quality of reflexivity in the second sense (i.e., the sense of 'using' information – a form of 'definitional' reflexivity) has changed – such that more and/or different kinds of understandings and information now order and define activity – and that this has changed the conditions under which reflexivity in the first sense (i.e., the continual, unacknowledged monitoring of conduct) takes place? In this case, the reflexive monitoring of conduct is conditioned by something that cannot be derived from the duality of structure: the conditions through which reflexivity in the second sense gives definition to activity are not the outcome of reflexivity in the first sense. Indeed, although it might be argued that reflexive monitoring is logically (and ontologically) prior to 'definitional reflexivity', this is not the same as saying that both, logically, are mutually implicated in global modernisation. Indeed, it could be argued that definitional reflexivity (sense two) diminishes the capacity or the quotidian effectivity of reflexive monitoring (sense one). By intervening into and reordering activity, definitional reflexivity may lead to ritualised, coerced or distorted forms of reflexive monitoring.

In this case, it might be suggested that what is distinctive about modernity is not the reflexive monitoring of conduct but the conduct of reflexive monitoring: how reflexive monitoring is *in fact* undertaken or achieved; *what* mutual knowledges are constituted or renewed in the interstices of institutional and everyday life. To be modern may be to conduct one's reflexive monitoring of conduct in particular ways.

In spite of these ambiguities, I propose that Giddens' structurationism depends upon this dualistic interpretation: *two distinct types of reflexivity* mediate everyday and institutional life in modern social systems but further problems arise immediately if this is the case. These can be illustrated by asking whether or not 'definitional reflexivity' is a feature of non-modern cultures. If reflexivity in this second sense is in fact a feature of both modern and non-modern situations then what, sociologically, is the difference between 'modern' and 'non-modern' social orders according to the perspective of structurationism? If, on the other hand, 'definitional reflexivity' is not a feature of the non-modern, then on what historical basis was new knowledge and information incorporated and assimilated into everyday and institutional contexts and how did this incorporation give rise to a world distinct from its past?

These questions go to the heart of both dimensions of structurationism's ontology and theory of modernity – the *uniqueness* and the *transformability* of the modern order. There are no logical or ontological grounds on which to argue that 'definitional reflexivity' developed with modernity. Therefore, the uniqueness of the modern must lie precisely in the *form* of this *second type* of reflexivity and not in the fact of reflexivity as such. In this case, the historical existence of modern social orders – their embeddedness in specific time–space relations – is not dependent on their own thoroughgoing reflexivity. Rather, the modern form of reflexivity (in the second sense) is a historical outcome of social changes that have affected both institutional and everyday contexts *in spite of* the mundane reflexivity (in the first sense) that is shared by traditional and modern forms of social action. Separating out a specific form of modern reflexivity from the structurationist ontology of recursively produced social systems can help to explain aspects of the ecological crisis, or the 'end of nature', as a product of that modern reflexivity.

Environment

One of Giddens' central achievements in his recent work has been to acknowledge the crucial significance of environmental and ecological change for any sociology – political, economic, cultural or otherwise – of late modernity. There are two key aspects of the approach he develops. First is an emphasis on environmental and ecological threats as 'high consequence risks' (1990a: 124–34; 1991: 113–24, 243; 1994a: 219–23), which underpins the proposition that the post-traditional order is one characterised not so much by 'the end of history' as by the 'end of nature' (Giddens 1991a: 137, 165–6; cf McKibben 1990). The second aspect is a conception of environmental and ecological activism as expressing a 'life politics' as opposed to an 'emancipatory politics' (Giddens 1994a: 198–228), which underpins the proposition that ecological politics is the exemplar of a politics 'beyond left and right'. I will discuss some issues in Giddens' political philosophy below. Here, I want to explore the relationships between Giddens' conception of a 'post-natural' society and the claim that modernity is characterised by global 'high consequence' risks.

For Giddens, the 'natural' has been profoundly and irreversibly recast through human intervention. Contemporary society is a 'post-natural' as well as a 'post-traditional' world. It is a world characterised by a fully 'humanised' or 'plastic nature' (1994a: 101). This conception itself represents a profound shift in Giddens' ontology of modernity. Whereas the theory of structuration initially distinguished sharply between society and nature, its later application to political questions – of environmental change, genetic manipulation, reproductive technologies, and so on – overhauls the earlier proposition. Compare, for example, *New Rules of Sociological Method* (1976) and *The Consequences of Modernity* (1990a):

> The difference between society and nature is that nature is not man-made, is not produced *by* man. Human beings, of course, transform nature, and such transformation is both the condition of social existence and a driving force of cultural development. But nature is not a human production; society is. (1976: 15)

> In the industrialised sectors of the globe – and increasingly elsewhere – human beings live in a *created environment*, an environment of action which is, of course, physical but no longer just natural. Not just the built environment of urban areas but most other landscapes as well become subject to human co-ordination and control. (1990a: 60)

Today, human beings no longer live in a contradictory relation to nature (1979: 161), nor in a nature that is 'refractory to the human will' (1977: 294), but in a 'nature that no longer exists', 'that is devoid of nature', a nature that is 'no longer natural' (1994a: 11, 206, 209) and 'has become dissolved' (1996: 31) into the social systems of modernity. The condition of the modern world, exemplified above all in relations with nature, is one of manufactured uncertainty: a condition that has arisen directly from human intervention into the natural and social parameters of human life.

In earlier formulations, then, *society* is made to happen as a skilled performance on the part of its members; *nature*, on the other hand, is an independent condition of action that can be 'transformed' but not 'performed' or 'accomplished'. This distinction applies both to 'external' (ecosystemic) and 'internal' (bio-anatomical) nature and is what 'sets off' the 'second nature' of human beings from the (first?) nature which they are simultaneously 'in and of' (1979: 161). In later formulations, Giddens proposes that 'nature' has become socialised to such an extent that it is no longer inhabited by people at all. Instead, modern individuals exist in the created environments of a reflexive modernity (1994a: 165), environments that consist in a nature that has become 'transformed into areas of action where human beings have to make practical and ethical decisions' (Beck, Lash and Giddens, 1994: vii). Nature, here, is *neither theoretically nor ontologically* an independent, refractory or contradictory condition of action and interaction: it is, instead, a (re)produced dimension of action. In structurationist terms, it amounts to a *medium and outcome* of human practice, a structuring property instantiated in a routinised world of social conduct, with the consequence that 'no attempt to reanimate nature will reintroduce nature as it used to be' (1996: 32). Let us, then, bite the structurationist bullet and contend that socialised nature – the created environment – is a skilled accomplishment, performed routinely and regularly in a denaturalised, detraditionalised, internally referential modernity.

The advantage of this theoretical step is that the environment can be theorised as a fully sociological phenomenon. It can be argued that the relationships between individuals and what used to be the 'natural' world are more open in modernity than ever before because individuals accomplish both external and internal nature through the structuring properties of reflexive social institutions that are global in scale. The environmental risks of modern society are 'high consequence', both globally and personally, *precisely because the environment is both medium and outcome of human activity*. Whether referring to global warming or *in vitro* fertilisation, anorexia, ozone depletion or genetic engineering, Giddens proposes that the contemporary world is an experimental world that engenders both epistemological uncertainty and ontological angst. The expert knowledges on which modern technological, social and economic systems rely, of which both natural and social sciences are important examples, offer no guarantees that disaster is not around the corner. The final certainty provided by expert knowledges is that the consequences of the socialisation of nature and of the creation of environments are ultimately uncertain. Thus, individuals are condemned to choosing courses of action whose ramifications are always and irremediably risky.

This is a sophisticated and original formulation, one that places at centre stage the (largely unintended) consequences of human interaction on the post-natural world, whilst emphasising the 'high consequences' of many of the risks and threats to the planet thus engendered. Difficulties remain, however, with both the ontological and theoretical dimensions of this position. One way of coming to terms with the problems is to take a detour and consider the existence of structures that are the products of human activity but which, at least initially, seem to persist in spite of either the reflexive monitoring of conduct or the reflexive use of information in the reordering of activity.

In structuration theory, structures (or structuring properties) are recursively constituted in interaction. It follows that individuals are not mere products of structural forces and that structures do not exist independently of human action. However, looked at in reverse, since individuals recursively (re)produce structures then structures must be open to or must express at least some part of people's agency and individuality. The question is, *what part* of people's individuality, or *what part* of human agency, is reproduced in the structures of the phenomenal world that form the objective contexts of human activity? Examples of such produced structures include buildings, railway lines, roads, telephone boxes or electricity pylons, although any kind of produced structure would serve the same exemplary purpose – including 'landscapes' or, certainly in the North Sea oil fields, 'seascapes'. The sociological existence of these objective structures can be conceptualised in a number of ways but for reasons of brevity and focus I will contrast Giddens' perspective with that of Marx.

For Marx, physical structures – indeed, all physical objects – produced by humans in capitalism always have a dual essence. On the one hand, as capitalist commodities, they express the social relations of production of capitalism. On the other, as physical products of human action they are made of or constituted by human labour. Since all production is a labour of transformation then the existence of all produced physical objects and structures consists in an amount and relation of that labour. The part of human individuality or agency expressed by such structures is 'labour'. This is a sociological account of the phenomenal existence of non-human objects and structures that are produced by human beings or, in other words, a social ontology. The production of such objective structures as roads or electricity pylons, by labour is what distinguishes them as products of human activity, distinct from the products of non-human forces. Theoretically, for Marx, because capitalism hides the labour relation that produces such objects behind the commodity form, then human beings are alienated from the objective consequences of their own activity (their own agency) and in consequence are alienated from their own 'nature' (their own creative individuality).

When Giddens theorises structures/structuring properties, he is not referring to things like roads or electricity pylons or even landscapes, but to instantiated social relations. However, a theoretical ontology of modern society needs an account of the difference between the objectivity of what people do produce and the objectivity of what people do not produce. Without such an account, structurationism loses its ontological credentials and becomes a version of deontics, instead: a logical formalisation of the ethics of conduct in a pregiven objective world. In structurationism, the everyday world of objective structures comprises not a ratio of labour but a ratio of trust. The part of individuality and agency that is reflected through the structuring properties of social systems is the active placing of trust in abstract systems: the money that pays for and the expert systems that ostensibly guarantee (but ultimately, existentially, fail to do so) the objective reliability and permanence of the world. But note that, for Giddens, 'trust' is not placed in the objective structures themselves; instead it is placed in the systems that guarantee their solidity and reliability. This is a critical reversal of the Marxian view. Whereas, for Marx, capitalism hid the social relations of production behind the objective form of the commodity, for Giddens modernity hides the commodity-object behind the social relations of trust: the object loses its objectivity and is manifested as a social relation (of trust and risk) instead. Theoretically, the facticity of the road, the pylon, and so on – what the road or the pylon is in itself – is separated entirely and radically from individuals and their agency: the object expresses nothing of the individual at all and everything of the abstract system.

But note that if the objective world is outside of the individual – that is, if the objectivity of the world in itself bears no relation to the individual – then it cannot simultaneously comprise a skilled performance on the part of interacting individuals. I want to suggest that, if the structurationist ontology is taken to its logical conclusion, then the skilled performance, the accomplishment of modern, reflexive interactional and institutional systems is the *negation of the objectivity of the world*, including both its natural and social objectivity. Modern reflexivity consists in the denial of any form of social or natural interconnection: the manufactured uncertainty, the created environments of modernity simultaneously render the world as a human creation and deny individuals any objective stake in that creation. If the structurationist ontology correctly identifies the social reflexivity of modernity, it also reveals a dualism of subject and object in the dissolution of nature.

It is my view that structuration theory does indeed identify this dualism of subject and object. It provides the starting point for a critical sociology of an objective world that is both post-natural and 'post-traditional' but this is not because it overcomes the structure–agency dichotomy in social theory. On the contrary, it is because it provides theoretical resources for understanding how structures that are specifically modern – or 'post-traditional', in Giddens' terminology – extract the agency of individuals and groups from the ordered systems in which their social activities are organised. Giddens' assessment of a post-natural social system can be used to illuminate why the ecological crisis is fundamentally a political problem. The social reflexivity of a post-natural world is a specific form of rationalisation that removes the last vestige of individual power over the pace and direction of socio-environmental change.

Identity

How is identity manifested in the world? And how is the world manifested in identity? Giddens' sociological project offers at least a partial solution to the apparent opposition of these questions. His attempt to link the social and political contours of modernity with the cultural and psychological contours of self-development represents an innovative account of the relationships between identity and institutions. Just as the *Constitution of Society* worked through the disciplinary boundaries between sociology and human geography, so *Modernity and Self-Identity* and *The Transformation of Intimacy* work at the borders of sociology and psychology. The reason for this boundary-crossing, I suggest, lies in Giddens' determination to construct a sociology of modernity in which feelings and emotional routines can be connected to the contours of institutional and social change in the contemporary world. This focus on the sentience, rather than merely the rationality, of sociological agents responds positively to feminist critiques of malestream sociological theory (see for example, Waerness 1984) which contest the 'over-rationalised' conception of the social actor in sociology. In more critical terms, Giddens' use of the concepts of self and identity represents a response to post-structuralist and post-modern concepts of subjectivity and the latter's realisation in discourse. In developing the positive and the critical dimensions of his exploration of modern identity, Giddens draws on G.H. Mead's social psychology of the self and aspects of the psychotherapeutic tradition in order to retain a concept of an 'inner core of self-identity' (1991a: 100). Ultimately, however, I will suggest that this notion of an 'inner core' is sociologically unconvincing. Instead, I will propose that, just as structuration theory exposes a dualism of subject and object in the dissolution of nature, so it exposes a dualism of self and identity in the abstract systems of a modern social order.

Ontologically, Giddens grounds both 'self' and 'identity' in reflexivity. This grounding, however, is different in each case and parallels the conceptual dualism of reflexivity discussed above. 'Self' is a construct grounded in reflexivity in the first sense which I discussed above – the sense of the reflexive monitoring of action as a mundane, practical means of being in touch with the *phenomenal* world – which is why the routine maintenance of 'normal appearances' is dependent on the bodily 'bracketing out' of the self (1991a: 58). 'Identity', on the other hand, is a construct grounded in reflexivity in the second sense – the sense of using knowledge and information as a means of defining and ordering activity and one's presence in the *social* world – which is why self-'identity' corresponds with self-'image' (1991a: 58). The theoretical bridge between the two forms of reflexivity is constructed out of 'trust'. The problem is that whilst Giddens provides a detailed picture of the constructs – of self, identity and trust – he does not specify who or what is doing the constructing. The ontology states that everything is constructed, but the theory develops no account of the relationships between constructor and constructee. Does the self construct the identity, or does the identity construct the self? Is trust constructed on the foundation of self-identity or is self-identity constructed on the foundation of trust? The response of structuration theory is the concept of 'mutual implication': self, identity and trust are mutually implicated in their co-construction but are they implicated as constructors or constructees?

One way of seeing the importance of these questions is to consider the 'body' in Giddens' approach to self-identity. In spite of the many and diverse references to the body, the sociological entities of which Giddens writes have a distinctly non-corporeal existence: structuration theory attends to the body as an abstract system and not to bodies as pained, chained or claimed entities in the world. Giddens is not theorising the particularity of bodies – the bodies of the slave or the condemned, of lesbians, labourers, racialised and stratified collectivities – but *the* body, or *the embodiment* of modern personhood. Like the structuring properties of language-use, bodies are vehicles or media for realising something which they themselves are not. To put the matter in structurationist terms, bodies instantiate the absent properties of the self anew on each occasion of their social use. Hence, the body has to be routinely controlled, created and designed. It is not a possession but an 'action system' that comprises an 'essential part of sustaining a coherent sense of self-identity' (1991: 99). The body is a practical mode of handling the world: shaped, oriented, preened and punished in the service of psycho-social coherence. Failures of such practical management – or 'authentic reflexive monitoring' (1991a: 107) – display personality disorders and pathologies of various descriptions: anorexia nervosa, narcissism, paranoiac and schizoid states, for example. The 'normal' self is a bracketed practical attitude in which the bodily display of self is a known but unremarkable, seen but unacknowledged, condition of going on in the world. Being 'safely' in the body – being a competently embodied self – is the absence of routinely accountable embodiment: the body brackets the self in situations of co-presence.

Although set against the backdrop of modernity's 'post-traditional existential terrain' (1991a: 80), the relationship between self and body is the foundation of Giddens' theory of self-identity which, in turn, is dependent on systematised trust relations. Giddens contends that 'bodily and psychic ease with the routine circumstances of everyday life . . . is acquired only with great effort' (1991a: 127). The effort consists in the construction of a protective cocoon of trust that stands guard over the self (1991a: 3, 129, *et passim*) in normal circumstances. The construction begins in infancy when the child learns that the primary care-giver is 'trustworthy' – that is, the child learns to trust the care-giver's return and the care-giver's satisfaction of the child's bodily, emotional and social needs. The child's early experiences of stability and dependability contribute to an emerging sense of ontological security on the basis of which trust can be placed in a larger number of differently significant others as the scale of the child's sensory environment increases. Over time, the child, and then the adult, places trust in more and more others whose relationships to the individual become increasingly distant and increasingly mediated. Trust comprises an 'effort bargain' with, or a 'leap of faith' in, first, care-givers, then more distant others and ultimately modern institutions and systems (1991a: 23) and is the 'condition of the elaboration of self-identity' (1991a: 41). Trust is 'diffused' throughout the everyday and institutional contexts of modernity, providing a substratum of non-consequential uneventfulness in which individuals carry on with their lives. This generalised trust, whilst not without dilemmas, enables 'contacts and exchanges "at a distance"' (1991: 134) and simultaneously brackets or discounts possibilities that are 'irrelevant to the individual's self-identity' (1991a: 129).

Note, here, that the *Umwelt* of modernity, as Giddens discusses it, is paradoxically a world of self-effacement. For, just as the body brackets the accountability of self-identity in the mediation of presence, so the cocoon of trust brackets the accountability of self-identity in the mediation of absence: the diffusion of trust is the social (re)production of the protective cocoon as a world in which the self is not accountable. I suggest that, in these respects, a modern identity is 'self-less'. It is an identity which abstracts or removes the self from any *social* connection either with the body or with trusted individuals and institutions. Structuration theory, in this construction, reveals the radical split between people's own feelings and senses of personal existence (their idea of or belief in an inner core) and the identities through which they can engage with other people and with the institutional complexes governing modern life. In short, it exposes a dichotomy of self and identity – a dualism of intensionality and extensionality – in the abstract systems of a modern social order.

The Politics of the Modern

> There is a remarkable similarity between what a good relationship is like, as diagnosed in the literature of therapy and self-help, and the properties of formal democracy in the political sphere. (1996: 221)

Giddens' assessment of contemporary political philosophy and practice is rooted in his prior analysis of the consequences and conditions of modernity that I have discussed above. Although the political has always been an aspect of his engagement with social theory it has become an increasingly central element of his writings across the 1990s. It is not my intention here to explain the rise of this political project in his work. Rather, I want to situate Giddens' conception of modern politics in the context of his modern social theory. I suggest that doing this shows why Giddens' political project is a critical project in the sociological sense of that term: it reveals important processes and sites of social change and the ways that the activities of individuals and institutions influence that change. At the same time, however, I will argue that Giddens' political assessment of contemporary society lacks a theory of power and that developing such a theory is a necessary step if structurationism is to furnish effective grounds for responding to important political questions of the day. My aim is not to dismiss or denigrate Giddens' political position. Developing a coherent theory of power is one of the most difficult tasks in the sociological enterprise but I propose that, currently, the terms of reference of structuration theory do not provide for a concept of power that enables sociologists to explain relations of domination, subordination and inequality. Paying attention to such relations is a more illuminating strategy for theorising contemporary political practice than the focus on dialogic democracy. The discussion will explore some of the ways that the critical agenda of Giddens' political writings is in tension with their normative agenda. I begin my discussion by commenting on the emotionality and humanisation of modern politics before going on to address power in structuration theory.

For Giddens, modernity is a world seething with feeling. Every relationship, every action and experience is an emotional investment: from the individual's point of view, the matter of life is passionately anchored. To theorise politics without accounting for the emotional substance that provides its personal significance is to abstract the private from the public. It is to replicate the classical liberal conception of society as an arrangement of independent spheres of rights and responsibilities, duties and attachments where state and family, personal and political, private and public represent opposing arena of action and development. Giddens' recuperation of aspects of philosophic conservatism is an attempt to overcome such dualistic divisions and explore the relationships between the intensional intimacy and the extensional diffuseness of modern politics. The 'utopian realist' project he advances comprises a model of the connection between autonomy and solidarity in the modern world and recommends the pursuit of dialogic democracy in both the personal and public spheres. The realist, or 'realistic' (1990a: 155), part of the project is based on the analysis of actual social processes (1994a: 249), whilst the utopian part represents an apparent will to dialogue. The ideal type or model (dialogic-democratic) connection between autonomy and solidarity in the modern world is the 'pure relationship', to which I return below.

The contemporary world is fully humanised. Human beings intervene, on a global scale, into every corner of social life and nature: the conditions of experience and action are the media and outcome of that intervention. Yet, rather than leading to 'mastery' over and certainty in the world, the process inspires security and risk in equal measure, leading to a condition of manufactured uncertainty. Technological intervention into nature and the body provides comforts and cures as well as dangers and threats, revealing both the positive and negative consequences of a scientific culture. Social intervention into lifestyles unleashes new opportunities for personal development and disturbs the social relations that once provided the contexts for that development. The 'detraditionalisation' of the world consists in the disclosure of all social and natural horizons, their revelation as social choices and not as fixed limits of opportunity and change.

In such circumstances, dialogue is an increasingly important feature of social activity. It is facilitated by processes of globalisation but is rooted in the emergence of the pure relationship. According to Giddens, pure relationships originate primarily in the domains of sexuality, marriage and friendship (1991a: 98). They are characterised by commitment, trust, exploration, intimacy and a lack of traditional constraints on what can and cannot be achieved through the relationship. In the negotiation of such relationships, individuals expose the changeability and impermanence of traditional identities, roles and expectations and contribute to a remoralisation of personal life. At the same time, these characteristics of intimate relationships also define significant processes of public democratisation (1992: 188). Globalisation of communications media and a global cosmopolitanism create common dialogic spaces where different traditional roles, identities and expectations meet. With no shared tradition on which to draw – where any tradition becomes one option among others – the importance of trust, commitment and exploration are brought to the fore. The alternatives to dialogue include hostility and war, cultural isolation and fundamentalisms of many kinds. In contrast to these refusals of dialogue, the pure relationship signals the purchase of universal values of autonomy and solidarity, freedom and democracy in personal and public life.

Thus, dialogic democracy – or the 'democratisation of democracy' – is a critical social process: it emerges in the context of changes at the micro level (in the negotiation of intimate relationships) and at the macro level (in the cosmopolitan confusion of alternative traditions and normative frameworks and in the globalisation of uncertainty and shared risks). Like the structuring properties of social systems, dialogic democracy is both a condition and outcome of social action but, unlike those properties, it is in a basic sense the product of choice. There may be pressures towards dialogue in modern social systems but only in the context of countervailing tendencies towards fundamentalism and violence. Fostering the conditions under which the former might prevail over the latter is the normative agenda of the utopian realist project. In order to respond to critical processes of social change in ways that secure dialogue and trust, Giddens proposes a programme of 'generative politics', a programme that depends upon creating active trust in government institutions, regenerating civic culture and responsibility, and is 'the main means of effectively approaching problems of poverty and social exclusion in the present day'. The political programme hinges on three important requirements: a redefinition of 'welfare' to a concept of 'positive welfare', a generative model of equality, and the promotion of an autotelic self (1994: 180–94), which latter refers to a person who can expect and confront risk, 'translate potential threats into rewarding challenges' and manage stress.

However, the normative agenda, here, runs counter to the critical agenda in a number of ways although, for reasons of space, I will comment on only two. First, whilst it may be the case that generative politics is one means of *addressing* questions of poverty and exclusion, a concept of generative politics does not *account* for poverty and exclusion. The generative politics approach to political questions again encounters the problem of deontics that

I discussed above: whilst the political concepts supply resources for comprehending a pregiven world of poverty and exclusion, they do not identify the political causes of poverty and exclusion and, by extension, provide no warrant for assuming that generative politics will lead to *effective* responses to those conditions. It may be, for example, that the emergence of the autotelic self is part of the problem, rather than part of the solution: how does a sociologist or political theorist distinguish the positive from the negative consequences of confronting risk, translating threats into challenges and managing stress? This question reveals a second way in which the critical and normative agendas of generative politics are confused. The activity of managing stress is presumably intended to signal the capacity of individuals to deal with their 'inner core' of emotions and feelings, but emotions are not fixed, immutable characteristics of individual selves. They are, rather, part of the social fabric in which selves are formed, maintained and changed. Contemporary social institutions comprise emotional régimes or matrices in which feelings and emotions are organised in the service of instrumental goals. The management of 'stress', or any other emotional condition, is a socio-political transaction in a hierarchically ordered world. The sociology of emotions (after Hochschild 1983) explores the ways that emotion management services the requirements of economic, political and social institutions and acts as a means of sustaining or reconfiguring power differentials between different social groups.

A critical sociology of contemporary society must situate power at the heart of any theorisation of social change and social experience. Without a theory of how power differentiates or dominates social groups, or subverts social processes, the normative agenda of any theory – including structuration theory – cannot be distinguished from its analytic agenda. Thus, in the case of generative politics it is difficult to disentangle the extent to which the autotelic self, for example, is a consequence of specific social changes, promoting certain forms of social interaction and development, and to what extent it is a normative goal, vaunted in the desire to promote autonomy over heteronomy, individuation over sociation. In contrast to the bootstrap theory of the autotelic self – a form of self which emerges as a bare consequence of micro and macro social change – one might propose that the autotelic self is a political counterpoint to the 'heterotelic self', a form of self that promotes heteronomy over autonomy, sociation over individuation. On this basis it can be suggested that the social reflexivity of modernity expresses a form of power that destroys the heterotelic self or weakens the associative bonds of heteronomous social development. To the extent that the autotelic self is fostered through a programme of generative politics, then this programme may be said to be complicit with the subordination of heterotelic relations and interactions that socialise, rather than individualise, threats, risks and stresses.

Power, here, is not merely transformative capacity. It is, rather, the exercise of domination over certain kinds of relationships, norms, interactions and practices. The social reflexivity of modernity, as a form of power, can be understood as the active dislocation of heteronomous social selves from the contexts and relationships that sustain them and the reconfiguration of those selves as autotelic isolates in abstract systems of social control. Under such circumstances, it can be argued that a critical sociology of modern society that begins in the terms of reference of structuration theory identifies the emergence of the autotelic self as the consequence of a *degenerative* political programme. The normative agenda of such a sociology may then assert the primacy of a *regenerative* political project aimed at fostering the conditions under which democratic dialogue may be related to the diverse experiences and demands of hierarchically ordered and politically differentiated social groups.

Concluding remarks

In this chapter I have provided a brief introduction to some of the main strands of Giddens' social and political writings. I have not been able to address all of the themes and interests that he has developed in three decades of sociological scholarship. Instead, I have focused attention on some of the insights that structuration theory can provide into processes of reflexivity, environmental change, identity-formation and political domination. In doing so, however, I have observed that the aim of structuration theory to overcome the dichotomy of structure and agency has, rather, displaced it onto a series of related conceptual dualisms. The displacement should not be considered simply and only in negative terms, as an inability to resolve a classic sociological conundrum. I have used the dualistic character of structuration theory to explore critical dimensions of social, ecological and political change in the contemporary world.

Theorising modern social life is a difficult and intricate task. It involves attention to the details of social conduct and interaction, the operation of social institutions, the process of social change, the political contours of heterogeneous social formations and the relationships between self, identity, environment, action, agency and structure. To develop a programmatic sociology that is able to encompass all of these dimensions of contemporary society is a huge undertaking and one that invites debate and controversy. Any intellectual discipline that is alive and flourishing necessarily welcomes such debate as a stimulus to the continued search for new perspectives on the world and new kinds of explanation through which to address the complexity and diversity of its subject matter. Anthony Giddens' sociology has certainly furnished grounds for wide-ranging debate as well as contributing to a reformulation of the discipline's intellectual and political location in contemporary Britain.

CHAPTER 2

Radical politics – neither Left nor Right?

Ted Benton

In contrast to some other European countries, Britain's political culture remains markedly anti-intellectual. It is to Anthony Giddens' great credit that he has succeeded in becoming acknowledged as a public intellectual. Very few of his generation of sociologists and social theorists have been able to deploy the resources of their specialist disciplines in such a way as to connect with the public arena of political debate. Giddens' special achievement has been to link such issues as the crisis of welfare, ecological degradation, family policy, and democratic reform with wider philosophical/theoretical speculation about the nature of our contemporary civilisation and the trends and opportunities within it. Inevitably, such an ambitious sweep lends itself to easy over-generalisation and superficial judgment. There is no doubt that Giddens is very vulnerable to such complaints on the part of the specialist practitioners of the numerous disciplines across whose boundaries he bravely trespasses. Though I have some sympathy with these complaints, my discussion here will seek to avoid the more small-scale doubts and difficulties, in favour of a more wide-ranging evaluation of Giddens' political thinking, as exhibited in his *Beyond Left and Right* (1994a). In the course of the discussion I will present the outlines of an alternative approach, focusing particularly on the interpretation of green social and political thought and practice.

The core of Giddens' argument is that we have entered upon a phase of history in which the main inherited political traditions of left and right, of conservatism and socialism, as well as the broader framework of liberal democratic capitalism, have become exhausted. At the same time, we live in a 'run-away' world, characterised by social disintegration, escalating inequalities, the threat of ecological catastrophe, and the emergence of dangerous 'fundamentalisms'. The need for radical politics is urgent, but the contradictions of neo-liberal radicalism and the exhaustion of the socialist tradition debar them from answering to this need. Fortunately, at least one of the forces that renders socialism obsolete, 'social reflexivity', together with its manifestations in progressive social movements, may come to the rescue in the form of what Giddens calls 'life', or 'generative', politics. Giddens draws upon his understanding of the social movements in suggesting a reconstituted radical politics that preserves some of the core values hitherto associated with socialist thought whilst also drawing on what he refers to as philosophic conservatism (1994a). Whether or not the 'modernising' leaders of the British Labour Party were Giddens' deliberate addressees, there is a clear affinity between 'New Labour' and the general tendency and tenor of Giddens' political argument (see Rustin 1995). That said, Giddens' radicalism remains much more far-reaching than anything yet put onto the political agenda by the Blair/Mandelson axis.

In what follows, I explore at a little more length the main elements in Giddens' argument. I then consider some reasons for disputing his claim that the political traditions of Left and Right are exhausted. The focus here will be on a defence of the continuing pertinence of socialism, both as a resource for explanatory analysis and as a critical normative perspective on contemporary society. This leads on to a broadening of the theoretical frame, to a questioning of the key concepts – 'tradition', 'modernity', 'simple' and 'reflexive modernisation', and 'globalisation' – through which Giddens constructs his account of current social processes and the futures they make possible. Here, it is argued that an alternative approach that gives a more central explanatory role to the transnational dynamics of capitalist accumulation and associated forms of organisation of political power has more purchase on the problems of ecological and social disintegration in a 'runaway' world. If this is right, then the critical focus of the socialist traditions on capitalism and its social and ecological consequences is endorsed. For this, as for other strategic reasons, socialist analyses and perspectives must be considered indispensable to any projected reconstitution of radical politics. However, it is accepted that Giddens is right to claim that radical politics stands in need of reconstruction, in the light of issues posed by green, feminist and other social movements, and in the face of the deeply problematic heritage of past attempts at socialist construction.

Politics and 'modernity'

The central organising concepts in Giddens' analysis situate the present in terms of two related contrasts. The first is between 'traditional' or 'premodern' societies, and what he calls 'modernity'. The second contrast is between phases of modernity: an earlier phase of 'simple' modernisation, and, our current phase, 'reflexive' modernisation. The term 'modernity' designates the complex of institutions that emerged in the West three to four hundred years ago, and which has since spread across the globe. This complex of institutions has four 'dimensions':

1. 'Our' relation to nature, characterised by the growing role of science, technology and industry.

2. An economic order, typically capitalist, but with a now defunct communist variant.
3. The organisation of political/administrative power, characterised by surveillance, and increasingly taking the form of representative liberal democracy.
4. Control of the means of violence, generally monopolised by the nation state.

'Modernity' is founded on a sharp historical discontinuity with all previous social forms. It is marked by its restless dynamism, and its ruthless undermining of tradition. It is made possible by what Giddens thinks of as a separation of space and time and their constitution as 'empty dimensions', so permitting the 'stretching' of social relations over time and space. Key to understanding this paradigmatically modern shift away from localised, face-to-face forms of organisation of social life are 'disembedding mechanisms', such as money, and 'expert systems' (such as transport and communications technologies, which form the context of everyday life, but whose mechanisms we do not understand or control). The undermining of tradition also implies the end of nature, conceived as something 'given', independently of human agency. The risks and dangers encountered in pre-modern societies were 'external' in origin, by contrast with an intensifying process of 'manufacture' of risks under modernity. It is not that modernity is more risky than the pre-modern world, but rather that the *source* of risk has shifted to society itself, and to modern science and industrial technology in particular.

In its earlier phase, modernity engendered its own traditions: those associated with occupational communities and class identities, and with the social division of labour between men and women. Even science and technology were treated as traditions, as possessing their own self-guaranteeing authority. The political traditions of conservatism, liberalism and socialism made sense and were appropriate to that earlier phase of 'simple modernisation', but have become disoriented and eventually exhausted in the course of the last half century as a result of intensifying social processes that Giddens thinks of (*contra* the post-modernists) as a radicalisation of modernity itself. These interconnected processes are globalisation, de- (or post-) traditionalisation and social reflexivity, and their combined consequences are sufficient to define the emergence of a new historical phase: 'high' modernity, characterised by 'reflexive modernisation'. On the nature of globalisation, there is a shift of emphasis between Giddens' earlier *Consequences of Modernity* (1990a) and *Beyond Left and Right*. In the former work there is a qualified endorsement of 'world system' theory as an account of economic globalisation, together with an insistence that other, non-economic aspects of globalisation were of importance. In the latter, Giddens seems more concerned to emphasise the role of communications technology and cultural globalisation, and to distance himself from economic analyses. He also emphasises the contradictory character of globalisation, sometimes appearing as a force for global uniformity, sometimes as evoking localist or fundamentalist responses; both as exemplified in the universality of the nation state, and as at work in undermining its significance. (Whether a concept designating such a kaleidoscopic diversity of mutually contradictory attributes can do any useful theoretical work is a question I will put to one side for now.)

One consequence of globalisation is cosmopolitanism, and the increasing difficulty of maintaining any tradition 'in the traditional way'. By this Giddens means that all traditions now are faced with the demand that they justify themselves in dialogue with other traditions in the public space. Detraditionalisation in this sense combines with globalisation to increase the scope and significance of 'reflexivity', which Giddens (1991a) also treats as a generic feature of all human social action. By reflexivity he means the continuous reordering and reconceptualising of action in the light of actors' monitoring of its conditions and consequences. The circumstances of manufactured risk, and uncertainty in all domains of life, together with the dissolution of traditionally or naturally 'given' identities and destinies imposes on both institutions and individuals immensely expanded opportunities and requirements for engaging in reflexive conduct. So far as individuals are concerned, the formation of self-identity is now a thoroughly open-ended 'reflexive project' of self-constitution.

The onset of reflexive modernisation disorients the established political traditions of Left and Right, resulting in paradoxical realignments that Giddens (1994a) sees as mere symptoms of their exhaustion, and growing inappropriateness to the new conditions of social life. On his account, conservatism, in the shape of neo-liberalism, has become radical, whilst socialists have retreated from their former claim to be the vanguard of historical progress into a conservative defence of the welfare state. This apparent paradox is explained in terms of the exhaustion of the mainstream traditions. Conservatism as the defence of tradition in the traditional way can no longer be sustained in the face of detraditionalisation and reflexivity, whilst neo-liberalism must collapse under the weight of its own contradictions. However, one of the legacies of conservatism, what Giddens calls 'philosophic conservatism', survives to make an important contribution to the politics of the future. Liberal democratic capitalism is inadequate to the challenge of global ecological limits and is incapable of generating sufficient sources of social solidarity. In turn, socialism can at long last be consigned to the dustbin of history. The collapse of the European state-centralist régimes, and the reorientation of the remaining Asian ones to the world market and capitalist development only confirms the long-established critique, associated with Ludwig von Mises and Hayek, of centralised planning. Reformist socialism is also in crisis, in part because of the decline in class identity and associated forms of collective action, and in part because of a crisis in the welfare state. This latter is only partially a result of fiscal pressures, and is more centrally a consequence of the way reflexive modernisation has altered the problems that the welfare state was designed to solve.

However, the death of socialism and the demise of neo-liberal radicalism do not entail the end of radical politics. Giddens discerns in the growth of social movements such as feminism, ecologism and environmental politics, the peace movement and so on, as well as 'self-help' groups of various kinds, the emergence of a new radicalism, neither of the Left nor of the Right, but drawing on both philosophic conservatism and some of the values of the socialist tradition. The radical politics of the past was primarily 'emancipatory', struggling for freedom from various forms of domination or oppression. Giddens notes that inequality and domination remain pervasive features of reflexively modernising societies, so that there remains a place for emancipatory politics. However, it is now joined by 'life politics', which are about how we should live individually and collectively in the context of a world that demands more and more conscious choices. Giddens also introduces the notion of 'generative' politics, as concerned with 'making things happen', by which he seems to envisage forms of linkage between grass-roots mobilisations and institutionalised politics.

Understandably enough, Giddens says relatively little about how the newly emerging radicalism might contribute to the reshaping of social life. In *Consequences of Modernity* it is made clear that there can be no 'guarantees' of the historical emergence of any particular future. However, it is still worthwhile to envisage possible futures ('utopian realism') in terms of detectable trends in actual social development. In that book, Giddens suggests that the contours of a possible future 'post-modern' society can be made out. In *Beyond Left and Right*, the preferred direction of change is spelled out at some length in the currently fashionable topic of welfare reform, and there is a more substantial engagement with the content of ecological politics. Though the formal commitment to a transcendence of capitalism remains, there is no further discussion of how this might be achieved, or how, short of such a transcendence, the other items in Giddens' wish list might be realised. There is, however, some further elaboration of the notion of a 'post-scarcity order'. Here, as in the previous work, we are told only that this will owe as much to ecology and philosophic conservatism as it does to socialism, but there remains little or no discussion of the institutional forms through which the production of material wealth and the meeting of subsistence needs might be organised. Since Giddens' extensive discussions of generative and life-political approaches to positive welfare, and his approach to ecological politics, depend rather crucially upon transformation of the currently dominant economic, cultural and military/political priorities of capital accumulation, this surely deserves some serious attention.

Role reversal and political exhaustion

This takes me on to critical evaluation of Giddens' argument. First, however, some points of agreement. Many of the changes in current social and political life identified by Giddens are matters of common experience. Giddens is, I think, right to argue that the rise to prominence of the questions posed by feminist, green and other social movements poses deep challenges to the inherited political traditions of Left and Right. In particular, a socialist politics that remained innocent of these questions would, indeed, deserve to be cast into the rubbish bin of history! He is also, I think, right to abandon what he calls 'providentialist' views of historical 'development', the notion that history has its own, generally beneficent, direction. However, such a providentialist 'meta-narrative' is not essential to socialism, nor, indeed, to Marxism, given Althusser's controversial reading of Marx as an anti-historicist. More centrally, I shall be arguing that, despite his disclaimers, Giddens himself remains committed to key elements of a linear, developmental view of history. Finally, in his attempt to specify the sorts of relationships and values which could take us beyond the human suffering and ecological destruction imposed by 'productivism' and consumerism in the context of global poverty, there is much in common between Giddens and the on-going dialogue within the green Left. Indeed, Giddens seems to draw (if rather selectively) from this dialogue, in ways which call into question his self-description as 'beyond Left and Right'.

Giddens softens up the reader in preparation for his 'exhaustion' argument by noting a paradoxical reversal of roles: conservatives as radicals, socialists as conservative defenders of the 'status quo'. Here, as in so much of Giddens' argument, the phenomenon is recognisable enough, but his characterisation of it is questionable. The reversal of roles is a consequence of profound shifts in power relations between Left and Right, and signals no significant shift in value perspectives, at least so far as the Left is concerned. The Left has never been uncritical in its relation to 'actually existing' welfare states, and indeed, has been an important source for the sorts of critique of bureaucracy, paternalism, exclusion and dependency in some modes of welfare 'delivery' upon which Giddens himself draws. Where the Left has defended the welfare state against neo-liberal attacks it has generally done so in the belief that it offers protections not otherwise available to the most vulnerable in society and because, for all its limitations, it embodies values of social integration and public responsibility that have always been at the core of socialist thinking (see Townsend 1995). It is certainly true that there are commonalities between those values and the traditional conservative reaction against capitalist commercialism, but that has been long recognised and is in no sense an indicator of 'reflexive modernisation'.

The radicalism of the neo-liberal Right is another matter. There clearly are important respects in which it departs from traditional conservative values. Its radical individualism, to the point of denial of the very existence of society, is at odds with traditional concerns with social integration on the basis of paternalism, deference and status-hierarchy. The same applies to its confident abandonment of moral concern for the disintegrative and polarising consequences of unrestrained market forces. However, the sense of paradox is lessened if we distinguish between the political Right and conservatism (the identification of the Left with socialism is, of course, equally tendentious, given the historical significance of the anarchist movements, as well as contemporary liberation movements which often orient themselves on the Left, without necessarily identifying with socialism). Pre-war Nazi and Fascist movements, as well as resurgent racist and authoritarian movements in our own time, are unmistakably of the Right, but clearly also are committed to radical social change. The emergence of the New Right, in the shape of 'Thatcherism', in the British Conservative Party can be seen as a largely contingent and localised phenomenon. So far, other European conservative parties, often Christian Democrat in their ideology, have been much less inclined to adopt the politics of the New Right. The intense conflict that was associated with the Thatcher 'revolution' within the United Kingdom Conservative Party is also an indicator of its essentially alien character in relation to the broad traditions of conservative politics.

However, the 'reversal' thesis is merely a prelude to Giddens' more thoroughgoing claim to have revealed 'plainly enough the exhaustion of the received political ideologies' (1994a: 10). What he calls 'old conservatism' can now be pronounced dead because the institutions it stood for have been swept away and no one now can seriously defend their resurrection. It has given way to three inheritors – philosophic conservatism, neo-conservatism and neo-liberalism. Of these, neo-liberalism collapses under its own contradictions, whilst neo-conservatism and philosophic conservatism, if drawn upon critically, do have a place as necessary components in the political response to reflexive modernisation. However, in linking philosophical conservatism with Wittgenstein, Rorty and others, it is arguable that Giddens empties political conservatism of almost all content. It becomes little more than the assertion of the importance in social life of tacit, unarticulated local knowledges as against the imposition of change based on abstractly rational formulas. It is true that Hayek deployed these ideas in his critique of centralised planning, but others (most effectively O'Neill 1998) have pointed out that the expansion of capitalist markets is similarly destructive of such localised tacit knowledges. What Giddens calls philosophic conservatism has no special affinity with political Right or Left. As for neo-conservatism, the attempt to revitalise institutions such as religion and the patriarchal family as focuses for meaning and solidarity, Giddens distinguishes the defence of such traditions 'in the traditional way' from dialogic justification of them in a cosmopolitan cultural context. The former is 'fundamentalism', and carries the danger of violence, whereas the latter may have a positive contribution to make.

In choosing to define the continuing legacy of old conservatism in terms of the valuing of 'tradition' (in the abstract) as against, for example, its commitment to patriarchy, patriotism, militarism, racial superiority, deference to authority, and homophobia, and in his apparent assumption that survival for movements of the Right requires rejection of the taint of Fascism,

Giddens seriously understates the continuing significance of reactionary and authoritarian political and social movements. These are lumped together in the residual category of 'fundamentalism' on the basis of their supposed defence of tradition 'in the traditional way', but are not acknowledged sociologically as conscious normative orientations that offer often persuasive diagnoses of contemporary sources of suffering and resentment. The strength of the Christian Right in the USA, the growth of popular support for the National Front in France, and the electoral strength of the reformed Fascists in Italy (see Magri 1995) are a few of the most obvious examples that suggest that the political Right is far from exhausted.

As for the dismissal of socialism, rather more needs to be said. In my discussion it will be important to keep in mind four distinct elements of the socialist legacy: the core value-commitments, the explanatory theory (of which the diverse traditions of modern Marxism are an important part, though by no means the whole), the collective agencies and strategies for realising socialist values and, finally, the institutional forms through which those values are to be realised. Giddens does not always recognise these distinctions and, where he does, he often defines socialism in an idiosyncratic and tendentious way. Internal diversity in the broad tradition of socialism is reduced to a dualism of revolutionary socialism, as exemplified by the former state centralist régimes, and reformist socialism, associated with western social democracy. The twentieth-century socialist critics of both, most notably the traditions of 'western Marxism' and the New Left (as well as the important traditions of associationist socialism – see Wainwright 1994, Hirst 1994, O'Neill 1998) remain largely unacknowledged, despite Giddens' evident dependence on many themes originating in those circles.

Giddens' conclusion that socialism is 'exhausted' and unviable rests on four main premises. First, globalisation undermines the conditions for macro-economic regulation of the neo-Keynesian type by nation states. Second, traditional class identities and forms of collective action are dissolved as a result of all three processes that define reflexive modernisation, so undermining the base of social support for reformist socialism, and rendering implausible the view of the working class as a historical agent. Third, the endemic crisis of the welfare state is such that socialist defences of it are both futile and wrong-headed. Finally, and perhaps central in importance for Giddens, reflexive modernisation is held to confirm Hayek's neo-liberal epistemic argument against central planning (see O'Brien and Penna 1998: Chapter 3). I offer some brief elaboration and criticism of each of these claims in turn.

Globalisation

Giddens' discussion of economic globalisation, like that of many other sociologists, is rather ill-defined and unconnected with any rigorous use of evidence. Recent work by Hirst and Thompson (1996) and others presents evidence to the effect that the proportion of GDP made up of internationally traded goods in the industrialised economies does not show a long-run secular increase, as globalisation theory predicts. On the contrary, the recent trend towards more international openness in these economies follows a prior phase of relative closure, and is now roughly equivalent to that prevailing at the end of the nineteenth century. This research also shows that capital flows, measured in value terms, take place overwhelmingly between the already industrialised countries and a small number of 'newly industrialising' ones. That is to say, most of the international mobility of capital takes place within and between the major trading blocs. This suggests that high levels of structural unemployment and labour market 'flexibility' in the industrialised countries cannot be easily attributed to transfer of jobs to low-wage economies. It also suggests that pressure to cut welfare benefits, limit tax burdens, deregulate labour markets and so on in the name of international competitiveness have to be understood more as ideology than as genuine recognitions of structural constraints imposed by globalisation.

Relatedly, the extent of economic openness should not be regarded, as Giddens seems to do, as an autonomous historical trend unconnected to the strategic policies of key nation states and economic interest groups. To the extent that the economies of the industrialised countries are more open to international competition and capital flows it is because their governments have designed international trading and investment régimes for that purpose. This can just as easily be seen as an exercise of national sovereignty as an abandonment of it. So far as governments of the New Right have been concerned, deregulation has been consistent with their economic ideology, and has greatly empowered them in their attempts to weaken labour movements and reduce state sponsorship of social provision *within* their national boundaries. As Lydia Morris (1997: 206) points out in a study of the bearing of 'globalisation' on migration: 'In so far as multi-state collaboration has been established, it is through intergovernmental meetings premised on national sovereignty'. In short, 'globalisation' is an important strategic weapon in the hands of politically and economically powerful groups and institutional complexes, not a secular tendency of a certain phase of 'modernity'.

The death of class

The topic of the continuing pertinence of class in sociological analysis has been hotly debated in recent years. Giddens' position seems to be that reflexively modernising societies remain capitalist in their economic organisation, and that capitalism is inseparable from the class division between capital and labour. High modernity remains class society. However, the disruption of local occupational communities, the growth of reflexivity in relation to masculinity and other traditional sources of class identity, the growing importance of consumer choice in the construction of self-identity and so on have severed the links between the occupancy of class positions, on the one hand, and the formation of class identities and class-based collective action, on the other. Again, the available evidence does not support these generalisations (see Lee and Turner 1996 for excellent statements of both sides in this argument). Empirical studies in the United Kingdom provide evidence for the continuing salience of class as a source of social identity. International studies of voting behaviour show little evidence for class de-alignment in political orientation. More informally, the language of class continues to pervade everyday interpretations of events, and surfaces regularly in media coverage of political debate: the much reviled 'fat cat' beneficiaries of the privatised utilities in the United Kingdom, the recurring refrain of the opposition between the 'haves' and the 'have nots' in the recent election campaign. There has, indeed, been a major reduction in both trade union membership, and overt industrial action. However, it is important not to over-interpret this phenomenon. It follows historically very high levels of industrial militancy in the 1970s, and a crucial defeat in the national dispute in the mining industry in 1984.

A period of relative quiescence of less than 15 years is a weak evidential basis from which to infer a long-run historical trend. Demoralisation consequent on the concerted use of state power to defeat the miners, the effects of neoliberal economic policies on industrial employment, deregulation of labour markets and successive waves of anti-union legislation provide alternative ways of explaining the observed decline in industrial militancy in the United Kingdom, rooted in relatively localised and historically contingent economic and political circumstances. A good deal of the decline in union membership can be explained in terms of shifts in the occupational structure away from traditionally unionised sectors, but it is important also to recognise that there remain some 7.2 million union members. In other European countries, the labour movement continues to show very considerable mobilising power, as evidenced in recent campaigns in Germany, Italy, France and elsewhere against proposed cuts in social spending in preparation for European Monetary Union. In short, the labour movement retains a very extensive social basis, and has very considerable potential mobilising power.

What is clear, however, is that in the United States since the 1930s, in the United Kingdom currently, and possibly in some other European countries, the coalitions which made neo-corporatist policy making unavoidable have broken down. Whilst labour movements remain very powerful, it is clear that governments determined to do so can govern without their tacit consent. However, in strategic terms, this is a situation not well characterised as signalling the demise of class politics. For one thing, it is arguable that coalitions of the Right and centre Right continue, now in a more overt and often ruthless way than before, to pursue the class politics of capital. For another, the continuing presence of strong working-class identities and organising potentials together with an increasingly diverse social movements sector suggests the alternative possibility of a new coalition of the Left. There is, again, nothing new in this. Where socialists have gained state or governmental power in the twentieth century, they have always done so on the basis of coalitions between industrial workers and other social groups, such as poorer peasants and rural labourers in Third World countries, or public sector white-collar workers and liberal professionals in the industrialised countries. There remain, of course, serious questions about the feasibility and character of any proposed new coalition of the Left, though detailed discussion of these is beyond the scope of this chapter (see Red–Green Study Group 1995 and Benton 1997).

The crisis of welfare

The third source for Giddens' 'exhaustion' argument in relation to socialism is the crisis in the welfare state. For Giddens, the main reason for this crisis is not the commonly acknowledged fiscal one but, rather, his claim that the problems the welfare state was designed to solve have now, under 'reflexive modernisation', radically changed their character. Giddens argues that the post-war settlement assumed lifelong male waged employment, stable nuclear families, in which the wife and mother was mainly engaged in domestic labour, sustained out of the male 'family wage', and broadly predictable lifetime health risks. Globalisation makes for 'flexible labour markets', whilst detraditionalisation leads to the dissolution of old-fashioned gender divisions and family forms. At the same time the epoch of 'manufactured' risk, and, especially, the increasing significance of 'high consequence' risks due to new industrial technologies, exceeds the sort of actuarial calculation upon which health service provision has been based. Giddens adds to this diagnosis of crisis a series of critical comments to the effect that welfare states have not generally succeeded in their redistributive aims, and that they have tended to render recipients of benefits passive and dependent.

I do not have space for a full engagement with Giddens' views on the proclaimed crisis of welfare, but some brief comments are necessary. If Giddens is to use this as part of his case for the exhaustion of socialism, he first has to establish an identification of modern welfare state institutions with socialism. It is true that large measures of welfare reform and extension in the United Kingdom were carried through by post-war Labour governments, but they built upon prior liberal thinking and practice. Moreover, significant elements in social democratic and socialist programmes for the extension of welfare during that period, such as fully socialised health and educational provision, as well as programmes of preventive medicine, environmental health and health education were abandoned or compromised in the face of resistance from powerful vested interests. It is arguable that many of the perceived problems in some areas of current welfare provision derive from failures to carry through socialist proposals in those areas, from subsequent distortions in modes of provision imposed by those same vested interests (most obviously and devastatingly, by the pharmaceuticals industry), and by governments fundamentally opposed to residual socialist aspects of welfare provision (such as universal benefits).

Most obviously, the continued existence of privileged private provision in both health and education has enabled better resourced and more influential groups in society to by-pass state provided services (an aspect of the continuing pertinence of class division that seems to have escaped Giddens' attention). This has arguably deprived the latter of powerful pressures for resources and standards that would have been forthcoming in fully socialised systems. In addition, given the public provision of education, training, and many material facilities that go on to be utilised by the private sector, it is arguable that the latter is directly subsidised by the former in a way that makes a significant contribution to the financial dimension of the perceived crisis. Finally, to the extent that the welfare crisis is linked to tax-resistance on the part of higher income earners, this may also be rooted in the availability to them of private-sector options. Nevertheless, for all the specific complaints made about treatment in the National Health Service in the United Kingdom, there remains a public consensus over its unmistakably socialist central normative principle, namely, treatment on the basis of need, and independent of ability to pay. So powerful is public commitment to this principle that even the most vociferous advocates of neo-liberal economics never dared to confess its abandonment in public (though in practice, of course, the principle has been subject to a long-run process of erosion since the establishment of the National Health Service). The much-feared tax-payers revolt, and the unquestioning acceptance that 'the costs of public health services outstrip the capabilities of governments to pay for them' (Giddens 1994a: 225), fail to take account of the immensely greater cost of privatised systems, their manifest injustice, and the evidence that many western publics are prepared to bear the tax burden necessary for improved public services such as health and education. Not only do attitude surveys bear this out (see Jowell 1997) but, for example, the most dramatic electoral gains were made in the United Kingdom election of 1997 by a Liberal Democratic Party committed to increased taxation to fund public services.

Two further processes that Giddens discusses at length in his exploration of 'reflexive modernisation' both offer strong confirmation of the continuing pertinence of the socialist commitment to inclusive public provision. First, the 'high consequence risks' that Giddens takes to be characteristic of this historical phase are not only undelimitable in space and time, but also in their incidence across social and economic divisions. If, as Giddens (and Ulrich Beck, his mentor on this issue – see Beck 1992) claims, the rich and powerful are no less at risk from nuclear accidents, global climate change and so on than are the poor and weak, then the rich and powerful themselves have an interest in the pooling of risk and the costs of responding to it that is entailed by universal public provision. The second case is the Human Genome Project (see Chapter 5), which Giddens discusses at some length. His apparently uncritical acceptance of the genetic determinism underpinning the absurd claims being made on behalf of this project is hard to square with Giddens' view of the contemporary self as an intentional product, such that even the body is 'no longer "nature"' (1994a: 224). However, even if we consider the implications of widespread acceptance of the determinist ideology (see, for a thoroughgoing critique of genetic determinism, Rose 1997) that one's life expectancy and vulnerability to specific diseases will soon become predictable with 'scientific' precision, then this becomes a new basis for discrimination in employment, and in access to private insurance. Again, a fully socialised pooling of risk is the only reliable defence against the opening up of a massive new dimension of injustice, exclusion and social fragmentation in late capitalist societies.

Tacit knowledge

The fourth prop to Giddens' claim that socialism is 'exhausted' is his acceptance of Hayek's epistemic argument for the unworkability of centralised economic planning. Giddens' use of this argument, however, has an oddly contradictory twist. We are told that under conditions of 'simple modernisation' with relatively stable and tradition-bound consumer preferences, centralised planning, such as characterised the Soviet Union, can be successful. However, these are precisely the conditions under which consumer choices are most bound by the unarticulated 'tacit' knowledges which Hayek thought made centralised planning impossible. For Giddens, paradoxically, centralised planning comes under pressure as consumers become more self-conscious and 'reflexive' about their preferences, that is, as the latter become less governed by unarticulated 'tacit' knowledge. Suitable use of new communications and information technologies, which so excite Giddens' sociological imagination in other respects, could surely, under conditions of enhanced social reflexivity, replace the supposedly indispensable 'signalling' function of markets?

But, more seriously, this view of markets, endorsed by Giddens, is a travesty of the workings of contemporary capitalism. The supposed role of consumer choice presupposes a methodological individualist and voluntarist model of consumers, whilst the account of the responsiveness of firms to the vagaries of consumer preferences appears innocent of differentials of power and knowledge between consumers and the often highly concentrated large-scale producers and distributers in modern capitalism. Moreover, the extent of involvement of national and local states, as well as international regulative organisations such as the North American Free Trade Association, the European Union and the World Trade Organisation in shaping the boundary conditions under which market exchanges and capital flows are conducted, largely beyond the reach of any democratic accountability, and overwhelmingly in the interests of big capital, render the assumptions underlying the epistemic defence of the market utterly untenable. The Giddens/Hayek defence of the market has about as much relevance to contemporary capitalism as did the Webbs' eulogy of the Soviet Union to the then-prevailing Stalinist autocracy.

However, this is not the fundamental objection to Giddens' reliance on Hayek's supposed refutation of socialism. Still more serious is that he, like Hayek, identifies socialism with a 'cybernetic' system of centralised economic control. This entirely leaves out of account long and diverse traditions of democratic, decentralist and associationist socialist thought that have both opposed Soviet-style régimes, and proposed alternative visions of socialised economic life. Giddens himself quotes Kautsky (the leading Marxist thinker of the Second International (1889–1914)) as suggesting that 'The most manifold forms of property in the means of production – national, municipal, cooperatives of consumption and production, and private – can exist beside each other in a socialist society' (Giddens 1994a: 58). That in fact this did not happen in the Soviet Union under the Bolshevik monopoly of state power seems to be understood by Giddens as a refutation of Kautsky, but it could only be taken as such if one supposed that things could not have been otherwise in the Soviet Union, and could not have been otherwise in any other attempt at socialist construction. But the historical determinism implicit in such a view is not argued for, and nor does it fit well with the views Giddens expresses elsewhere about human agency and historical openness. Where Giddens does come to a consideration of socialist attempts to think beyond the simple opposition of market and plan, he quickly concludes: 'There is no Third Way of this sort, and with this thought the history of socialism as the avant-garde of political theory comes to a close' (1994a: 69).

Nowhere in this discussion does Giddens face the implications of his wholescale dismissal of socialist economic thinking for the central question of his own project. If the key problems we face derive from a 'run-away world', a 'juggernaut', running out of control, then this is only his recognition, less precisely expressed, less adequately theorised, of what socialists have seen as the consequence of anarchic and unaccountable forces of capital accumulation on a global scale. Giddens' discussion side-steps the immense strategic problems that these vast concentrations of economic and political power pose for his own vision of a 'post-scarcity order' no less than for a socialist future. As Michael Rustin succinctly puts it:

> This post-socialist analysis, in both the theoretical form it has been given by Giddens and in its marketed version as New Labour image-making, has a quality of 'turning a blind eye' to problems and realities to which no one currently has a solution. The most important of these remains the control and ownership of capital, and its embodiment in large-scale private property. (Rustin 1995: 23)

Tradition and modernity

My defence of the continuing purchase of socialist traditions of thought and practice calls into question the theoretical frame through which Giddens periodises the present phase of history, and thinks about its possible futures. As we have seen, despite his own disclaimers, Giddens advocates a 'stages' view of history (see also Morris 1997: 193, Rustin 1995) in which an institutional complex that he calls 'modernity' is everywhere displacing predecessor forms, which he designates 'traditional' society. Modernity itself begins 'simple', but under its own developmental tendencies becomes 'reflexive'. Reflexive modernisation erodes boundaries between discrete 'societies' under the pervasive influence of 'globalisation', which is itself a force for 'de-traditionalisation' and intensified 'reflexivity'. Occasionally Giddens claims to foresee (1990a: 3) the outlines of a future 'post-modern' society, but this is not to be identified with the views of those who think the present should be so described.

Giddens' commitment to a linear-developmental view of historical change has many parallels with conventional 'development' thinking (see Woodiwiss 1997), as well as with some versions of historical materialism (elsewhere criticised by Giddens). One feature shared with these other forms of 'social evolutionism' is a tendency to see western societies as the source of a historical dynamic of world-historical significance. For Giddens, the global spread of the influence of western 'modernity' remains unexplained, except that we are told it is made possible by global communications. Whatever its limitations, historical materialism, in its classic forms, at least offered an explanation in terms of the requirements of capital accumulation, imperial conquest and subsequent patterns of economic dependency between centre and periphery. The continuing history of bloody struggle, exploitation, oppression and war that have characterised this process disappear, in Giddens' account, in favour of a rather anodyne account of the 'peculiar dynamism' of modernity. This, we are told, derives from a separation of time and space, and the 'disembedding of social systems'. But is this more than an obscurely abstract euphemism? Is it supposed to carry explanatory power? If so, then it needs far more theoretical elaboration and empirical substantiation than it has so far been given.

Arguably, another consequence of Giddens' conceptual privileging of specifically western institutional forms is the astonishingly reductionist lumping together of all non-western as well as 'pre-modern' social forms into the single category 'traditional orders'. This has several damaging consequences for his understanding of the current period and the political possibilities inherent in it. One of these is the very unsatisfactory conceptualisation of 'tradition' itself. Giddens recognises, despite his 'discontinuist' emphasis on the contrast between the traditional and the modern, that 'modern' societies also have their traditions. So the contrast becomes more to do with the way traditions are defended: 'in the traditional way', or, under conditions of modernity, especially 'high' modernity, through dialogue with other, rival traditions. What it is to defend tradition in the traditional way is never fully spelled out (nor is the related notion of a defence of 'nature in the natural way'!). Presumably Giddens has in mind something like the Weberian category of traditional action as unreflective, and habitual repetition. This is, however, a highly questionable way of understanding traditions and how people relate to them as providers of social identities, resources for social understanding, and normative guidance. It understates the extent of internal diversity, historical fluidity, adaptability and self-reflection endemic in all traditions, and it presupposes a historically unsupported view of the 'pre-modern' west as culturally homogeneous and cut off from engagement with non-western thought and traditions.

There is also a link between this sociologically dubious idea of tradition 'defended in the traditional way' and his tendency to demonise what he calls 'fundamentalisms' in the current period of reflexive modernisation. There is a real danger here of uncritical acceptance of current media stereotyping of Islamic and other non-western sources of resistance to the globalisation of western visions of 'modernity'. Whatever normative stand one takes in relation to such movements it is dangerously mistaken to see them as unreflective and mindless resistances to an inevitable cosmopolitanism. Relatedly, too, Giddens' tendency to assimilate all non-western social and cultural forms into the catch-all category of the 'traditional', combined with his assumption that the dynamic of historical 'development' comes from the West, leads him to an unquestioning privileging of western social movements as the key to a future 'beyond Left and Right'. There is no serious sociological attention to the immensely diverse class, ethnic and cultural sources for movements and alliances that have emerged, and continue to emerge, in non-western societies in response to the penetrations and transformations wrought by globalising capitalism and consumerism. The Indian farmers' movement, the Himalayan 'chipko' movement, transnational coalitions of indigenous peoples, rural social movements in South America, the colossal experiment in greening agriculture and medicine in Cuba, and so on, may hold keys to prospects for transformed social and ecological relationships that cut across and make nonsense of the simple opposition between 'tradition' and 'modernity'.

But there are problems, also, with the account Giddens offers of 'modernity' itself. The label implies the identification of a specific institutional complex in terms of a historical chronology, and so betrays his unacknowledged social evolutionism. For Giddens, as for other contemporary sociologists, 'modernity' has become a convenient term to replace 'capitalism', tainted by its association with an unfashionable political orientation, and with a discredited 'economic determinism'. The wish to avoid economic determinism is understandable enough, but there may be more than one way of doing it, and it is arguable that the theoretical baggage that comes along with adopting the evolutionist 'tradition/modernity' couple represents an even more serious danger. As we have seen, Giddens characterises modernity in terms of four 'institutional dimensions', each with its endemic oppositional social movement: movements for democracy and civil liberties in response to political/administrative system, the peace movement in response to the military, the labour movement in response to capitalist economic organisation, and the green movement as a response to the industrial mode of relationship to nature. It is acknowledged that the feminist movement does not fit the schema, cutting, as it does, across each of the institutional dimensions.

There are some shifts of emphasis between *Consequences of Modernity* (1990a) and *Beyond Left and Right* (1994a) such as a notable down-playing of the significance of the labour movement, and a partial correction of the surprising omission in the earlier work of the institutional complexes through which social and cultural reproduction takes place. In the discussion of the crisis of welfare in *Beyond Left and Right* Giddens does discuss changing family forms and relations, as well as health care provision, but there remains little or no discussion of educational institutions or communications media as a distinct 'institutional dimension' (notwithstanding his mention of the latter in relation to 'globalisation'). However, Giddens continues in the later work to identify social movements in relation to specific institutional dimensions, and offers no theorisation at all of the structural or causal connections *between* 'dimensions'.

Given, also, Giddens' interest in 'risk, danger and trust', it is not surprising to find discussion, much of it loosely following the work of Ulrich Beck, of risk and hazard in 'high modernity'. Like Beck, Giddens contrasts 'traditional' with 'modern' societies with respect to the hazards to which they are vulnerable. Formerly, risks, such as flooding, epidemics, climatic disasters and so on, were 'external', naturally caused. With industrialisation and 'simple modernisation' the risks and hazards to which we are vulnerable are increasingly generated by society itself, and so can be referred to as 'manufactured'. However, with the onset of 'reflexive modernisation', these risks become extended in their spatial, temporal and social scope. They potentially affect everyone, and may be literally incalculable. This newly emergent category of what Giddens calls 'high consequence risks' arises in the 'risk environments' provided by the four institutional dimensions of 'modernity': global environmental problems arising from industrialism, global poverty from capitalist economic organisation, the threat posed by weapons of mass destruction in the domain of control over violence and the denial of democratic rights in the domain of administrative power and surveillance. As we have seen, the social movements (or, rather, the more benign ones whose significance Giddens acknowledges) are also linked, as forms of resistance, to each of these institutional dimensions and the 'manufactured' risks emergent within it.

Giddens and the greens

In Giddens' view, the pervasiveness of high consequence risks, and the movements that emerge in response to them are manifestations of growing reflexivity, entailing both a negative and a positive moment. As well as opposing ecological destruction, for example, the green movement is part of a process of reposing the existential and normative issues repressed by 'simple' modernity: centrally, 'How shall we live'? Hence, Giddens' characterisation of an emergent 'life politics', complementary to rather than replacing the older emancipatory politics (which, it is conceded, still has work to do). However, as we shall see, this does not imply a straightforward endorsement of either the green or other new social movements.

Giddens devotes a chapter to his critical engagement with green theory, noting that green politics has no special affinity with Right or Left, and so conforms to the theme of his book. However, the greens are as much an expression of social problems as a solution to them. He accepts the green distinction between 'environmentalism', which seeks to solve environmental problems within the existing framework by the further development of science and technology, and 'ecology', which, in Giddens' account, tries to address practical and ethical issues 'in terms of natural criteria or the recovery of lost natural harmonies' (1994a: 207). The latter perspective is commended for raising ethical questions, but criticised for its 'incoherences' and 'lapses' (1994a: 208). These include a mistaken tendency to identify biological with cultural diversity, to idealise the ecological friendliness of societies with 'a low level of technological development', to favour small, rural communities at the expense of the positive values Giddens associates with urbanism, and to call for decentralisation when clearly strong measures to control environmental destruction are needed. These criticisms do tell against particular writers but, as Giddens himself notes, there is enormous diversity in green politics and social thought. Each of these criticisms has its counterpart within the green debate itself.

There are, however, two further criticisms that require more detailed comment. The first concerns the tendency of many radical greens to see their analysis and value perspective as requiring some sort of revolutionary overthrow of existing institutions in favour of a radically different order. He quotes Jonathan Porritt and David Winner: '. . . a non-violent revolution to overthrow our whole polluting, plundering and materialistic industrial society and, in its place, to create a new economic and social order which will allow human beings to live in harmony with the planet' (in Giddens 1994a: 209). Giddens thinks this is contradictory because it undermines green emphases on continuity and inter-connectedness. Greens would reply that the thesis of inter-connectedness is precisely why a radical change of direction in human society is required. The theme of continuity is Giddens' own inclusion, motivated by his wish to link ecological politics with strands of traditional conservatism. But green commitment to qualitative social change is also open to criticism because of its implausibility. Giddens takes it to be self-evident that such a radical project is not 'remotely feasible', but gives us no general account of the socio-political reasoning behind his judgment. Indeed, if reflexivity and detraditionalisation are as all-pervasive as his argument suggests, there would appear to be no outer limits to the horizon of historical possibility. Moreover, it is arguable that Giddens' own rather sketchy account of a 'post-scarcity order' presupposes equally profound socio-economic and cultural changes, but lacks the realistic acknowledgment that runs through much green thinking of the sheer power of the forces opposed to any such radical change.

A more serious difficulty for Giddens' theoretical framing of the green movement is the clear implication, even in the account that he gives of it, that it is far more than a form of resistance to industrialism, considered as one institutional 'dimension' of 'high modernity'. Virtually all green social and political thought works with some sense of the *interconnectedness* of the processes Giddens' social theory holds apart: the direction of scientific and technical innovation; capitalist economic growth-dynamics and the pursuit of profit at the expense of both humanity and nature; the deployment of surveillance; direct violence and other forms of coercion on the part of states, as well as private organisations against grass-roots movements; the global promotion of consumer culture; and, in many accounts, gender and racial domination. It is precisely this sense of interconnectedness that leads radical greens to see a need for the kind of deep-rooted change that Giddens believes to be unfeasible. The main point, here, is that green thought and practice cannot be confined to the 'single issue', single dimensional role to which Giddens' theorisation of the social movements consigns it. Radical green movements, like many labour-movement organisations, feminists and others, are 'totalising' movements, in the sense that they are able to utilise direct experience, cognitive and cultural resources that necessarily exceed the boundaries of any one institutional dimension.

One example here is the recent and continuing campaign against live animal exports. Interviews conducted with protesters (see Benton and Redfearn 1996) at the port of Brightlingsea revealed that participation in direct action for the first time had made possible significant shifts of self-identity which in turn, in some cases, had led to revaluation of previously held political values and alignments. One Conservative voter, for example, had been led by his disgust at media misrepresentation of his own protest action to wonder whether he had been right to believe 'what they said about the miners as "rent-a-mob"'. As this suggests, protesters also became adept at critical evaluation of media representation in ways that carried over into other areas beyond their own campaign. Above all, however, it was escalation of police control methods that transformed protesters' wider social and political outlooks. In the words of one elderly campaigner: 'I feel they have taken away all our rights that we fought for in 1939. The right for us to be free: free speech, free to do what we like, but we haven't been free to walk on the road.' Another newcomer to protest action said: 'And you start questioning more and more things, 'Where's democracy?', and so, now ... well, it's made us much more politically aware, I think, as a result ... I think all sorts of people are going to be questioning all sorts of things' (Benton and Redfearn 1996: 56). Some protesters were, indeed, initially motivated by a desire to defend civil liberties against police action, rather than by concern about the treatment of farm animals. But this issue itself had led many protesters over the long months of the campaign into a much deeper understanding of the linkages of agricultural policy, dietary imbalance, food processing and marketing, the rural environment and so on with large-scale maltreatment of animals.

All of this suggests that there is, in Giddens' account of the social movements, an under-theorisation of the dynamic cultural and cognitive processes through which they are formed, maintained and transformed. This is, indeed, something which his own emphasis on reflexivity ought to have suggested to him. Moreover, once we recognise the open and dynamic character of these cultural processes, it becomes possible to approach a sociological understanding of the possibility of realignments, coalitions and fusions as between different movements and campaigns. A very striking case is the coalition recently formed in the UK with the struggle of more than three hundred sacked Liverpool dockers as its focus. Roads protesters, trades unionists, civil liberties activists, anti-racist campaigners and radical environmentalists joined subsequent protest action. Similar coalitions have also formed around civil liberties and other issues. Giddens' sequestering of diverse movements from one another, itself a consequence of his sequestration of the four 'institutional dimensions of modernity', arguably renders invisible the processes that make such coalitions possible, and so cuts him off from an analysis of their political character and potential. In particular, such an analysis would expose the limitations of his approach to the question of the continuing relevance of the Left/Right division in politics. For example, the 'Reclaim the Future' alliance of radical environmentalists in support of the dockers consider that all actions they are engaged in take place in the context of a social system dominated by the drive for profit against the needs of people and the environment, whether there be an anti-roads campaign, an industrial dispute or an animal rights campaign. Such analyses as these emerge from the dynamics of processes of social struggle, reflection upon that practice and dialogue about it on the part of activists. In this particular case, we have a statement that endorses the core propositions of the 'traditional' Left, but transforms much of its strategic vision (for example, in its implicit denial of the privileged role of any single one of diverse sources and sites of activism).

A further criticism Giddens makes of ecological politics concerns its tendency to see solutions to ecological crisis in terms of a 'return to the security of nature' (Giddens 1994a: 220). He endorses Beck's comment that:

Nature is not nature, but rather a concept, norm, memory, utopia, counter-image. Today, more than ever, now that it no longer exists, nature is being rediscovered, pampered. The ecology movement has fallen prey to a naturalistic misapprehension of itself . . . 'Nature' is a kind of anchor by whose means the ship of civilisation . . . conjures up, cultivates, its contrary: dry land, the harbour, the approaching reef. (Giddens 1994a: 206)

That nature is now thoroughly socialised, that the ecological crisis has been brought about by 'the dissolution of nature', and indeed, that nature no longer exists, are recurrent themes in Giddens' commentary on ecological politics. It seems clear that if nature no longer exists, then a return to it must be, as Giddens points out 'not really feasible'. However, alongside these irrealist remarks about nature, we find acknowledgments that humans in the last few decades have had a much larger impact on the natural world than ever before (1994a: 203), that there are boundaries to human control of nature (1994a: 211), that ecological crisis 'is a material expression of the limits of modernity' (1994a: 227), and so on. Nature has things done to it by us, sets limits to what we can do, and requires protection, but no longer exists!

Giddens' confusion here mirrors the widespread tendency to use the term 'nature' in a wide variety of different and often conflicting senses (see Soper 1995). This confusion is amplified in his case by his failure to 'settle accounts' with the unsatisfactory state of sociological theory in this area. Sometimes this takes the form of unacknowledged shifts between talk of cultural representations of nature to claims about nature itself, and *vice versa*. Elsewhere, appeal is made to an inherited nature/society dualism, as in the opposition between 'external' risks (effects of nature) and 'manufactured' risks (effects of society). At one point, interestingly, Giddens points to the difficulty of disentangling what is natural from what is social, and speaks of 'ecosocial systems' (1994a: 210). However, he does not seem to recognise that such a notion calls into question the basic concepts of his own analytical framework. Such a view, far from insisting on the end of nature as 'given independently of human intervention' (1994a: 206), would, on the contrary, have to theorise human social practices as always conditioned, enabled and mediated by pre-given natural causal laws, mechanisms, substances and processes. The idea that nature no longer exists is an absurdly superficial empiricist identification of 'nature' with some primeval Eden. Since our hominid ancestors first took to their hind legs they have been restlessly transforming their environments, but only in accordance with nature's laws, and in virtue of their practical apprehension of the properties of the living organisms, objects and substances they found around them: organisms, processes, laws, substances and properties which long predated them and us.

When greens call for smaller-scale, ecologically benign technologies, for a mode of human social life that makes minimal demands on 'planetary life support systems' and makes room for the flourishing of other species, they are not naively calling for a return to a past 'pristine' nature. On the contrary, they are drawing upon a much richer and inclusive concept of interconnected complexity and dynamic process in nature. Giddens is trapped by his own unacknowledged linear-progressive view of history into seeing political visions as pointing only either forward or backward: either forward with the 'modernist' project of 'mastery of nature' (but, now, conducted in a 'caring' way), or (impossibly) backwards to (no longer existing) nature. That greens might be struggling to formulate *qualitatively different* visions of a possible future for human social life, conducted in a spirit of respect for the integrity of both our pre-given and humanly created contexts of life, cannot be fitted into this frame.

Risk, modernity and capitalism

I have discussed at some length two of Giddens' criticisms of green politics because I think they reveal significant limitations in his overall theoretical approach. First, his reductive association of particular social movements with abstractly segregated 'institutional dimensions' of 'modernity' involves not only a failure to recognise the breadth of analysis and vision developed by at least some movements, but also a failure to understand the causality of the *conditions* about which such movements make 'social problem claims'. For example, to see 'manufactured uncertainty' and high-consequence risks as consequences of modern industry and technology, understood as something separate from capitalist economic organisation, is seemingly wilfully to ignore the specifically capitalist direction of scientific and technical innovation and industrial application. In recent decades there has been a strong tendency for research in such ecologically significant fields as gene manipulation, pharmaceuticals, and agro-chemicals to be transferred from public sector to corporate Research and Development laboratories. What remains of public sector research is also overwhelmingly financed by private capital, or allocated according to commercial criteria (Webster 1991, especially Chapters 4 and 5). Also in these areas there is clear evidence of integration between the relevant government departments, regulatory bodies and business interests, often obscured from the public view, and insulated from democratic accountability (see, for example, O'Brien and Penna 1997, Shove 1995, Goodman and Redclift 1991, Shaoul 1997, Irwin 1995). This suggests that a non-reductive conceptualisation of the structural connections and patterned interactions between commercial strategies, scientific and technical innovation and application, and state institutions is required if we are to analyse the complex causality of 'high consequence risks'. This is precisely what is obstructed by Giddens' theorisation of 'modernity' in terms of discrete 'institutional dimensions'.

The case of the epidemic of BSE, and its hypothesised link with new variant CJD in humans, serves as an illustration here. In the late 1960s commercial pressures in the food production and processing industries led to the feeding of cattle with high-protein compounds derived from animal waste. In 1979, UK government-appointed experts warned that this presented a danger to human health, through the possible transfer of pathogens between species. Not only was this warning ignored, but the wider climate of deregulation, demanded by powerful business lobbies, and favoured by neo-liberal ideology, enabled the meat rendering companies to introduce new, cheaper technologies which processed animal feed at lower temperatures. This, of course, increased the risk of transfer of pathogens between species in the artificial food-chain. Since 1986 some 170,000 cases of BSE have been confirmed, amid repeated government assurances as to the safety of 'British beef'. Belatedly, the government introduced a series of measures designed to stop the spread of BSE among cattle and to exclude suspect offal from the human food supply. These measures were directed at the slaughterhouses, but were not enforced. Meanwhile the commercially powerful and highly monopolised meat rendering companies maintained pressures on through-put in the slaughterhouses that made compliance with government requirements extremely impractical. A subsequent report (Meat Hygiene Service 1996) exposed the fact that 50 per cent of slaughterhouses were failing to comply. The government's own Ministry of Agriculture, Fisheries and Food, whose responsibility it was to ensure that regulations were enforced, also stated to an investigation of the meat rendering industry by the Monopolies and Mergers Commission that it was 'the sponsoring department' for the industry (see Shaoul 1997). Repeated reassurances from government relied on the opinions of government-selected committees of experts, one of whom stated that a reluctant consensus was arrived at on the available evidence, effectively an informed guess, which had huge economic consequences one way or the other. As is well known, dissenting scientists suffered discrimination and vilification. The eventual announcement on 20 March 1996 that there was a likelihood of a connection between new variant CJD and BSE in cattle was followed by intense efforts to frame a major issue of public health as a matter, first, of the survival of the British beef industry, and subsequently, of resistance to a German-inspired European conspiracy against the British economy: it became a patriotic duty to eat beef!

As against Giddens' abstract separation of institutional dimensions, any adequate social scientific treatment of this complex story would involve analysing institutional linkages between government, its regulatory and advisory bodies, specific ministries, the public funding of scientific research, the political economy of the agricultural, slaughtering, meat rendering and food retail industries, and technical change in those industries, together with the modes of representation of all this in the media. Moreover, the immense causal importance of the shifting structures and priorities of the big agribusiness and related companies in shaping government policy and practice, the deliberations of committees of 'experts', and media representations is unavoidable. To represent episodes such as this as mere symptoms of a developmental phase of 'modernity', in which technological advance generates high-consequence risks, is deeply mystifying. It evades the responsibility to identify the complex and highly specific causal nexuses at work in each case, and avoids confrontation with the equally specific power relations and entrenched interests at work.

A further limitation in Giddens' overall theoretical position is brought out by his confused and contradictory remarks about nature, and the feasibility of 'returning' to it. Giddens shares with the most influential traditions in social theory a dualistic ontology in which society and nature are counterposed (but which readily gives way to a 'social constructionist' eclipse of the independent existence of the latter – see Benton 1994). This has been very important in enabling social scientists to assert the specificity of their disciplines and so resist biological determinist approaches to social life. However, as I have shown elsewhere (Benton 1991, 1993), this ontology becomes deeply problematic when sociologists address issues that inescapably cut across the nature/society boundary – such as health, environmental degradation, and gender divisions. One response to the problems that emerge here is to rely on a division of labour between the natural and social sciences, and to avoid comment on those aspects that can be assigned to the expertise of natural scientists. However, the natural sciences are themselves part of the subject-matter of the social sciences, and this tempts many sociologists into a 'social constructionist' extension of their disciplinary boundaries. Nature becomes a topic for social scientific investigation, but in the displaced form of a study of forms of *representation* of 'nature'. As we have seen, Giddens' discussion oscillates between these two strategies.

Though the social constructionist strategy is often justified as the adoption of an appropriate scepticism in the face of rival accounts of causal mechanisms, processes and so on in nature, it has the effect of an *a priori* exclusion from analysis of the part played by such mechanisms and processes in the conduct of social life. If natural processes and mechanisms are causally significant in the production of social outcomes, then to make a methodological principle out of ignoring them is bound to lead to distortions, which are, moreover, not open to empirical correction. A preferable alternative, I think, is a critical realist one that recognises the role played by ecological conditions, physiological processes and so on in social life, but adopts descriptions of them that are openly provisional and liable to be abandoned in the face of evidence. This approach is implicit in the above account of the BSE episode: the narrative makes no sense unless we are committed to the view that large numbers of cattle did contract a fatal disease, that the disease vector was an organic pathogen, that infection could be transmitted through compound feeds, that humans are susceptible to the pathogen or one of its mutant forms, that the physical operations (quite independently of their social meanings) carried out in slaughterhouses make a difference to the entry of the pathogen into human diets and so on.

It follows from this that the implicitly historical materialist account of the episode sketched above in contrast to Giddens' version of modernisation theory needs to be 'rendered' still more materialist: we need to recognise not just the causal linkages between state institutions, capitalist firms, media representations and technical change, but also the linkages between all of them and their physical, organic, and so on contexts, conditions and media. Moreover, we need to do this in a way that avoids reduction of any of these inter-connected conditions and processes to the others. Both sociological and biological reductionism involve distortion and misrepresentation of these complex interactive processes. These considerations are prompted by both feminist and green social theorising, but do not necessarily entail commitment to those normative standpoints. However, it is already clear that such an approach does not involve the 'naturalistic misapprehension of itself' of which the ecology movement stands accused. On the contrary, the ecological perspective brings into focus the intellectual limitations of (unstable) social constructionism in relation to nature.

Conclusion

I have tried to show that the reversal of roles between Left and Right is less paradoxical than it appears to be in Giddens account. Then, by way of a critical discussion of Giddens' treatment of globalisation, class, the crisis of welfare and the epistemic critique of socialism, I have attempted to show the continuing relevance of both the explanatory and the normative heritage of the Left, especially the socialist Left. The argument then opened out into a more general critique of the theoretical framework of 'reflexive modernisation', which grounds Giddens' projected radicalism 'beyond Left and Right'. In the course of this critique I have indicated, without fully specifying it, an alternative theoretical framework, drawing upon a critically reworked historical materialism, feminist and green social theory, and critical realist theory of knowledge.

In its emphasis on the causal role of the dynamics of capital accumulation, and of state policies favouring the class interests of capital, this theoretical framework is unmistakably drawn from the intellectual resources of the Left, but critically revised and renewed in the light of the issues posed by 'new' social movements. To consider whether this critical renewal of the analytical and explanatory resources of the Left should, as Giddens might argue, be understood as itself a move beyond Left and Right, it will be necessary to turn very briefly to a more explicit discussion of normative issues. In part what is at issue turns on whether the feminist and green social movements upon whose theorising and practice my arguments have drawn are themselves seen as aligned with the Left. There is, I think, growing evidence of a transnational re-alignment between social movements, in which unregulated and globalising capitalism is seen as the principal cause of escalating economic polarisation within and between countries and regions of the world, actual and impending ecological destruction, and growing social fragmentation. This very basic orientation is now shared by many socialists and trade union activists, radical ecologists, ecological feminists, civil liberties campaigners and many others. The normative orientations of these movements are overwhelmingly anti-capitalist, they prioritise need over profit, and favour social solidarity, equality and the sharing of social wealth. In these respects the normative commitments of the Left remain very much alive.

However, there are distinctive values – such as respect for the intrinsic value of non-human nature, and positive valuation of diversity (as distinct from mere toleration of it) – which constitute significant new moral insights introduced by the social movements. These were not part of the 'mainstream' of past socialist practice, so do they displace the old Left/Right opposition? In my view they are new cultural orientations, indispensable to the renewal of the Left. It is self-evident that such new value orientations could not be reconciled with the continuing traditions of homophobic, racist and patriarchal conservatism on the Right. Neither, given the sort of analysis of our current situation sketched above, could respect for diversity and the valuing of non-human nature align itself with the currently prevailing political consensus around permanent subservience to the interests of unlimited capital accumulation, even to the social and ecological abyss. On this analysis, the divisions between Left and Right, transformed as they are, cut deeper than ever. The need for a pluralistic and vital new Left has acquired a quite special urgency as unbridled capitalism threatens global disaster for humans and our fellow species alike.

CHAPTER 3

Beyond emancipation? The reflexivity of social movements

Paul Bagguley

Giddens' work on late modernity, reflexivity and self-identity is becoming increasingly influential among sociologists of social movements. Some recent theoretical and empirical studies of social movements frequently cite Giddens' recent work as a key support of their arguments. However, their use of Giddens is often in a kind of 'legislative' mode of argument, and Giddens' analysis is used to provide an intellectual legitimacy for their arguments. At present there seems to be a lack of critical engagement with his work among analysts of social movements. Indeed, for some authors Giddens' discussion of 'life politics' has become a kind of domain assumption for defining any recent social movement that is not directly concerned with class (Cox 1997: 2, McNeish 1997: 9, Taylor and Whittier 1995: 181). Here I want to open up a more critical, but still productive, engagement with Giddens' recent writings as they relate to social movements. How useful are Giddens' analyses of late modernity for the sociologist of contemporary social movements?

Below I outline the development of Giddens' thought in relation to social movements. Regarding his most recent analyses, my main point is that what he sees as somehow specific to the life politics of contemporary social movements – reflexivity and the transformation of self-identity – are generic features of social movements. In particular social movements sometimes provide socially unregulated milieux within which people intentionally and unintentionally undergo self and collective transformation. Furthermore, I intend to show that Giddens' account of reflexivity and life politics provides us with limited conceptual tools with which to analyse these phenomena.

My argument is both theoretical and empirical. Whilst I want to make some general claims about the transformation of identity in the context of social movements, I also draw upon empirical research to substantiate these claims. In particular I shall draw on two studies that have as their central focus the impact of social movements on their participants. The movements are separated in time by 20 years and in space by several thousand miles.

Whilst one concerns primarily 'race', but also, I would claim, class, the other principally focuses around militarism, patriarchy and sexuality. The former is *Freedom Summer*, Doug McAdam's (1988) study of 1,000 middle-class white students from the northern states of the USA who spent the summer of 1964 registering Blacks to vote, and teaching basic literacy to poor rural Blacks in Mississippi as part of the civil rights mobilisations of the 1960s. The second source is Sasha Roseneil's (1995) account of Greenham Common women's peace camp, where for much of the 1980s up to several thousand women permanently camped outside, and occasionally 'invaded', the United States Air Force cruise missile base at Greenham Common in Southern England, as part of the peace mobilisations of the 1980s. Whilst being quite different in terms of topic, location, time, and form of collective action, they both exemplify in unparalleled empirical fashion the transformations of individual and collective identities.

The emergence of life politics

In a similar vein to Ulrich Beck (c.f. 1996), Giddens has increasingly focused his attention on the personal aspects of politics, what Beck calls sub-politics, and what Giddens refers to as life politics. Whilst this is related to ideas around the pluralisation of life-worlds, and self-reflexivity, Giddens' discussion of life politics also has close affinities to Habermas' (1989) discussion of the life-world and new social movements, as well as certain themes discussed by social movement scholars, such as Melucci (1988). These theorists counterpose some notion of the private, the interpersonal, to the public, the system level, and so on in order to analyse new social movements. Habermas examines the seam between system and life-world in his analysis of new social movements, whilst Beck and Giddens similarly examine the relationship between an increasingly risk-producing, globalising modernity and life politics. Whilst Beck and Habermas see more of a contradiction between the rationalities of the system and the life-world, the public realm and private decisions, Giddens seems to suggest a less contradictory or conflictual relationship between globalisation and self-reflexivity.

However, this present concern with reflexivity, self-identity and life politics marks a shift from the manner in which Giddens examined the relationships between social movements and modernity in the 1980s. In those writings Giddens linked his discussion of social movements to the four dimensions of modernity, that he saw as the fundamental institutions of modernity with their own specific axes of domination. There he argued that the institutions of state surveillance gave rise to free speech and democratic movements around political rights. Another aspect of state power – the military – gave rise to peace movements that Giddens sees as oriented towards civil rights. The broader systems of industrialism and capitalism were also the bases for distinct social movements. In the case of industrialism the ecology movement associated with an alternative culture emerged, whilst, unsurprisingly, capitalism is contested by labour movements articulating economic rights.

Giddens' discussion of social movements at this stage is apparently dictated more by his analysis of the institutional parameters of modernity than by any consideration of social movements. Since he theorises four dimensions of modernity, it seems to follow logically that there should be four principal social movements that correspond to these dimensions. Giddens does mention other movements, such as feminism and anti-colonial struggles, but they are inexplicably disconnected from the classification of the institutions of modernity and their movements. The exclusion of such movements seems to be primarily pragmatic (see, for instance, Giddens 1985: 318). However, a little further into his discussion he suggests that movements such as feminism can be distinguished in a variety of locations in relation to the four dimensions of modernity, without corresponding to any one dimension (1985: 320–21). This suggests to me that there is a problem of greater conceptual significance. It suggests that the model of modernity is not exhaustive of the possibilities when it comes to identifying the range of social movements. It appears that Giddens is trying to 'read-off', in a far too structural and almost reductionist fashion, the range of social movements of modernity from the basic four institutions of modernity that he has defined in an *a priori* fashion. Whilst Giddens has identified a plurality of dimensions of modernity, this plurality is perhaps too restrictive, crucially omitting gender relations. However, in his discussion of late modernity, reflexivity and social movements, he does attempt to address gender relations more centrally.

In other respects the account developed by Giddens in *The Nation-State and Violence* seems peculiarly British and rooted in its time – the 1980s. During the 1980s Britain saw a remarkable mobilisation of the peace movement, but would one give the peace movement such a prominent place in a similar classification during the 1990s? Furthermore, one could question the kinds of rights and culture associated with the specific movements. Civil rights only really come to the fore in the peace movement as a result of the policing and repression of the forms of protest that they developed, and civil rights often become points of contest between social movements and the state, whatever the original issue. Yet movements explicitly concerned with 'civil rights' that have had a significant historical impact in certain societies, such as movements for extensions of the franchise in Britain or Black civil rights in the USA, do not have their historical significance reflected at the conceptual level of Giddens' analysis. Furthermore, why should only the ecological movement be associated with an alternative culture? All of these movements develop alternative cultures, and such alternative cultures may be a defining characteristic of all social movements. There are of course other striking absences from Giddens' account: how does one theorise the place of Islamic movements in relation to this account of modernity and its social movements, for example?

Despite these weaknesses, this 1980s approach to social movements developed by Giddens does have the methodological advantage of suggesting that there are certain fundamental institutional features of contemporary societies that are contested by social movements. This provides us with a useful step towards a sociological understanding of these movements by pointing to the institutions and social relations that they are seeking to transform. However, given that feminism, for instance, was such a significant movement of the 1970s and 1980s it is surprising that Giddens did not consider gender relations as some kind of institutional dimension of modernity with its own corresponding social movement. The case of feminism becomes even more intriguing in his more recent work on reflexivity and life politics, for he argues that feminism seeks to connect life politics with emancipatory politics, but at the same time Giddens counterposes life politics to emancipatory politics (Giddens 1990a: 157).

What is apparent is that there is a disjunction in the ways in which Giddens thinks about social movements. In his 1980s writings about modernity and social movements, conflicts were seen as rooted in the specific institutional dimensions of modernity, with New Social Movements among the primary challenges to the basic institutions of modernity. However, his 1990s writings seem to suggest that new forms of political life – 'life politics' – are emerging precisely because individuals are 'cut free' from the institutionalised settings of action within modernity. Here he introduces a distinction between emancipatory politics and life politics that in some respects reflects others' (Melucci 1988 for instance) distinctions between old and new social movements, or materialist and post-materialist politics. Giddens argues that emancipatory politics was principally concerned with freedom from tradition and religion. It was concerned with liberation from social constraints and giving people more control over their lives. Linked by the principle of autonomy, Giddens sees emancipatory politics as having been focused on the constraints of exploitation, inequality and oppression through the imperatives of justice equality and participation. Underlying this is a periodisation of social change moving from traditional societies, through modernity, to what Giddens at various times has termed 'radicalised modernity' (1990a: 150), 'late' or 'high' modernity (1991a: 4), and 'reflexive modernisation' (1994a: 80).

Giddens sees modernity's main characteristic as being incessant social change through technological innovation, and the constant dismantling and rebuilding of social institutions. Modernity is also a global phenomenon taking the form of global markets, global culture, global communications, and global politics. These features are seen as historically unique, as specific to the era of modernity, open-ended, unpredictable and uncontrollable by human agency (1991a: 151–4).

One of the main consequences of this social system is detraditionalisation. Modern societies are post-traditional societies according to Giddens, as there are no uniformly accepted core values and norms that might provide clear guides for individual decisions, actions and patterns of conduct. There are no absolute moral guidelines passed on from previous generations, because modernity constantly challenges and transforms traditional values, norms and forms of conduct (1994a: 57). Alongside this detraditionalisation goes a pluralisation of life-worlds. People now live and act in many different social settings. Life-worlds and social settings are seen by Giddens as 'sites' of 'face-to-face' interaction, that are segmentalised and separated from each other. Furthermore, these separate life-worlds are associated with particular kinds of lifestyle (1991: 83). This produces a world where:

> social bonds have effectively to be *made*, rather than inherited from the past – on the personal and more collective levels this is a fraught and difficult enterprise, but one also that holds out the promise of great rewards. It is decentred in terms of *authorities*, but recentred in terms of opportunities and dilemmas. (Giddens 1994b: 107)

As a consequence, knowledge and beliefs are both contingent and contextual. Since there are numerous segmentalised settings for producing new, different forms of belief and culture, there are no longer any universally accepted absolute truths, so that science is constantly challenged by alternative forms of knowledge. This contingency and contextualisation of knowledge and belief also extends to cultural, political and moral questions. However, Giddens suggests that late modernity does not just involve a segmentalisation of life-worlds, but, in a contradictory process, our everyday experiences are increasingly mediated, as well as based on face to face interaction. We experience many other cultures, events and ideas through the global mass media. These highly mediated, pluralistic experiences and interactions construct new identities, and new bases for social differences (1991a: 86–7).

Thus, modernity is profoundly 'disembedding'. Prior to modernity, beliefs and social relations were embedded in particular places and particular times, and were rooted in local cultures. Disembedding refers to how social and cultural relations are spread to different times and different places. The specific mechanisms through which this happens are money and markets on the one hand, and the global dissemination of knowledge on the other (Giddens 1990a: 21–9). Finally, a central feature of modernity is reflexivity, and in contemporary societies, reflexivity has become an even more chronic feature, meriting the term late modernity (Giddens 1990a: 45–53). Generally, reflexivity is understood in the following terms:

> The reflexivity of modern life consists in the fact that social practices are constantly examined and reformed in the light of incoming information about those very practices, thus constitutively altering their character . . . only in the era of modernity is the revision of convention radicalised to apply (in principle) to all aspects of human life, including technological intervention into the material world. (Giddens 1990a: 38)

At this level what defines modernity for Giddens is reflexivity, and this is the crux of his contrast between traditional and modern societies. He sees traditional societies as relatively unchanging, with little routine examination and transformation of established beliefs, institutions and practices (1990a: 37, 39–40). However, Giddens' analysis utilises two distinct notions of reflexivity: institutional reflexivity and self-reflexivity. The former examines how knowledge about social life is used in ways that organise or transform social life. It appears that this notion of reflexivity is grounded in, or is a development of, certain aspects of Giddens' earlier notion of the 'double hermeneutic – where social scientific knowledge about society may "re-enter society", leading to changes in people's actions' (1976: 162). Institutional reflexivity is a key feature of modern organisations, and instances include modern government and private corporations.

Self-reflexivity is what has preoccupied Giddens' recent work. Again it has roots in his more abstract social ontology, especially those parts where he discusses agency as the 'reflexive monitoring of action' (1990a: 36–7). The crucial theoretical development here is to see the agent – the self – as the object of reflexivity, rather than the action produced by the agent and its social context. Consequently his analysis shifts to examine how people reflexively produce narratives of the self. This involves seeing '. . . *the self as reflexively understood by the person in terms of his or her biography*. Identity here still presumes continuity across time and space: but self-identity is such continuity as interpreted reflexively by the agent' (1991: 53).

Here I think that Giddens' theoretical developments are of particular significance, as self-reflexivity is a feature of modernity where the self becomes a reflexive project. In traditional societies reflexivity is limited to interpreting and applying traditional values – an instance of the reflexive monitoring of action – but in late modern societies the producer of action, the agent, the self, becomes the *object* of reflexivity. Consequently Giddens has, as Alexander (1996) puts it, 'historicised' reflexivity. As we proceed from traditional social forms through modernity and onto high modernity, social conditions require us to be more reflexive about ourselves in ways that were simply not possible in traditional contexts.

The five features that indicate the emergence of a 'high-modernity' – the post-traditional society, the pluralisation of life-worlds, the contingency of knowledge, mediated experiences and the disembedding of social relations – force people to be self-reflexive, or to make choices. Self-reflexivity involves the constant production and revising of 'self-narratives'. The stories of who you are can be chosen from an endless range that may be placed before you. Individuals are forced to choose lifestyles that are not about superficial consumption, but are expressions of self-narratives. In this context the lifestyle is a routine of dress, eating, forms of behaviour and places for meeting others. Nevertheless, this is constantly subject to revisions. For Giddens this is not just a relatively superficial cultural phenomenon, but a distinct form of 'life politics'.

In relation to this periodisation, emancipatory politics is concerned with the liberation of people from tradition on the one hand, and the overcoming of social inequalities of resources and power on the other (Giddens 1991a: 210–15). Giddens argues that these familiar themes of enlightenment politics are being superseded in contemporary 'high' modernity by what he terms life politics. In essence he is arguing that social movements are now moving beyond the concerns of emancipation. This means there is now a new politics of choice in the context of people's biography, and it consists of '. . . political issues which flow from processes of self-actualisation in post-traditional contexts, where globalising influences intrude deeply into the reflexive project of the self, and conversely where processes of self-realisation influence global strategies' (1991a: 214).

What does this mean in terms of substantive political issues? Most centrally it concerns the question of self-identity:

> The narrative of self-identity has to be shaped, altered and reflexively sustained in relation to rapidly changing circumstances of social life, on a local and global scale. The individual must integrate information deriving from a diversity of mediated experiences with local involvements in such a way as to connect future projects with past experiences in a reasonably coherent fashion. (Giddens 1991a: 215)

This kind of politics is only attainable in late modernity, made possible by the partial success of emancipatory politics, by our freedom from tradition. Giddens further suggests that there are four aspects of life politics: *nature,* around which moral issues such as human–nature relations and environmental ethics revolve; *reproduction,* encompassing issues such as abortion and genetic engineering; *global systems,* to which questions of technological progress and the role of violence in human relations are related; and finally *the self and the body,* which gives rise to questions around animal rights and individuals' rights over their bodies. Throughout there is an emphasis on the relations between the abstract systems of modernity and the self: 'Thoroughly penetrated by modernity's abstract systems, self and body become the sites of a variety of new lifestyle options. In so far as it is dominated by the core perspectives of modernity, the project of the self remains one of control, guided only by a morality of authenticity' (Giddens 1991a: 225).

As an analysis of contemporary political issues this seems to me little more than a classification, with some suggestive lines of explanation as to why these aspects of life political movements have become important questions. Intermediate structures of power and domination seem to be overlooked as Giddens posits the 'micro' interactional order of life politics directly in relationship to the 'macro' global processes of late modernity (Hay *et al.* 1994). In addition, the model of the reflexive self is highly instrumental and ascetic or self-disciplining. As Giddens puts it in the above quote 'the project of the self remains one of control' (1991a: 225). This is what I object to when I claim that Giddens' account is too instrumental, too 'intentionalist', for it to form an adequate basis for the transformation of identities in social movements – such transformations are not simply under the control of individuals. Giddens' mode of explanation displays striking parallels with Habermas' system/life-world model, where the systems of the market and bureaucracy are forever encroaching on our interpersonal life-worlds, such that we seek alternative social models in the form of various kinds of communicative rationality. However, there is one crucial difference: Giddens does not perceive globalisation as an encroachment on, but as an opportunity for, increased freedom, for increased self-reflexivity. Whereas Habermas might be presented as analysing a dialectics of modernity, Giddens sees no dialectic, no real significant contradiction, just an increasing reflexivity of the self enabled by the globalisation of late modernity. Furthermore, even as a classification, Giddens' discussion of life politics is not entirely coherent or empirically convincing. Why should global systems be related to technology? Why should technological development be related as an issue to questions of genetics, or ecology, or rights over the body?

Reflexivity, agency and structure

Giddens' account of late modernity and reflexivity has been addressed by a number of critics, and two themes run through their comments. First, the most frequent criticism is that his recent work neglects issues of power, domination and social inequality. Frequently connected to this is the claim that his concept of reflexivity is individualistic in both its theory and its politics. Consequently it is seen by some as closely related to classic liberalism or even contemporary neo-liberalism (May and Cooper 1995).

Secondly, it has also been suggested that Giddens' notion of reflexivity is instrumentalist and scientistic (Lash 1994). This is reminiscent of earlier arguments that his concept of agency was highly rationalised, and that it presumed a model of the self that was peculiar to the public life of modern societies. (Kilminster 1991). A related, but rather different, angle of attack on these issues might be to suggest that discussions of an increase in reflexivity in the late twentieth century overlooks the phenomenon of habit or routine in everyday life and social action (Campbell 1996).

Whilst these arguments have a certain cogency, it might be objected that they do not entirely undermine Giddens' sociological project, and that they could be deftly handled by some minor changes of emphasis in Giddens' analysis. Indeed Lash (1994) attempts something like this by producing a model of different kinds of reflexivity. However, Giddens' recent work on reflexivity raises certain fundamental problems for his earlier work on the duality of structure, and the relationship that he posits or, rather, attempts to dissolve, between agency and structure.

Put simply, my general point is that Giddens' account of self-reflexivity signifies a breakdown of his overarching theory of structuration and the duality of structure. The concept of the self-reflexive individual of late modernity posits a dualism between agency and structure, involving the reflexive agent now increasingly liberated from structural constraints, 'free' to choose and construct her identity. Furthermore, what Alexander (1996) has criticised as the historicisation of reflexivity by Giddens, in my view, implies a shift from the duality of structure of traditional society to a dualism of agency and structure in post-traditional social orders. More generally, I would suggest that to understand reflexivity and the transformation of identities within social movements, we have to see structure and agency in a more dynamic, dualistic way as suggested by Archer (1995) and Mouzelis (1991). This assumption of 'dynamic dualism' is what underlies my later discussions of the reflexivity of social movements and the complex manner in which identities are transformed.

The question of the character of social movements is of course caught up in the centre of these power and domination, structure and agency controversies around reflexivity. However, they are rarely the focus of explicit, sustained discussion in these critical accounts. In some circumstances Giddens (see, e.g., 1985) puts social movements into a central place in his sociology in that he attempts to conceptualise them and their role in modern societies. He is perhaps the only British sociologist outside the Marxist tradition to attempt such an original grand theorisation of the role of social movements in relation to social change, one that is comparable say to the work of Habermas or Touraine for instance. Nevertheless, with the development of his account of late modernity and reflexivity – his reflexive turn – Giddens' analysis of the character and role of social movements in contemporary societies has similarly shifted. This shift revolves around his claim that life politics has emerged alongside emancipatory politics. What I want to attempt now is a recasting of reflexivity and identity transformations in a manner that I think will prove more useful for the sociological analysis of social movements.

The reflexivity of social movements

In this section I want to consider how reflexivity, the reflexive monitoring of action, is a defining characteristic of all social movements, and cannot be used to distinguish life politics from emancipatory politics. Further, as self-identity has always been transformed among participants in social movements, equating this with life politics introduces an unsustainable distinction between types of social movement by ignoring the way in which social movements emerge and develop historically in waves or cycles. Historical work on social movements shows how they appear in apparent waves or cycles

(Tarrow 1995), such that there is no easy dichotomy between 'old' and 'new' social movements as is suggested in Giddens' account of the emergence of life politics. However, Tilly (1996) suggests that each cycle or wave of protest may bring with it a new repertoire of collective action. These are new routines of engaging in political struggle, new way of defining issues (for instance in terms of 'civil rights'), new forms of organisation and association, new ways of protesting (the invention of demonstrations and strikes for instance). These constitute a whole new mode of interaction between struggling collective actors, but they all involve reflexivity and the transformation of identities. However, the reflexivity of social movements and the processes that transform identities in social movements are *not* the same thing. As all social movements involve the 'reflexive monitoring of action', as Giddens calls it, greater or lesser degrees of reflexivity are not useful ways of distinguishing different kinds of social movement.

In response it might be suggested that life politics constitute a new repertoire of collective action. However, it can also be argued that these themes of the transformation of self-identity were prominent in early nineteenth century social movements. These movements have been examined in the most sustained way in relation to these issues by Craig Calhoun (1995). Although Calhoun's arguments are principally aimed at 'new social movement' theorists such as Melucci (1988), who claimed to have identified new forms of politics operating outside of formal political channels and principally concerned with ethical, cultural and identity issues, it is clear that they can also apply to Giddens' analysis of life politics. Briefly, Calhoun shows that the themes of identity and self-realisation, the defence of diverse life-worlds, the politicisation of everyday life, non-hierarchical forms of organisation, unconventional means of contention, and networks of people committed to diverse but overlapping political concerns were all characteristics of early nineteenth-century social movements. In Giddens' terms what Calhoun is discussing is 'life politics', yet these instances of 'life politics' were occurring in early nineteenth-century England. In addition, Tucker (1991) has also shown that both nineteenth-century syndicalism and contemporary labour struggles around workers' control share the 'life politics' concerns of morally justifiable ways of life, self-actualisation and personal autonomy. Finally, transformations of self-identity also occur in that arena of classic working-class protest, the strike. Lane and Roberts summarise the impact of strike action on the formerly acquiescent workforce at Pilkingtons in Britain's industrial North in 1970 as follows:

> To some the strike was an education; it opened their minds; it broadened their horizons; it gave them new insights into themselves and into the society in which they lived. During the dispute some individuals began to think and argue about issues that they had never previously attempted to understand; they discovered abilities within themselves that formerly they never knew they possessed. (Lane and Roberts 1971: 104)

Implied by the above arguments are two broad claims opposed to Giddens' analysis of social movements, self-reflexivity and late modernity. In relation to social movements at least, Giddens is wrong to 'historicise' reflexivity. I believe it is simply implausible to suggest that reflexivity is a social product specific to the late twentieth century, and that this reflexivity is somehow only characteristic of contemporary social movements engaged in life politics. Reflexivity is a characteristic feature of all social movements, since they are fundamentally about reflecting and acting upon people, their conditions of existence and their identities.

The distinction between emancipatory politics and life politics cannot be sustained, at least in the way that Giddens construes it. Such a binary opposition between emancipatory and life politics does not seem to me to be justified. Although the post-1960s wave of social movement activity is highly suggestive of such a distinction, a closer perusal of social movements historically shows this to be yet another wave in the cycle of collective action.

In a manner comparable to self-identity, new collective identities have always been constructed in social movements, but this is lost in Giddens account of life politics. Group identity is more significant than self-identity for a number of reasons. First, group identities endure through time and over space much more than self-identity does. Self-identity is tied to the individual in a way that group identities are not, as they are transmitted between individuals over time. Secondly, collective actions are only possible with the existence of some kind of group identity, some minimal identification with common goals. Thirdly, collective action based on group identity is more likely to have significant social effects than relatively isolated individual actions based on self-identity. Finally, self-identities in Giddens' sense utilise group identities as the means of their construction. His analysis of the pluralisation of life-worlds considers how individuals now have access to many potential group identities, and consequently have to construct their own self-identity. This entails a causal and analytical primacy of collective or group identities that Giddens does not consider in any real detail. It suggests that the focus of the analysis should be the development of new collective identities as much as self-identity.

In contrast to Giddens, who appears to be saying that social movements merely exhibit the reflexivity of late modernity, I wish to argue that there are various forms and levels at which *all* social movements are reflexive. The concept of reflexivity, somewhat modified from Giddens' use of the idea, is useful for thinking about various aspects of social movements.

Most significantly I think we have to recognise the role of collective reflexivity as distinct from self-reflexivity in social movements. Social movements as phases of *collective* action involve a collective reflexive monitoring of action by the individuals involved. They are acting reflexively *together*, rather than as isolated agents. Social movements, through the individuals that constitute them, engage in a continuous '. . . monitoring of behaviour and its contexts' (Giddens 1990a: 37). Social movements are centrally an expression of collective reflexivity and not just an aggregation of, nor merely an arena for, self-reflexivity. Similarly, the construction or transformation of the self or self-narratives in the context of social movements is not just a product or expression of self-reflexivity. That notion alone I find too instrumental in its connotations. It suggests, in Giddens' account at least, that any transformations of identity in social movements are directly the product of each individual's intentions, where these individuals have 'chosen' an identity from the many they have before them. But where I am most drastically at odds with Giddens' discussion is in my emphasis on *the unintentional transformation of self-identity through collective action*. It is a common occurrence in social movements for individuals to find themselves transformed in quite unpredictable and unintended ways through their involvement in conflict with others, and through induction into the habits of social movement activity. This might be seen as socialisation into the tradition of the movement and centrally revolves around what others in the movement expect of a participant. In the rest of the chapter I demonstrate the significance and centrality of unintended transformations of self and collective identities within the context of social movements.

The transformation of identities in social movements

The unintentional transformation of selves through involvement in collective action is an empirical process that requires careful conceptual analysis in order to tease out its various aspects. The key to understanding this claim is to consider the following question: do people join social movements with the intention of transforming themselves or transforming the people around them? I wish to argue that their intentions are to transform other people and social circumstances more generally, and that self-transformation often occurs through conflict with those opposed to the movements, or with institutions seeking to repress it, usually the state.

Induction into the habits of a social movement constitutes another way in which self-identity may be transformed. Presenting a certain 'self' within a social movement is essential to fitting into its routines and its 'tradition'. This applies both politically and culturally. In some sense this is closer to Giddens' view, although I would like to suggest that we think of it a less 'intentionalist' connotation. The transformation of identities in social movements thus involves the following. First, there is some original reason for becoming involved in the movement based on an interpretation of its stated aims or collective identity. Secondly, as people become involved in the movement there is often a growing awareness and critique of the wider social context within which the movement is acting. Thirdly, at the level of self-identity, transformations occur through conflict with the movement's opponents and through interactions with other movement participants.

A particularly useful empirical study that illustrates my thoughts in these respects is Roseneil's (1995) analysis of Greenham Common women's peace camp of the 1980s. Greenham Common was one of the locations for the siting of United States' Air Force cruise missiles between 1983 and 1991. The principal form of opposition to this was the peace camp set up by women. From the evidence presented by Roseneil, we see that many women's original intentions in participating in the camp was opposition to nuclear weapons, yet, as a direct consequence of their participation, some women experienced a dramatic transformation of their sexual identities – from heterosexuality to lesbianism, among other transformations. This process is analysed empirically in some detail by Roseneil, and I summarise it here in order to develop my particular theoretical claims.

Superficially Roseneil's analysis of the experiences of the women at Greenham would appear to provide empirical support for Giddens' account of life politics and the transformation of the self. Yet, on closer inspection we see that something more complex happened, involving a transformation and fragmentation of the collective identity of Greenham.

The Greenham Common women's peace camp began as a result of a march of women from South Wales to Greenham Common. The march's principal 'collective identity' *as those on the march presented it to the outside world* was primarily one of maternalist opposition to nuclear weapons (Roseneil 1995: 34). The major public justification of the march was women's concern for their children's futures in a nuclear world. However, this collective identity, the public justification for the action, *became increasingly feminist over time.* Furthermore, the women who set up the peace camp participated in the first instance for quite diverse individual reasons, such as the fact that it was a women's action not run by men, or that it was direct action against nuclear weapons. Nevertheless, the vast majority of the original marchers were recruited through established social networks in the feminist and peace movements. Initially Roseneil's analysis suggests that the public collective identity was not reflected in the reasons for many individuals' original participation (1995: 34–7).

After the initial establishment of the camp Greenham attracted the participation of thousands of women, as permanent residents, visitors or just members of support groups around the country. Among this core group of residents and visitors to the camp, that form the focus of Roseneil's analysis, quite diverse reasons are given for going to Greenham, which, by the time it had become established and more widely supported, had a confirmed feminist, 'women-only' collective identity. Whilst many were attracted by the fact that Greenham was a 'women-only' action, personal change became important to a significant minority of women involved. In the longer run the 'fun' of living at Greenham and its significance as a lesbian community, where lesbianism was a normal taken-for-granted sexual practice, also attracted some women. However, Roseneil shows that for most women opposition to nuclear weapons was the most significant reason for participation: 'Many went to Greenham primarily to oppose Cruise missiles, with no conscious notion that they would be fundamentally changed by the experience' (1995: 57).

The experience of Greenham not only offered opportunities to explore alternative identities, but also transformed women regardless of their intention to transform themselves. Those who originally became involved for 'maternalist' reasons, or saw Greenham as an expression of their self-identity as 'mothers', were most affected by the impact of Greenham on their self-identity. Roseneil shows how the internal social relations and social processes within the peace camp had a transforming effect on women's consciousness. Their participation in decisions enabled by the informal, diverse, network-like structure of the movement had an empowering effect, and led to women reflecting upon men's domination of wider social and political structures. According to Roseneil, the fact that Greenham was a women-only movement led to the women forming strong *affective* bonds with each other. Greenham's principle of concern with the ecological impact of the nuclear state, and their own peace camp, resulting in new ways of thinking about the natural environment. The women also developed a global consciousness of their action and wider position in the world through the international network of supporters and allies that grew up around Greenham. Finally, as Greenham had a strong lesbian community, it challenged heterosexual women to think about their own sexuality as well as lesbianism for the first time (Roseneil 1995: 145–49). Among her interviewees Roseneil found that, whilst 14 were lesbians at the time of going to Greenham, 21 were lesbians when interviewed some years later (1995: 178). These kinds of processes of self-transformation show how people are transformed by fitting into the culture, routines and habits of a social movement.

However, women's consciousness and identity at Greenham were not transformed just by the internal social relations of the women's peace movement. Roseneil also argues that their conflicts with authority, especially various levels of the state, had a significant impact. Conflict with wider private and public patriarchal authorities in the form of opposition to the women-only policy of Greenham from men in the wider peace movement, as well as male partners, heightened women's consciousness of the patriarchal domination of public and private life. The sexualised violence that they experienced from the police and soldiers drew their attention to issues of sexual violence against women, whilst their experience of the criminal justice system when they were arrested led to a radical re-assessment of the state (Roseneil 1995: 149–54). These kinds of transformations of self and collective identities illustrate my claim of unintentional self-transformation through the experience of conflict with opponents. As Roseneil makes clear, this involved a complex, active inter-play of women's individual and collective agencies, the agency of powerful opponents, as well as relatively fixed and enduring structural features of the situation.

My second empirical example is drawn from the civil rights protests of the 1960s in the USA. The Freedom Summer mobilisation of white middle-class students into Mississippi in 1964 by the Black civil rights group the Student Non-Violent Co-ordinating Committee (SNCC) also illustrates the phenomenon of unintentional self-transformation through the experience of conflict with opponents. One of the most significant aspects of Freedom Summer that had an impact on the volunteers was the scale of violence in opposition to what they were attempting to do: 4 participants killed, 4 critically wounded, 80 beaten, 1,000 arrests, 37 churches bombed or burned, and 30 Black homes or businesses bombed or burned (McAdam 1988: 96).

The students volunteered for Freedom Summer for a wide variety of reasons: religious, patriotic or socialist values, often shared with their parents. Many were already politically 'active' in some way, though often not in the civil rights movement. However, McAdam shows that the broader consequences of these experiences of the intensity of opposition from the white establishment was an increased political radicalisation among the volunteers. They became increasingly critical of the racialised social and political structures of the USA. Particularly important were the experiences of Federal complicity in the white power structure of the southern states, and in the actions in opposition to Freedom Summer (1988: 127). The experience of living in a rural Black community, seeing at first hand its material poverty alongside its cultural solidarity and resistance, also had an impact on the Freedom Summer volunteers (1988: 86–92). This is also a good illustration of my claim about the unintentional self-transformation that results from the experience of conflict. However, McAdam makes a further significant point: it was not only the attitudes, ideology or identity of the volunteers that was changed but their *preparedness to take political action*:

> . . . it was not only the attitudes of the volunteers that were changed by the summer, but their willingness to act on those attitudes. This is not a trivial point. When we speak of the Sixties as a 'political' era, we are really making a statement about the level of political *action* during the period rather than the content of political attitudes *per se*. In this sense, the most important legacy of Freedom Summer may lie in the 'positive impulse to action' it furnished the New Left. (McAdam 1988: 131–2)

This is an aspect of self-identity that Giddens oddly overlooks. Whilst his analysis suggests a greater preparedness to act in refashioning ourselves, he does not suggest that sub-politics and its impact implies a greater preparedness for broader, perhaps unrelated, political action.

More complex are the effects of the internal social relations and dynamics within the Freedom Summer projects that I have described conceptually as induction into the habits of the movement. In a positive sense the 'anarchic consensus' style of decision making within the SNCC organising Freedom Summer came to be 'copied' and applied in the student, anti-Vietnam War and feminist movements that partly flowed out of the Freedom Summer experience (McAdam 1988: 166, 184–5). The communal style of living in Freedom Summer projects might just be seen as typical student collective households, but McAdam argues that these styles of household organisation had a political rationale rather than an economic one, and, furthermore this political rationale for household organisation was subsequently imitated across the USA later during the 1960s and 1970s (1988: 140–2). Even the styles of dress and speech of the Southern Black SNCC leaders were imitated by the young middle-class whites. For young educated middle-class whites to wear blue jeans and use Black working-class vernacular speech was quite shocking to mainstream society even as late as 1964. More contradictory and controversial are the complex inter-racial and sexual relationships that developed during Freedom Summer (McAdam 1988: 142–4).

Many of the Freedom Summer volunteers described to McAdam how Freedom Summer was their first experience of open sexuality that in the 'Sixties' later came to define its broader cultural reputation. 'Sexual inhibition' was something seen to be overcome, and the experiences of the summer fed into the later politicisation of sexual questions. The many inter-racial sexual relationships added even more to the political combustion in the eyes of wider society, but also within the civil rights movement. The controversies around inter-racial relationships, as well as the rather patronising attitude of some of the white volunteers to the local Black civil rights activists, played a role in the development of Black separatism. Moreover, the sexism experienced by women on Freedom Summer gave rise to the initial mobilisation of late twentieth century radical feminism, including explicit comparison of women's position in the sex-caste system with Blacks in the race-caste system of the USA (McAdam 1988: 178–9, Echols 1989: 23–36). This consequently raised the question of political 'self-transformation'. In the course of the attempts to transform the people and social relations around them, some Freedom Summer volunteers came to see the necessity for self-transformation:

> The ideology of liberation came to be *applied* personally as well as politically over the course of the summer. The volunteers came to believe it was just as important to free *themselves* from the constraints of their racial or class backgrounds as it was to register black voters. *They* became as much the project as the Freedom schools they taught in. A stress on self-awareness and personal liberation suffused the project. Later both elements would be incorporated as important behavioural cornerstones of the counterculture. (McAdam 1988: 139)

Like Roseneil and many other social movement theorists (see Barker 1999 for an extended discussion), McAdam stresses the way in which the movement functioned as a social 'space' outside of the taken-for-granted structures of society. Through such processes of 'stepping outside of structures' in order to reflect upon them, self and collective transformation may occur. McAdam argues that for many of the Freedom Summer volunteers the project was:

. . . an intensely stressful, yet exhilarating, confrontation with traditional conceptions of America, community, politics, morality, sexuality, and above all else,
themselves. What the volunteers were beginning to experience . . . was, to use
Peter Berger's term, 'ecstasy', that giddy, disorienting sense of liberation that
comes from 'stepping outside . . . the taken-for-granted routines of society' . . .
It was not so much a case of the volunteers *choosing* to take this step, as being
compelled to do so by virtue of their contact with a project staff that had itself
become more radical and alienated as a result of three long years of struggle in
Mississippi. (McAdam 1988: 67, emphasis in the original)

Again we have this theme of a complex interplay of agency and structure combined with attendant unintended consequences. What both Roseneil
and McAdam have demonstrated in the cases of different movements in
different places, and at different times, is that the transformation of self and
collective identities is an unpredictable and complex process. Consequently,
I would suggest that it is one that cannot adequately be understood in
terms of life politics and self-reflexivity. Finally, I would contend that these
studies support my claim that social movements and the collective actions
that they generate by definition involve a collective reflexivity through strategic interaction with opponents and/or the state.

Conclusion

Giddens' discussion of life politics and social movements seems too individualistic, as social movements are both collective and individual projects.
Social movements are more than the sum of the reflexive projects of the
individuals from which they are constituted. At this level social movements
are an emergent property of the interactions of the individuals that constitute them. Social movements have their own reality above and beyond the
individuals who participate in them at any particular time. The individualistic character of Giddens' notion of reflexivity has its roots in his generic
concept of agency. At the most general conceptual level this is purely individualistic (Kilminster 1991). As others have noted, Giddens only conceptual-
ises agency as individual agency yet is quite prepared to use collective action
concepts in the analysis of particular social changes, such as the emergence
of citizenship (Mouzelis 1991).

I have argued that the notion of 'life politics' of the late twentieth century, and the way in which Giddens contrasts this with the emancipatory
politics of the nineteenth century, restates the ideal typical division between
old and new social movements, between class politics and identity politics.
I have argued that this is historically inaccurate, as others (Calhoun 1995,
Tucker 1991) have shown how the features of life politics can also be found
in the nineteenth century. Furthermore, features of life politics also characterise working-class politics, so the distinction between emancipatory and
life politics has no real empirical validity.

On another level I have contested Giddens' account of reflexivity in the context of social movements. As he sees self-reflexivity and the transformation of self-identity as somehow characteristic of life politics, this implies that emancipatory politics are not reflexive, or do not involve the transformation of self-identity. In contrast to these claims I have argued that all social movements are characterised by a *collective* reflexivity, in Giddens' sense of the 'reflexive monitoring of action'. Indeed, I have suggested that social movements are sites where people both individually and collectively are often at their most reflexive in this sense. Finally, I have argued that the transformation of identities is not as straightforward as Giddens suggests. In his account self-identities are transformed through the realisation of the individual's intentions. I have argued that the *unintentional* transformation of identities is what usually happens within social movements. As individuals in social movements interact with other participants and with their opponents they find themselves transformed in ways that they did not originally intend.

CHAPTER 4

Exploring post-traditional orders: Individual reflexivity, 'pure relations' and duality of structure

Nicos Mouzelis

Giddens' theory of reflexivity is a central theme of his broader theory of transition from traditional to post-traditional social orders. Traditional orders are characterized by codes of 'formulaic truth' that routinise social conduct in a meaningful, emotionally satisfying manner. Following traditional rules and routines gives dignity to their adherents and moral authority to those who guard and interpret such rules. 'Detraditionalisation', on the other hand – via such processes as disembedment, increase of mediated experience, pluralisation of life-worlds, and the emergence of contingent knowledge – creates a situation where routines lose their meaningfulness and their unquestioned moral authority. They become mindless habits or compulsions that may give temporary relief from the insecurities of late modern life, but cannot and do not lead to a meaningful existence (Giddens 1994b).

However, according to Giddens, the social and moral vacuum created by detraditionalisation is not filled simply by compulsive routines. An alternative possibility is the reflexive construction of one's 'biography' via an active choice from among the varied goals offered by late modernity, and by rational adaptation of one or other of the multiplicity of available means for the realisation of such goals. In other words, whereas in pre-modern contexts individual conduct – in such crucial areas as work, marriage, the socialisation of children, entertainment, and so on – was regulated routinely but meaningfully through traditional moral codes, in detraditionalised social contexts all the mechanisms of social regulation extrinsic to the individual become weaker, and people are forced to confront a situation that urgently asks them to make choices, to decide about their career, their lifestyles, their diets, the number of children they wish to have, the way they will raise them, and so on. In this situation *homo optionis,* faced with a geometrically rising number of choices in all institutional spheres, can either escape from 'the tyranny of possibilities' by compulsively adhering to meaningless routines, or decide actively to construct their life projects by a process of creative self-reflection (Giddens 1994b: 70 ff).

During the earlier phases of modernity the emergence of this type of individual or self-reflexivity was not as marked as it is today. At that time, traditional certainties were replaced, at least in part, by the collective certainties of class, party and nation, and to some extent such configurations were able to provide non-traditional, extrinsic mechanisms of self-regulation and identity formation. In late or high modernity, however, these in-between arrangements became peripheralised by the rapid processes of globalisation. Individuals, more than at any time before, are today facing the unprecedented situation of an 'empty space' that demands to be filled by either meaningless compulsions or, via individual reflexivity, by the active choice of goals/means and the construction of their own self-projects. Whilst Giddens introduces a distinction between individual and institutional reflexivity, my concern in this chapter is to consider same issues relating only to the former.

Two types of self-reflexivity

For some critics, the way in which traditional modes of regulation and the development of individual reflexivity have declined is not as unique as Giddens posits. Even in pre-industrial complex civilisations during periods of transition one can find processes that led to the weakening of traditional controls and the development of self-reflexivity (Rose 1996: 309). I myself, however, would rather agree with Beck (whose theory of individualisation has received similar criticism) that it is only in late modernity that the kind of individual reflexivity he and Giddens talk about has spread 'from the few to the many'. It is only during the present period of 'reflexive modernisation' that the demise of traditional certainties and the multiplication of choices has been forced not only on the elites but also on the masses (Beck and Beck-Gernsheim 1996). To be more specific, in relation to the radical undermining of traditional arrangements that globalisation brings about, the extraordinary mass production and distribution of self-help manuals (including the myriad guides on how to improve your muscles, your memory, your self-confidence, self-esteem, self-image etc.) constitute a unique phenomenon, whose importance and centrality for understanding our present predicament cannot be minimised by reference to similar practices having occurred in past civilisations.

For much the same reasons I also remain unconvinced by the argument that reflexivity is a constitutive dimension of all social action – whether traditional or modern – and that therefore, even in the absence of detraditionalisation, the application of formulaic truths to specific interactive contexts unavoidably entails choices, uncertainty, the reflexive use of means to achieve a given goal, and so on (see, for instance, Alexander 1982: 67). Although I accept the general argument that humans cannot but be self-interpreting and, therefore, self-reflexive, animals (Taylor 1985), and that, in an ethnomethodological sense, the ongoing construction of social reality always entails self-reflexivity, it does not follow that one cannot identify qualitative differences between the types of reflexivity to be found in traditional and late-modern contexts. In the former case the reflexivity Giddens talks about is restricted by the fact that the basic parameters of an individual's social existence are provided by formulaic codes and traditional routines and rituals; in the latter case this is so no longer, and individuals have to provide some of these parameters themselves.

It seems to me that a more constructive way of criticising Giddens' notion of individual or self-reflexivity would be to focus less on the uniqueness or spread of the phenomenon in time and space, and more on the one-sided manner in which the notion has been conceived. More specifically, if one accepts the crucial importance of the emergence of an unprecedented 'open space' in detraditionalised, late modernity – a space forcing the individual to take a myriad of decisions on matters that were previously settled more or less automatically by tradition – and if one also accepts that in such an open situation the two fundamental responses are mindless compulsion or self-reflexivity, then the following question arises. Does Giddens' definition of reflexivity exhaust the possible *non-compulsive* reactions to the extraordinary increase of choices entailed by late modernity? Might there not be, potentially or actually, other ways of reflexively reacting to modernity's 'open spaces'? I think that the answer to this question is 'Yes'. In order to show why, I shall start by pointing out the culture-specific, or more precisely western-specific, character of Giddens' view of reflexivity.

Whether one looks at the way Giddens links individual reflexivity with detraditionalisation or at the examples he provides, it is quite clear that his notion of reflexivity is *over-activistic*. Following the Protestant-ethic tradition, the reflexive individuals' relation to their inner and outer worlds is conceptualised in ultra-activistic, instrumental terms: subjects are portrayed as constantly involved in means–ends situations, constantly trying reflexively and rationally to choose their broad goals as well as the means of their realisation; they are also constantly monitoring or revising their projects in the light of new information and of the already achieved results. Whether the chosen goal is to get rich, become famous, win friends, or improve one's sex appeal, the way in which both the goals and means are selected entails a type of reflexivity that excludes more contemplative, more 'easy-going', less cognitive ways of navigating reflexively in a world full of choices and individual challenges.

To reformulate the question: since the setting of goals and the choice of means for their attainment is no longer given or facilitated by traditional codes, is Giddens' type of activistic, instrumentalist, 'means–ends'-based reflexivity the only alternative to escaping into compulsion? Is it perhaps possible to resort to some non-compulsive, reflexive attitude that does not seek (via rational choices) actively to *construct* life orientations, but rather allows in *indirect, passive manner* life orientations and other broad goals to *emerge*? Is it not possible for modern reflexivity to be compatible with a kind of existence where, instead of actively and instrumentally trying to master the complexity of growing choices, one chooses (to use Pierre-August Renoir's expression) to 'float as a cork' in the ocean of post-traditional reality? Could it be that reflexively achieved individual freedom and autonomy in a detraditionalised situation may entail, following Simmel and Heidegger, the ability to get rid of the 'tyranny' of purposiveness based on calculation, planning, and ratiocination? Could it be that it entails the transcendence of the never-ending rational setting of goals, the fulfilment of which only leads to new goals *ad infinitum*? Could it be, finally, that one might be profoundly reflexive without becoming engulfed by the business of incessant means–ends decision making? Could it be that non-western cultures (e.g. Islamic, Confucian)[1] might offer possibilities for a type of *post-traditional* reflexivity that is not based on the European Renaissance and Enlightenment model of a human being? Could it be that individual reflexivity in the era of globalisation can take less or non-Promethean forms?

In order to answer the above questions one should first of all examine a type of reflexivity that is the exact opposite of Giddens'. In its non-secular form it exists in all the great mystical traditions of both East and West (Jones *et al.* 1986). To limit ourselves to the Christian tradition, Eastern Orthodoxy (much more so than Protestantism or Catholicism) emphasises the impossibility of relating to the divine via rational/cognitive means (Zizioulas 1993), and suggests that the more one attempts to approach God rationally, the more this becomes impossible. Cognition is useful only when used in a negative, *apophatic*, rather than a positive and affirmative, *cataphatic* manner.[2] Reason can help only through awareness and removal of the various obstacles (e.g. selfish practices, various forms of escapism etc.) that prevent the human soul from opening up to divine grace. Apophaticism aims at cleaning out the material and spiritual self so that the believer becomes an 'empty vessel' ready to receive divine illumination. The actual reception in no way depends on calculation or means–ends schemata. These are involved only *negatively*, by being useful for removing obstacles, so that the divine–human rapprochement can take place in a setting where any form of instrumental calculation, any form of ratiocination, is absent.

In Eastern Orthodox Christianity, apophatic theology was closely but not entirely linked with *hesychasm* (*hesychia* meaning quietness), a spiritual movement that acquired importance in the late Byzantine period. Its major representative at that period was St Gregory Palamas (Meyendorff 1974), whose writings rested on three basic themes. The first was that God in his *essence* is unknowable, and therefore one cannot say anything about what he is. Second, if on the level of his essence God is absolutely transcendental, on the level of his *energies* he is absolutely imminent: human beings experiencing the divine do so less as a result of mediation (e.g. via the scriptures, theology, rituals) but in unmediated, direct, personal, 'face-to-face' manner. Third, this direct relationship between human and divine can be facilitated by various techniques (such as posture, breathing, repeating the Jesus prayer) that aim at quietening the mind, so freeing it of categories, images, concepts, thoughts, and so on. Thinking, even *phantasia* (i.e. imagination) must be subdued, otherwise one becomes 'not a Hesychast but a phantast' (quoted in Ware 1986: 247).[3]

One could argue, of course, that the *via negativa*, the apophatic method, is more prayer than self-reflexivity, if for no other reason than because it entails a divinity which, somehow, plays a similar role to that of tradition: it assists the individual to make the necessary choices with the help of a mechanism that is extrinsic rather than intrinsic to the self. It entails, in other words, not a 'self–self' but a 'self–divinity' relationship, which is different from the self-referentiality of Giddens' notion of individual reflexivity.

However, the *via negativa* can also take secular forms that shift the focus from self–God to self–self relationships. For instance, the bulk of the psychoanalytic tradition is based on the idea that the role of the analyst is not to instil new goals or life purposes in analysands; it does not purport to help them directly to solve the moral or practical problems of everyday life. Rather, the role of the analyst is to help analysands to become aware of the variety of repressed and/or defensive mechanisms that are life-destroying, and that prevent the *emergence* of non-pathological life patterns. Once analysands achieve this awareness and experience directly the above mechanisms, the goals and means appropriate for them emerge without any cognitive intervention from either themselves or the analyst.

This is even more so when one moves from psychoanalysis to self-psychoanalysis – a technique that Freud himself practised, and that is becoming increasingly popular today. In self-analysis, the aim is to remove through self-awareness obstacles such as compulsions and defence mechanisms, so that 'what is to be done' is not constructed rationalistically by the subject but emerges spontaneously and unproblematically.

The above type of reflexivity I would call apophatic, in contrast to Giddens' 'cataphatic', affirmative activistic reflexivity. The subject turns away from tradition, divine revelation, formulaic truths and all other extrinsic sources of goal formation, in order to focus on the self in such a way that decisions and life-goals *'appear'* or *emerge* rather than having to be actively *constructed*. In a certain sense, therefore, it can be argued that self-analysis, as practised by Freud and many others, is a secularised form of the religious *via negativa*, a secularised form of apophaticism.

Radical, secular, apophatic reflexivity: the work of Krishnamurti

Stripping the religious connotations from apophatic reflexivity is a feature of not only Freud's written work and practice; in much more radical fashion it can be found in the work of Jiddo Krishnamurti.[4] Although his books are popular and well-known among spiritual seekers all over the world, since his work does not have a 'scholarly' character, it remains little known among academics. This being so, as well as the fact that Krishnamurti's notion of non-religious, apophatic reflexivity is central for my argument, I shall have to present a fairly extensive outline of his thought.

For Krishnamurti, spirituality has nothing to do with beliefs and formulaic truths (neither religious nor secular). Beliefs, divine revelations, sacred texts, as well as rationalistically derived moral codes, are not only quite irrelevant in the search for a spiritual, meaningful existence today, but they actually *constitute serious obstacles* to such a search. It is for this reason that Krishnamurti's writings scrupulously avoid any reference to God, or to whether or not there is life after death, as well as to other eschatological or existential questions. Concern with the future (in this life or after death) is an excellent way of escaping the present, the here-and-now, and in that sense it is profoundly anti-spiritual. Therefore, if Giddens' notion of reflexivity entails, to use his own terminology, a 'colonisation of the future' (Giddens 1991a: 111ff), Krishnamurti's notion of reflexive spirituality entails a 'colonisation of the present'. Krishnamurti equally rejects any attempt to elevate his own theory into an organised system of beliefs and practices, into a spiritual tool-kit for guiding his followers to a meaningful existence. His constant advice is that one should accept nothing, whether it comes from him or others, without first 'testing it', without seeing what it means in terms of one's own experience.

Krishnamurti sees himself as simply someone who helps his fellow human beings to look at themselves in a highly 'apophatic' manner. For him, looking inwards becomes creative and fruitful only when ratiocination, planning, and cognitively constructed means-and-ends schemata are peripheralised, and this includes not only all beliefs and preconceived ideas, but also all linguistic categories, and all conceptualisations acquired through the various processes of socialisation. This purgative, negating, apophatic reflexivity is a necessary precondition for the emergence of the spiritual, for the emergence of an internal awareness where decisions (on both goals and means) emerge without the activation of conscious decision-making mechanisms (Krishnamurti 1954, 1956, 1975, 1978, 1985).[5]

This type of apophatic approach does not seem to be very different from what psychoanalysts do when they try to clear the ground of defensive preconceptions and misconceptions, so that the hidden or repressed parts of the self can emerge into consciousness. But Krishnamurti is opposed to psychoanalysis on the grounds that the psychoanalytic process is based on verbal exchanges, and verbal exchanges, just like beliefs, ratiocination and other cognitive processes, prevent the emergence of the spiritual. So although Krishnamurti's (non-)method shares with psychoanalysis the urge to explore what *is* rather than what *ought* to be, his exploration dispenses with verbal exchanges. Any verbal interaction between analyst and analysand, or any attempt by the former to use analytical tools in order to describe or explain latent or manifest aspects of the ongoing interaction, automatically sabotages the detached exploration of what *is*. It is through silent and continuous gazing inwards, rather than through talking, analysing, expressing feelings verbally and looking for repressed mechanisms, that the genuine exploration of the self proceeds.

To put it differently: Krishnamurti, following a variety of eastern and western mystical traditions, regards *thinking* and *being* as antithetical. The more the spiritual is sought via conceptual categories, reasoning, means-and-end schemata, the more it remains elusive and unapproachable. He even rejects all spiritual disciplines, such as meditating with the use of mantras aimed at stilling the mind. *Any spiritual system, method, or technique* eventually leads to a mechanised, routinised relationship vis-à-vis the self, and in that sense it becomes anti-spiritual. In other words, it is not possible to acquire spirituality as one acquires knowledge of a language, gradually, that is, and by the use of various meditative techniques or methods.

Spirituality for Krishnamurti entails the 'pathless way'. It entails seeing, observing what goes on inside the self in totally detached manner – detachment here meaning not simply setting aside all beliefs, misconceptions and ratiocinations, but also, as much as possible, clearing the mind of all thoughts (positive or negative), all labels, all complex conceptualisations.[6] It is in this way that the empty space is created within where the spiritual can emerge. When this happens, it invariably entails a sense of unlimited compassion (or love) towards the self, towards the Other, and towards all creatures (Krishnamurti 1978).

It is precisely this overwhelming feeling of compassion that becomes a spontaneous motivation or (non-)guide to practical action. When in a state of compassion, one does not need to consult ethical codes or rationally ponder alternative courses of action; one does not need to make conscious decisions at all. Decisions emerge automatically, for instance, one knows exactly, without any planning or calculation, what to do both vis-à-vis the self, vis-à-vis the Other, and vis-à-vis Nature.

It is precisely at this point that one moves from Giddens' cataphatic to Krishnamurti's apophatic reflexivity. The latter's notion of compassion – the result of silent, detached, choiceless, internal observation – operates like divine grace does in certain Christian traditions. In the same way that the believer, by means of a corrective, expiatory purification (for instance, by means of apophatic, negatory cleansing) becomes an 'empty vessel' ready to receive the divine, so, as Krishnamurti tells us, silent observation of what goes on inside the 'spiritual non-believer' prepares that person for the emergence of compassion which leads to the right kind of intra- and inter-action. The difference between the more traditional Christian apophatic method and Krishnamurti's teaching is that for the latter the source of energy and guidance is not external but internal.[7]

A final note on the concept of reflexivity. Giddens' and Krishnamurti's diametrically opposed notions of self-reflexivity, as presented here, are obviously *ideal types*. A perfectly self-reflexive individual in Giddens' sense would be something of a computer, applying 'operational research' calculations to his or her every move. At the other extreme, being, a perfectly self-reflexive individual in Krishnamurti's sense would entail the total and impossible rejection of all purposive planning and calculation, even in such practical matters as building a bridge or learning a skill. Quite obviously, both apophatic and cataphatic self-reflexivity are constitutive dimensions of all intra-action. They are both present in various degrees, whatever the type of communication one has with one's self. It is also obvious that for the achievement of certain goals – such as accumulating economic capital or learning to play chess – it is the activistic and instrumental elements that are more relevant or appropriate. The opposite is true with respect to goals – or rather states of being, the realisation of which are not a matter of will or instrumental rationality – for example being humble, or acquiring courage or compassion (see on this point Campbell 1996: 157 ff, and Elster 1983: 50).

Reflexivity and the 'pure relationship'

This brings me to Giddens' other fundamental notion, that of the 'pure relationship' – a notion closely linked up with that of reflexivity. If, in conditions of detraditionalisation, self-reflexivity entails a non-compulsive, intra-active, self-to-self relation, the notion of pure relationship entails a non-traditionally regulated, non-compulsively established interactive, self–Other relation (Giddens 1991a). As an intimate bond between two human beings, pure relationship involves *active trust;* it involves emotional disclosure, the opening up of one's self to the Other in a context of mutual respect for each other's autonomy and self-respect. According to Giddens, it is an intimacy not based on extrinsic considerations of either *Gemeinschaft* or *Gesellschaft.* Instead, it is a type of intimacy that rests on constant *dialogue* between two human beings who can fall back on neither kinship networks, traditional codes of conduct, nor Kantian moral imperatives to buttress and sustain their relationship.

From the above perspective, pure relationship comes very close to Martin Buber's dialogic, I–Thou relationship (Buber 1937, 1947, 1952). Having been influenced not only by philosophers like Nietzsche and Kierkegaard but also by Simmel and Weber, Buber had a strong sense of social interaction as crucial for an understanding of social and moral life. His views on ethics and spirituality (after a mystical and existentialist phase) took the form of a dialogical philosophical sociology (Mendes-Flohr 1989). In this, the distinction between the I–It and I–Thou relationships plays a fundamental part (Buber 1937).

The former is based on what Weber has called instrumental rationality: the self responds to something extraneous to it (a physical object, another person, God) in a manipulative, rationalising, or calculating manner. The ultimate aim in the I–It relationship is the attainment of control or domination.

By contrast, the I–Thou relation, when applied to the 'interhuman',[8] comes very close to Giddens' pure relationship. Here the Other is neither reduced to an object, nor viewed as an extension of the self. There is a type of inter-personal mutuality[9] in which each individual retains full autonomy while opening up to and deeply understanding the Other's situation. It is from this in-between, inter-human space of open, 'undistorted' communication that the ethical in particular, and meaningful life in general, emerges. To put this in negatory terms, the ethical and spiritual *emanates* from an inter-personal situation where the rationalising, calculating, planning, utilitarian element (which transforms the 'Thou' into 'It') is absent. In default of such elements the I is able, in an open-ended interactive situation, to confirm the worthiness of the Other, and to show trust by being fully *present*: for instance, by not withholding any part of the self from the 'meeting' or 'dialogue'. A genuine meeting, therefore, being based on an I–Thou relation, presupposes a non-instrumental confirmation of the Other, which is expressed through the self being fully present to the interactive situation (Silbernstein 1989: 129 ff).

In the light of the above, it is not surprising that Buber rejects categoric-ally any attempt to derive ethical rules of conduct from sacred texts, tradi-tional religious practices,[10] or logico-deductive reasoning. For him, any attempt at codification, classification, typification – regardless of whether inspired by religious or secular theorising – automatically precludes the genuine meet-ing or dialogue. By leading from the I–Thou to the I–It type of interaction, it eliminates the 'in-between' space where the ethical and the 'what to do' can emerge. Another way of putting this is to say that codes of conduct, whether constructed via religious or secular theorising, cannot provide guidance for a concrete encounter, because each encounter is unique, unrepeatable and, therefore, not subsumable to any general category or concept.[11] This means that genuine ethical guidance can only spring from the encounter itself, it cannot be extrinsic to it (Buber 1947, 1952).

Going back to Giddens now, it can be argued that, despite the fact that his problematic is different from Buber's, his notion of pure relationship approximates the latter's I–Thou relationship. Both concepts are highly self-referential, in the sense that they exclude modes of regulation extrinsic to the relationship. They both emphasise openness, dialogue, mutual trust, and respect for the Other's autonomy. However, there is a difference with respect to the linkages between self-reflexivity and pure relationship or, in Buber's terminology, between intra-human and inter-human relations.

Here Buber implies that an I–Thou, dialogic inter-human/inter-active relation entails treating one's self in a non-instrumental, and not I–It man-ner. Whether the 'object' is the self, the Other, or Nature, it is possible to relate to it in either instrumental or non-instrumental fashion (Silbernstein 1989). Treating the Other non-instrumentally entails treating oneself non-instrumentally. On this issue Buber's and Krishnamurti's thinking approxim-ate quite closely, although the weight they give to the self–self relationship is different. Krishnamurti emphasises more the intra-active and intra-human: a pre-condition for a non-instrumental interpersonal relationship is the non-utilitarian, non-instrumental relationship one has to one's self. In Buber's case, the self–Other rather the self–self relation comes first. It is the establishment of a dialogic, I–Thou involvement with another that leads to non-instrumental, self–self relationships. Thus, although Buber considers practices of internal contemplation as legitimate, they are pathological and narcissistic when they become dominant, when they lead to a hermitic, isolated type of existence. For Buber, self–Other non-instrumental relations are more important than self–self non-instrumental relations.

For Giddens now, self-reflexivity leading to an active, do-it-yourself type of 'biography' is not necessarily egotistic or narcissistic (Giddens 1991a: 178); it does, however, entail an instrumental relationship to the self. When the self becomes the object of strategies aimed at 'character-building' or at the development of such qualities as the capacity to 'win friends and influence people', then the self is being manipulated. (A similar argument can be and has been put forward with respect to one's body – Joas 1996: 167–84). If this is the case, how compatible is Giddens' self-reflexivity (which entails an instrumental self–self relation) with his notion of pure relationship entailing a non-instrumental self–Other relationship?

What I want to suggest here is that if one limits self-reflexivity to its activistic dimension, then there is a tension between this notion and Giddens' notion of pure relationship. At least in ideal-typical terms, there is more compatibility between a pure relationship based on mutual trust and an apophatic self-reflexivity, rather than an activistic instrumental self-reflexivity. The latter type of self-reflexivity shows greater elective affinity with a pure relationship (i.e. a relation regulated by considerations intrinsic to it) based on mutual *dis*trust and manipulation.

This leads us to the conclusion that just as there are two types of self-reflexivity, so there are also two types of intrinsically regulated, or pure, relationships: a pure relationship based on active trust and mutual respect of the Other's autonomy, and an equally pure relationship based on mutual distrust and the mutual manipulation of each Other's weaknesses and insecurities. Both types of pure relationship can exist in a relatively stable manner within detraditionalised contexts. There is no reason to link, as Giddens does, 'purity' of the self–Other relationship with the life-enhancing element of mutual, active trust. Absence of extrinsic mechanisms of regulation can just as easily lead to a stable, but at the same time sado-masochistic type of relationship.

Giddens could argue, of course, that there is always the possibility of actors who are instrumental towards their self and body without being instrumental vis-à-vis the Other's. Although this combination cannot be excluded, it seems to me more plausible to establish an elective affinity between a non-instrumental self–self relationship, that is, between apophatic individual reflexivity and a non-instrumental self–Other relation, rather than vice versa. Here, however, we come to matters that can be settled only empirically. What it is important to stress in this respect is that the concepts of reflexivity and pure relationship that are here being proposed allow us to launch *researchable* projects based on questions such as:

- In what institutional conditions does reflexivity take predominantly cataphatic, and in which conditions predominantly apophatic forms?
- What precise mechanisms does a society or culture provide that can help a social actor to switch from one type of reflexivity to another?
- Is the present popularity in the West of eastern religious traditions a yearning for an apophatic type of lifestyle or spirituality that organised Christian churches have failed to provide?
- Is the resurgence of mystical Christianity in several developed countries today (e.g. Spain) related to a reaction among the young to the type of logocentric, do-it-yourself life project that Giddens sees as the only non-compulsive alternative in the present context of radical detraditionalisation?
- Concerning intimate relationships today, apart from the obvious decline of traditional 'external' modes of regulation, are there any intra-active and interactive considerations 'internal' to the relationship that explain their extreme fragility?
- Finally, on the level of social theory (i.e. on the level of 'second-order' discourses), are there, in conditions of rapid globalisation, any affinities between post-modern, anti-foundationalism and apophatic discourses on spirituality?[12]

I think that questions like the above make it clear that a more adequate analysis of reflexivity and pure relationships in conditions of detraditionalisation requires both a distinction between activistic/purposive and apophatic forms of reflexivity, and a distinction between pure relationships based on mutual trust and those based on mutual distrust. These fundamental distinctions represent a set of heuristic tools that are better able to deal with the complexities and pathologies of late-modern existence, because they can grasp more adequately the type of non-compulsive intra-active and interactive relationships that come to the fore once traditional or collective certainties decline.

Reflexivity and duality of structure

If there is tension between Giddens' notion of individual reflexivity and his notion of pure relationship, there is flagrant contradiction between the former and the basic conceptual framework of structuration theory. As I have dealt with this problem extensively in previous publications (Mouzelis 1989, 1991), I shall be very brief here. By his structuration theory, and particularly by his concept of the duality of structure, Giddens tries to transcend the divide between objectivist sociologies (structural and structuralist) and subjectivist ones (interpretative sociologies). In an attempt to go beyond the subject–object divide, Giddens defines structure as rules and resources which, like Saussure's *langue,* exist outside time and space (Giddens 1984: 18 ff). In fact, he considers structure as a virtual system that is recursively instantiated as agents draw on it in order to act and interact on a routine basis. From this perspective, structure (i.e. rules and resources) as an object is not external to the subject, since it is inseparable from the agent's conduct. Subjects, according to the duality-of-structure schema, do not face structures as objects 'out there' that constrain their conduct. It is rather that structures are both the *means and outcome* of action. So, for example, rules about teaching help me to give my sociology class, while my actually giving the class reinforces the rules of teaching. Therefore, when I (a subject) draw on teaching rules (object), the *dualism* (i.e. the distance) between subject and object disappears. It is replaced by a subject–object duality: a situation where the object is not external to the subject.

However, the notion of lack of distance between subject and object fits only cases where actors use rules in a taken-for-granted manner. When they become *reflexive* about the rules they use – that is, when they distance themselves from them in order to analyse, criticize or change them – then we move from subject–object duality to subject–object dualism. To take my previous example again, when I use teaching-rules in a routine, taken-for-granted fashion, then the duality-of-structure schema is perfectly appropriate. When, on the other hand, I distance myself from such rules because I am no longer satisfied with them, when I consider modifying them, then subject–object dualism replaces duality.

In the light of the above there is no doubt that Giddens' reflexivity (individual and institutional) entails a subject–object dualism. For instance, the 'do-it-yourself biography' entails, to use Meadian terminology, an 'I' that takes critical distance from the 'me' in order to observe it, analyse it, and actively transform it.

On the other hand, apophatic reflexivity, as I have argued in my analysis of Krishnamurti's work, entails a reduction or disappearance of the subject–object, observer–observed, I–me distance. In so far as the I does not aim at directly manipulating, transforming the me, in so far as the former is not instrumentally oriented to the latter as an object, then subject and object approximate closely and the distinction between observer and observed is blurred. To put it differently: instrumental intra-action increases the subject–object distance; non-instrumental intra-action (i.e. a situation where one treats oneself in the I–Thou rather than the I–It mode) decreases the subject–object distance.

If this is accepted, then one can go on to argue that there is a fundamental contradiction between Giddens' duality of structure schema and the way in which he theorises reflexivity in late modernity. For the latter notion is based on a clear subject–object dualism, whereas structuration theory has as its founding principle the subject–object duality.

Conclusion

I have made the following points in relation to Giddens' theory of individual reflexivity in post-traditional contexts:

1. His theory of individual reflexivity over-emphasises the activistic, purposive, instrumental aspects of intra-active, self–self relationships, and under-emphasises their apophatic, non-instrumental, non-activistic aspects.
2. Because of this, he does not take into account that in detraditionalised contexts one can avoid compulsive routine not only via a predominantly activistic/purposive reflexivity, but also via an apophatic one. Of course, in different combinations or 'mixes', both types of reflexivity are present in all intra-active situations. The theorisation of both is absolutely necessary in order to make sense of the complex ways in which subjects face the 'empty space' of growing choices created by detraditionalisation.
3. There is an incompatibility between Giddens' notion of individual reflexivity, based as it is on instrumental self–self relationships, and his notion of pure relationships, which presupposes non-instrumental self–Other relationships. A way to deal with this difficulty is to admit that a pure relationship (i.e. a relationship regulated without reference to considerations extrinsic to itself) can stably exist not only on the basis of active trust, but also on that of active mistrust and mutual manipulation of each other's weaknesses.
4. There is also an incompatibility between Giddens' notion of individual reflexivity – a notion entailing subject–object dualism – and his structuration theory, which has the duality of structure at its centre.
5. If we take seriously into account the two (ideal) types of reflexivity and the two (ideal) types of pure relationship discussed above, we have a more adequate set of conceptual tools for analysing empirically the intra – and inter-active dimensions of social life in conditions of detraditionalisation.

Notes

1. 'The idea of the uniqueness of Renaissance man and the subsequent Eurocentric view of history based upon it has prevented the Islamic influence upon *studia humanitatis* to be taken seriously in the West until now, especially since the Islamic conception of man as in perfect surrender to the Will of God stands so diametrically opposed to the Promethean and Titanic view of man cultivated in the Renaissance' (Nasr 1996: 166).

2. In the Greek, *cataphaticos* entails the notion of affirmation, and is the opposite of *apophaticos*.

3. The link of hesychasm with certain Buddhist and Sufi traditions is quite obvious. There was a long controversy within the Church over the validity of the basic hesychast positions. Eventually, Palamas' standpoint was validated by the 1341 synod in Constantinople (Ware 1986: 249). A hesychast renaissance in the second part of the eighteenth century was started by a group of Mt Athos monks, who were reacting to the rationalism and scientism of the Western Enlightenment (Ware 1986: 256 ff). Today, the hesychast tradition not only survives but is doing quite well in Russia, Greece, and elsewhere (Dupré and Saliers 1990: 417–79).

4. At the age of 14 Krishnamurti was 'discovered' in India by the clairvoyant C.W. Leadbearer and brought up as a messiah by Dr Annie Besant of the London Theosophical Society. As is usual in such cases Krishnamurti's early teachings and 'divine revelations' led to the founding of a religious order with followers, rituals, funds etc. But unlike most spiritual gurus coming from the East he, after a profound existential crisis in 1927, rejected his messianic status and all the elaborate organisational and institutional arrangements that went with it. Switching to the other extreme, he developed a secular teaching in the spiritual and ethical sphere, which is profoundly anti-foundationalist (see Lutyens 1988).

5. Of course, Giddens' concept of practical knowledge also entails an absence of conscious decision-making mechanisms. The difference, however, between Giddens' and Krishnamurti's reflexivity is that the former entails taken-for-granted, routine operations (which means that there is no reflexivity), whereas the latter entails a special type of reflexivity, an inward, 'silent' gaze.

6. Obviously, on a certain fundamental level, even silent observation entails language and concepts and this Krishnamurti ignores.

7. This is of course also the position of certain radical-liberal theologians (see for instance Robinson 1963), who do not necessarily adopt an apophatic theology.

8. According to Buber, the I–Thou relation, as a non-instrumental orientation to something outside the self, applies not only to the inter-personal, inter-human space, but also to the relationship between the self and Nature, as well as the self and God. For some of the difficulties entailed in this broad definition see Levinas (1967).

9. Buber developed the concept of mutuality late in his work. He distinguishes I–Thou relations entailing mutuality between persons, from I–Thou relations that are on the 'threshold of mutuality', for instance, between the self and Nature, or self and God (Silbernstein 1989).

10. In his later work, Buber turned more decidedly towards a secularised, anti-foundationalist position, as he found it less and less necessary to support his ideas by theology (Silberstein 1989: 146 ff).

11. 'Between the I and the Thou there is no conceptual structure, no prediction, fantasy, purpose, desire or anticipation. All intermediaries are obstacles. It is only when these vanish that the meeting occurs.' (Buber, quoted in Levinas 1967: 144).

12. With respect to this last point, I do not think that it is mere coincidence that Derridean deconstruction has been seen and criticised as a secular form of apophatic theology (Derrida 1989, Foshay 1992). It is also no coincidence that

towards the end of his life, in dealing with issues related to the care of the self, Foucault began to speak of practices not only for subjugating the self, but also of practices of freedom, relating the latter to certain forms of meditation (Foucault 1986). Although post-modernism/post-structuralism has not been able to explain very well the constitution, reproduction, and transformation of late modern social structures (Mouzelis 1995), it has been rather more successful in raising pertinent questions about the spiritual crisis of our age (Berry and Wernick 1992).

CHAPTER 5

Life politics, the environment and the limits of sociology

Peter Dickens

Anthony Giddens has had a long-standing interest in the relationships between society and nature. My purpose in this chapter is to explore his influential work, to point out what I see as the contradictions and problems within it, and to set out a somewhat different conceptual framework for understanding what he calls 'life politics'. For illustrative purposes I will give special attention to the new reproductive technologies.

The intention of this paper is not to develop an *ad hominem* critique against Giddens. Rather, and precisely because of Giddens' highly influential position in sociology, I see Giddens' work as a symptom of a wider set of issues. These primarily centre on epistemological and ontological questions, which become especially acute as sociology moves into areas such as the environment or the human body, zones where the discipline's limitations become more transparent. The problem is particularly exacerbated by inconsistent definitions of 'nature'. Nevertheless, the position can be recovered by linking the insights of sociology and science within a critical realist ontology. This is a perspective which Giddens has rejected but, as this chapter argues, it is one which is implicit in many parts of his analysis.

Giddens argues that the significance of the ecological crisis and the end of nature (in the form of innovations such as genetic engineering as well as *in vitro* fertilisation) is that human society is encountering its limits as a social and moral order, limits reached through pervasive human intervention in both external and internal nature. A vast and intolerable array of choices now has to be made, about the purpose of life, about our relations with nature, with other people and our own bodies.

The argument of this chapter, however, is that the significance of the environmental crisis and of developments such as the new reproductive technologies is not that of a vast array of choices in a moral and traditionless vacuum, but that people in modern society are simply not allowed to *understand* their own bodies and the world around them. This is because of the active subordination of some types of knowledge and the fragmentation of abstract understandings of knowledge into a complex range of distinct academic disciplines. 'Life politics' is therefore less a question of consumerist 'choice' between a vast range of options and more one of democratising biology. This entails recognising and developing the latent powers of those whose understanding of the environment and of their own nature have been socially and politically repressed. This is certainly not to attack science. Rather, it is to insist on people being able to see the relationships between their own understandings and the more abstract understandings offered by science.

Epistemology and ontology

In an interview carried out in late 1983, Giddens was asked about his views on post-positivist social theory (Gregory 1984). In particular, he was questioned about his views of contemporary realism, as represented by, amongst others, Bhaskar (1978, 1989). In some of his early work Giddens had argued for a reworking of existing forms of realism and he felt that a 'modified' version of realism could have much to offer (1977, 1982). Asked in 1983 what he felt about the value of contemporary versions of realism, Giddens' response was that while social theorists needed to remain 'alert' to philosophical issues, there should be no 'collapsing' of the distinction between philosophy and social theory. So, although he was sympathetic to the work of Bhaskar and others, he was trying to 'bracket' them to some substantial degree:

> I think it is true that any version of social theory presumes some kind of epistemological position, some position with regard to epistemological debates – for example, whether there can *be* an epistemology in a traditional sense, about which I'm still a bit unsure – but I don't think it either necessary or possible to suppose you could formulate a fully-fledged epistemology and then somehow securely issue out to study the world. So my idea is to fire salvoes into social reality, as it were; conceptual salvoes, which don't provide an overall consolidated epistemology. (Giddens in Gregory 1984: 124)

Now it is obviously important to make a distinction between epistemology and social theory. There is indeed no way in which these can be 'collapsed'. On the other hand, Giddens' stance leaves us in some severe difficulties. We cannot afford to 'bracket' philosophical from theoretical questions, particularly now that the social sciences are increasingly engaging with questions of external and internal nature. There are, in short, real limits as to what can be said within social theory without very clear regard to epistemological and ontological reference-points to the actual, real, physical world-out-there. The argument of this chapter is that Giddens' most recent work is now quite clearly demonstrating what these limits are. The same point can be made about social theory as a whole. How can claims be made about human society's impacts on nature (including our impacts on our own nature) without some reference to the insights offered by the natural and physical sciences?

First, and as I will discuss later in more detail, there is a tendency in Giddens' most recent work to attribute over-simple priorities and values to human beings. People are in practice subjected to a complex and multi-faceted set of processes and relationships. To sum these up under the rubric of what he calls 'life politics' conflates the kinds of philosophical 'meaning of life' abstractions that Giddens outlines with the much more practical, concrete and day-to-day concerns with which most of us are concerned. To put this more simply, there needs to be much more evidence that people are indeed beset and worried by 'meaning of life' questions. Are these issues which particularly beset young people, for example? Or are they more the preoccupations of elites such as sociologists and other academics?

Second, and more immediately important to this chapter, there are real problems stemming from Giddens' current interest in 'life politics'. As I have suggested above, Giddens' 'salvoes' are increasingly hurled into a reality that is both natural *and* social. And this means that the absence of 'an overall consolidated epistemology' leaves real difficulties as to what is actually happening as human societies increasingly penetrate and engage with the non-human world.

Giddens (again in line with many other social scientists) is continuing to fragment knowledge into different disciplines, those for 'society' and those for 'nature' (for a further discussion see Benton 1991). Arguably these divisions were more acceptable at a time when society had not become so deeply involved in the manipulation of the natural world. But now, as a result of the very processes Giddens describes (the humanising of nature through such recent developments as genetic engineering and the new reproductive technologies), such rigid divisions must start to be broken down. Social science still needs to catch up with what is happening in reality. Certainly the different spheres of scientific activity (as represented by, for example, physics, biology and the social sciences) are important insofar as they remain organised around, and try to identify, causal mechanisms within their sphere of analysis. Physics would obviously be unwise to look to biology if it was attempting to understand the physical mechanisms underlying nature. Biology would be just as unwise to look to sociology. And sociology would be unwise to depend on physics and biology for a true understanding of its subject matter (though it would certainly be unwise to ignore these disciplines altogether).

But, all this said, the study of the physical and natural worlds now needs merging with that related to the human world. The issue of precisely *how* such merging is to be affected is perhaps the central matter of our age. This brings this chapter to its second concern. The ways in which abstract forms of knowledge are used politically by vested interests (including those surrounding the medical profession or the biotechnology industry) to dominate lay, local and tacit understandings is also a key element in human society's relations with external as well as internal nature (for an extended discussion see Dickens 1996).

Giddens on the environment and 'life politics'

Giddens' most recent writings, and the critique of his work in this chapter, needs placing in the wider context of his very extensive earlier work. His comparatively early analysis of urbanisation, for example, can now be seen as having a strong connection with his most recent books such as *Modernity and Self-Identity* (1991a) and *Beyond Left and Right* (1994a). In *The Nation State and Violence* (1985), for example, Giddens argued that a crisis of *anomie* in modern society is closely linked to the human construction of the environment. The suppression of relationships to the natural world combined with the decline of tradition have led, he suggests, to a form of alienation, one which denies human beings as themselves part of the natural world. There are close links here with Elias' much earlier work on 'the civilising process', with modernity (and the nobles of court society in particular) repressing the outward display of greed and other biologically inherited behaviours (Elias 1978). Similarly, environmental movements are envisaged by Giddens as an attempt to recover moral, existential and aesthetic relationships with the natural world, relationships which were allegedly extant in pre-modern societies but that have been subordinated by imposed manners and etiquettes. 'The end of nature' is therefore one central feature of Giddens' most recent work (1991a, 1994a), his argument being that this 'end', combined with the end of tradition, is causing a host of new questions about the meaning of human existence. 'Life politics' is therefore envisaged by Giddens as raising primarily ethical and existential questions.

The above links closely with his more recent books, particularly with *Beyond Left and Right*. But in this later work, Giddens' view has undergone an important modification. Influenced, it seems, by the work of Ulrich Beck, his analysis focuses much more on manufactured risk as generating new forms of social movement. In *The Consequences of Modernity* (1990a) Giddens outlined what he saw as the large-scale ecological problems confronting modern society. People have become much more aware of such risks, he argued, and such awareness has spread to the population at large. Furthermore, science and expertise have come under increasing evaluation and criticism. Science has proved itself unable to spell out the unintended consequences of human actions on the environment and this in turn has led to a widespread critique of Enlightenment forms of knowledge. So *this* line of analysis suggests a change of tack. Environmental movements are now seen as less a product of existential or 'meaning of life' anxieties and more a product of real processes and real effects (Goldblatt 1996). Manufactured risk (or an emergent era of 'manufactured uncertainty') is here seen as a characteristic feature of modernity:

> Life has always been a risky business. The intrusion of manufactured uncertainty into our lives doesn't mean that our existence, on an individual or collective level, is more risky than it used to be. Rather, the sources, and the scope of risk have altered. Manufactured risk is a result *of* human intervention into the conditions of social life and into nature. The uncertainties (and opportunities) it creates are largely new. They cannot be dealt with by age-old remedies; but neither do they respond to the Enlightenment prescription of more knowledge, more control. (Giddens 1994a: 4)

Giddens' work is therefore simultaneously straddling two lines of analysis. On the one hand environmental politics are uncovering previously repressed existential questions in a context of manufactured risk and the decline of tradition. On the other, they are seen as a result of real environmental degradation. But Giddens is never very explicit about this division.

In terms of unpacking the difficulties and contradictions in Giddens' writings, Soper's work (1995) is especially useful. Sociologists need to be very clear about what is meant by 'nature' in all these arguments and there are some complex conflations taking place in Giddens' work. Soper suggests that there is an unspoken merging of different meanings of 'nature' in much environmental analysis, arguing that there are three distinguishable but intertwined notions of 'nature' in much contemporary environmental politics and discussion. One is a metaphysical concept that is used to distinguish between humanity and the non-human. A second is a realist concept, referring to structures, processes and causal powers operating in the physical world and natural worlds to which humans are subject, and that cannot be escaped or destroyed. Finally, there is what Soper calls nature as a 'lay' or 'surface' concept, often used in literary discourse and everyday life. According to this last view nature, in contrast to the human-made physical landscape, has become increasingly despoiled, polluted and in need of human conservation. This is of course a legitimate and plausible understanding but it is some way from the realist notion of a nature with structures and powers that are being manipulated with the possible outcome of a 'risk society.'

McKibben's (1990) book, *The End of Nature*, which seems to have inspired much of Giddens' thinking, is not at all clear about which of these three distinct meanings is being alluded to, and there is a similar lack of clarity in Giddens' analysis. He is never clear, for example, as to what distinctions he is referring to with the concept 'nature'. What exactly is this 'nature' that is being destroyed or 'ended'? His discussion of the civilising process suggests, as did Freud, that human beings' animal nature is being repressed. Humanity, in short, is in the process of distinguishing itself from the rest of nature. In Elias' version this would include the peasants of mediaeval society. Soper's distinction between 'humanity' and 'nature' is clearly in play here.

But Giddens' insistence on imminent pollution, degradation and risk depends on a notion of real structures, processes and tendencies in both the human and non-human world. Real mechanisms are in place, resulting in potentially catastrophic outcomes for humans and other species. Here, therefore, Giddens is actively deploying a realist view. There are also occasions when Giddens seems to be referring to a 'lay' or commonsense notion of nature as something that does not include human beings and which is being despoiled. For example, 'the "end of nature"', he argues in *Modernity and Self-Identity*, 'means that the natural world has become in large part a "created environment"' (1991a: 144). This is Soper's 'lay' or 'superficial' category. It is the popularly held view of a natural world that has become humanised and in some sense despoiled.

The problem is, therefore, that the 'nature' being supposedly 'ended' takes many and different forms in different parts of Giddens' work. The distinctions are merged or not adequately drawn out, with confusion often being the result. In the end these problems can only start to be overcome by being reformulated and by being more explicit about these awkward matters.

The 'end of nature' and the new reproductive technologies

In Giddens' latest work, the question of whether environmental degradation is actually happening is made secondary relative to an alleged widespread concern amongst the general population (either as individuals or as collective humanity) to recover meaning in their lives through the recovering of lost values, priorities and the sense of self. This argument is particularly applied to the new reproductive technologies; again, Giddens suggests that existing tradition offers little guidance in this context. As a human race, he argues, we are having to invent or re-invent our own traditions as to how to handle these innovations. Furthermore, 'life politics' is, for Giddens, 'not one of *life chances*, but of *life style*. It concerns disputes and struggles about how . . . we should live in a world where what used to be fixed either by nature or tradition is now subject to human decisions' (1994a: 14–15, author's emphasis). Again, all this is in the context of a 'nature' (in this case a human nature) which has now become fully manipulated in a modernity that has denied these connections. Note that all three of Soper's understandings of 'nature' seem to be at work in a passage such as this:

> The ethical issues which confront us today with the dissolution of nature have their origins in modernity's repression of existential questions. Such questions now return with full force and it is *these* we have to decide about in the context of a world of manufactured uncertainty. The longing for a return to 'nature' from this point of view is a 'healthy nostalgia' in so far as it forces us to face up to concerns of aesthetics, the value of the past, and a respect for human and non-human sources of life alike. (Giddens 1994a: 217)

Giddens elaborates his theme with particular emphasis on the manipulation of nature in the form of the Human Genome Project. Giddens cites one recent scientific commentary on the Project in support of his argument. This suggests that it will have set out:

> a complete genetic blueprint for humanity, uncovering not only the differences between one human and another but also deep underlying similarities between humans and the rest of the living world. Yet at the end, after all that effort (the challenge it poses) . . . is to redefine our sense of our own moral worth . . . that human beings retain a moral value which is irreducible. (cited in Giddens 1994a: 217)

Again we are in difficulties here about which 'nature' we are talking about. At one point we are discussing genetic structure as the alleged causal mechanism underlying human and non-human life. At the same time we are discussing the distinction between 'the human' and 'the non-human'.

At this point Giddens' arguments start running into further, though related, difficulties. This is partly, it must be said, as a result of relying on a particular kind of (reductionist) science. The result is plausible but in the end misleading. First, it inadequately specifies what the form of the problem really is. The Human Genome Project and the potential or actual manipulation of genes does self-evidently mean that biology is being increasingly influenced by conscious human intervention. But this does not mean that nature is in any meaningful realist sense 'ended'. The situation is actually far more complex than this and, if we switch to an explicitly realist view, it also emerges as more interesting.

It must always be remembered that the causal powers of organisms (including the causal powers of human and other bodies to give birth) remain intact despite the various forms of manipulation that are now possible as a result of the genetic code being discovered and changed. It is therefore misleading, and frankly somewhat journalistic to suggest that nature has been 'dissolved'. Furthermore, a realist view of organisms, their underlying structures and emergent properties and the fact that such properties are likely to express themselves differently in different contexts, would have helped to overcome such an over-simplified view of biological processes. As we will see, there are particular implications of such a view for recent developments in the manipulation of human reproduction but for now let us explore this further with reference to the Human Genome Project.

A central consideration missing in many understandings of the Human Genome Project, and hence in Giddens' account, is that organisms (including human organisms) operate *within an environment*. DNA is a way of passing on information from one organism to the next. It is information that is certainly central to its future growth and development from one organism to the next. But the *actual* ways in which organisms grow and develop depend on their environment, their interaction with other organisms. The information passed on via DNA only takes a particular and concrete form as a result of the organism's relationship with its environment, that is, with other organisms. To be sure, organisms are not infinitely malleable by their environment. Their real, inherent, and hereditarily acquired characteristics invite different expressions of their forms as a result of their interactions with the environment but their variability is bounded. They cannot, as indeed common-sense would suggest, take any old form as a result of their interaction with the environment. But the key point about the reductionist 'genes as a complete blueprint of humanity' version of biology is that the dialectical interplay between organisms and their environment has gone missing.

Therefore, in addition to confusions over 'nature', Giddens does not sufficiently recognise debates *within* science about the causal mechanisms of a natural world that now includes both humans and non-humans. This must be partly excused as he has adopted the reductionist view that is certainly dominant within biology. But a view such as that of Wilkie's is now becoming hotly contested by other scientists. There is now no one single 'science', not even a single science of biology. It is now becoming increasingly clear, for example, that, despite what some influential biologists may continue to say, a genetic description of an organism in fact offers us only an extremely partial understanding of the behaviour and form of that organism.

So, assuming we are still adopting a realist view of nature, the focus should be much more on organisms and about their properties, causal powers and relations with their environment. Similarly, it becomes increasingly clear that the notion of genetic engineering 'ending nature' and opening up a huge array of 'choice' is a simplistic and quite possibly dangerous conclusion.

We should therefore be far more cautious than Giddens, and many leading scientists, about the implications of the Human Genome Project for our understanding of the underlying biology of humans and other life-forms. An organism-centred view of biology, and one that insists on seeing an organism's powers developing within its environmental context, has a long, scientifically respectable, but until recently quite neglected history. Its modern version goes back at least as far as Bateson (1894) and to D'Arcy Thompson's famous book, *On Growth and Form*, first published in 1917 (Thompson 1962). A similar strategy is now being actively developed by biologists such as Levins and Lewontin (1985), Kauffman (1993) and Goodwin (1994). Jones (1991) is another contemporary geneticist who pursues this alternative view very forcibly. He writes:

The world's most boring book will be the complete sequence of the human genome: three-thousand-million letters long, with no discernible plot, thousands of repeats of the same sentence, page after page of meaningless rambling, and an occasional nugget of sense – usually signifying nothing in particular . . . The gene sequencers are pursuing the ultimate reductionist program: to understand the message, we just have to put all the letters in order. There is an opposing view which suggests that, having sequenced the genome we may be in the position of a non-musician faced with the score of Wagner's Ring cycle: information, apparently making no sense at all, but in fact containing an amazing tale – if we only knew what it meant. (Jones 1991: 323)

Similarly, the euphoria surrounding the Human Genome Project, and its supposed opening up of many life chances and opportunities, is now coming under severe question. The issue is again that of the reductionism associated with the project, the assumption that an understanding of the genetic code is the same thing as an understanding of the organism itself and its wider relationships with its environment. At one time, for example, it was thought that there was a fully genetic account of sickle cell anaemia and that this affliction could be diagnosed before a child was born and possibly treated. But this has since proved to be a chimera. This is partly because this type of genetic reductionism does not consider physiological interactions within the whole body and is therefore an inadequate specification of the individual body. But again little is known about how individuals' genetic inheritance interacts with the environment within which they are developing. As Lander and Schork (1994) put it: 'Even the simplest disease is complex, when looked at closely. Sickle cell anaemia is a classic example . . . Individuals carrying identical (genes) can show markedly different clinical courses, varying from early childhood mortality to a virtually unrecognised condition at the age of fifty' (cited in Holrege 1996: 84).

In *Modernity and Self-Identity*, Giddens makes a similar error regarding 'life politics', this time with particular emphasis on the new reproductive technologies. Here again he refers to 'the disappearance of nature' (1991a: 219). At this point he seems to be alluding to Soper's second and realist account of nature, referring to the structures, mechanisms and causal powers of all organisms. The human body, Giddens argues, has been made the sphere of social life (perhaps now indeed the main sphere) within which human identities are made, with these possibilities a result of the complete penetration of humanity into nature. 'Biological' reproduction, he argues, 'is by now wholly social, that is, evacuated by abstract systems and reconstituted through the reflexivity of the self' (1991a: 219). Once more, this 'end of nature' is envisaged as opening up multiple decisions, futures and lifestyle options to the individual:

Reproductive technologies alter age-old oppositions between fertility and sterility. Artificial insemination and *in vitro* fertilisation more or less completely separate reproduction from the traditional categories of heterosexual experience. The sterile can be made fertile, but various permutations of surrogate parenthood are also thus made possible. The opportunity offered for gay couples, for instance, to produce and rear children is only one among various lifestyle options flowing from these innovations. The fact that sexuality no longer need have anything to do with reproduction – or vice versa – serves to reorder sexuality in relation to lifestyles (although, as always, in large degree only through the medium of reflexive appropriation). (Giddens 1991a: 219–20)

This supposed ending of nature has, Giddens again suggests, combined and coincided with the end of traditions and moral systems that provide clear guidelines as to what ought to be. Once more, 'the end of nature' has led, Giddens believes, to a profound anxiety within the human condition. If the body and biology are no longer a 'given' and no longer impose a pre-destined fate on individuals, we are apparently now spoilt for choice, with a whole set of large-scale moral issues and choices being left to be confronted by individuals and their immediate associates. What, if anything, does gender mean any more? What, if anything, does 'the family' consist of? What are the rights of human individuals, as well as of other animals?

The organism in context: feminist critiques of the new reproductive technologies

A critique of this position is somewhat similar to that of genetic engineering. It would again need to start drawing on an explicitly realist epistemology, one that focuses on the body as a whole, its underlying structures, its powers for growth, development and reproduction but, at the same time, the many different ways in which such structures and capacities can be managed and understood. This territory of the new reproductive technologies has already been actively explored by a large number of feminist writers (see, for example, Arditti *et al.* 1984, Corea 1985, Stanworth 1987, Hynes 1989, Scutt 1990, Rowland 1992). First there is again the whole question of whether nature has indeed been 'ended'. Many feminist activists and writers have understandably resisted reductionist and demeaning forms of science and this has in some instances led to a hostility towards the life sciences as a whole. An example is, of course, sociobiology, where genes were again seen as largely determining the behaviours of women and men.

As a result of hostility to reductionist forms of science, much feminist work has examined the ways in which the body has been socially constructed in lay or 'surface' discourse in the exercise of male power. But all this is not to say that there is no longer any corporeal body with powers of reproduction linked in complex ways to such powers. Because knowledge is socially constructed it would, of course, be wrong to draw the conclusion that an independent reality in nature does not exist. Again, technologies such as IVF have not in fact replaced or 'ended' this corporeal body. The biological body is still there, with its complex feelings and emotions as well as the physical and chemical structures of which it is composed. And of course, whatever changes are carried out on it, it again still reacts dialectically with its social and natural environment. The question is about much more than nature having simply 'ended'. And it is also much more precise. In modern industrial societies it is centrally to do with how bodies have been medicalised. It is concerned with how, for example, formal science enables the mechanisation of the birth process to take place and whether or not women are also allowed to develop their *own* understandings and control over their bodies, within the context of a predominantly male medical profession.

Despite such technological innovations as the new reproductive technologies, there very much remains a material reality to internal nature and to the body. Indeed, the new reproductive technologies centrally rely for their 'success' on the still-remaining, underlying, real causal powers of women's bodies. It is central to their operations that they have not in fact been 'dissolved', 'conquered' or 'ended'. This is not to say, however, that such words do not describe dominant and popularly expressed attitudes towards bodies and non-human nature. These are examples of the lay or 'surface' versions of nature to which Soper alludes.

There is of course an enormous diversity in women's experiences and emotions surrounding IVF and birth itself. But at the same time a necessary commonality has to be acknowledged; one based on the real material structures and processes within bodies that are subject to change (Rose 1987). But also it is necessary to recognise that such commonality can be managed and experienced in our society in a vast number of different ways. Some may be emancipatory to women and some, as many feminists would argue, may not.

So if a real nature persists and has not in any meaningful sense 'ended', what should we make of the assertion that on offer is a wide variety of lifestyle choices stemming from such 'ending'? As with genetic engineering, this again turns out to be a quite misleading simplification. It is a product of an overly reductionist and mechanistic view of nature, including human beings' own nature. Intervention in relation to the causal processes of nature has important concrete effects. That is to say it immediately affects *how* the underlying powers and processes actually operate in the real world. Physical, psychological and social 'side-effects' (the phrase itself parallels the frequent marginalisation of these outcomes) are necessarily created and experienced. And the more abstract understandings of nature that are the currency of a medical profession often provide little in the way of predictions and ground rules for managing the complex outcomes and experiences resulting from expert intervention.

In short, there are real limits to the extent to which the whole process can be adequately 'medicalised'. This is an issue that feminist work has given a good deal of critical attention. At one level it might seem as though, particularly for the medical profession and perhaps for those women in a position to afford private sector treatment, there are indeed multiple choices to be made. Pregnant women can apparently 'choose' whether or not to continue with their pregnancy. They can learn more about the foetus and then decide whether or not to continue. And they can make this decision on the basis of the medical knowledge of their child's sex supplied to them by specialists. IVF technology can be seen as allowing infertile women to choose new ways of attempting to become pregnant. And there are multiple choices as to how birthing can proceed. Women can have other women as bearers of their child. A vast variety of family form 'options' seem possible.

Again, all this apparent choice might all look like emancipation but the real position in practice is again not so simple. Informed choice again depends on knowledge, understanding and, ultimately, power. Given the 'side effects' resulting from interventions affecting nature's causal powers there are real and very complex difficulties entailed in applying the abstract consumerist model of 'choice' to all these options over ways of acquiring a child and giving birth (Rothman 1984, Rowland 1992). The 'choices' are in practice often very difficult to make. And, as part of the complex sets of emotions a person feels, there are critical *social* pressures involved in the use of, and abstention from, the making of decisions regarding the power of women to give birth. Furthermore, as many feminist commentators suggest, the choice may indeed have moved away from the parents, and from the woman in particular, towards the medical profession. Who in practice is really in control of such 'choice' over reproduction? Is it really the woman and her feelings involved? Or, again, is it powerful social institutions such as the predominantly male medical profession and its formidable armoury of scientific understanding? Is such choice not made within the context of ruling orthodoxies? In reality we are surely dealing with a complex combination of all these pressures. In short, the apparently unproblematic notion of individual 'choice' seems peculiarly inappropriate. Rowland, as a feminist who is very antagonistic to the new technologies of reproduction, puts her understanding of 'choice' thus: 'In reproductive technology the "choice" presented to infertile women is either to live the life of the infertile with all the social stigma and negativity which is currently attached to that, or to undergo abusive, violent and dangerous procedures in the attempt to have a child. This is not choice as feminists would construct it' (1992: 279).

Hynes makes a similar point:

> Women's options, as the media and medical promotional literature would suggests, are not expanding. What is expanding is the number of women for which the technologies are prescribed, and the biotechnologists' portfolio of technical and chemical procedures to stimulate ovulation, to capture eggs, to fertilise eggs, to implant embryos. The technical and career options of the new reproductive technologies practioners are expanding. The amount of research and number of papers and symposia are expanding . . . (Hynes 1989: 140)

Furthermore, some humans may of course not be born with the powers or capacities to reproduce children at all. For them the new technologies are not only not offering choice. They can well be offering cruel delusions. As Rothman puts it:

> Just how many dangerous experimental drugs, just how many surgical procedures, just how many months – or is it years? – of compulsive temperature-taking

and obsessive sex does it take before one can now give in gracefully? When has a couple 'tried everything' and can finally stop? All of the technology still leaves many couples, about a third or more of those treated for infertility, without a pregnancy. At what point is it simply not their fault, out of their control, inevitable and inexorable fate? (Rothman 1984: 32)

So a simple picture of 'choice', with emancipated parents making agonising 'lifestyle' decisions in the face of multiple options and with no tradition to guide them again severely distorts the picture. It ignores the power relations surrounding the new technologies, the social constructions of these choices, the complex and contradictory emotions involved, the causal powers of nature and the many different ways in which a body's capacity to reproduce offspring are managed in a modern world with its complex divisions of labour and power relations. It also ignores the position of the surrogate mothers and the indignities, pain and emotions which they go through. Their protected 'rights' to have someone else's child has been called 'junk liberty' (Corea 1989).

All this is not to say that parents (and again women in particular) are devoid of human agency or the capacity to control their own bodies. Rather, as indeed Giddens suggested in his earlier work on social structure and human agency, agency is constrained, as well as enabled, by social structures, rules and resources (Giddens 1976). Furthermore, human agency in the form of the women's movement is now trying to change the institutions and power relations affecting women's lives and bodies. And, latterly, the women's movement has had a major role to play in resisting the reductionist forms of biology with which we are taking issue here. The new focus on the organism and its interactive interplay with the environment is, in part at least, a tribute to the demands of the women's movement (see, for example, Birke and Hubbard 1995). It is they who have demonstrated that a particular kind of abstract and reductionist science has consistently marginalised more qualitative forms of understanding that concentrate on organisms as a whole and their complex interplay with other organisms.

The implications of all the above for Giddens' argument are very important. If we again adopt an explicitly realist view of nature (one distinct from Soper's other two categories) we can clearly see that it has distinctly not 'ended'. It is not infinitely malleable and in practice such 'ending' does not open up a series of straightforwardly emancipatory choices for human beings. Given this view, the whole argument begins to fall apart. So-called 'life politics' (including broader environmental questions) may for some few people involve purely existential questions about the meaning of life in the context of repressed biological instincts. It may also be about the idea of supposedly pristine nature being lost. But if the literature from feminist theory is right, it is just as much, if not more, about real living bodies and about power and knowledge in the social world. It is, for example, about reducing the power of a scientific profession to make far-reaching and dangerously reductionist claims about genes or about their capacity for fundamentally changing life through IVF. It is also about linking general knowledge about genetic structures and about parts of bodies to organisms as a whole and to their environment. And, it must be said, it is about theorists in the *social* as well as the natural sciences providing their own kinds of reductionism; tacitly claiming, that is, that *they* have a monopoly of understanding of both the social and the natural worlds and that science has little to teach them.

In manipulating nature's causal powers the one thing we can be most sure of is that we can be sure of very little. We simply do not have sufficient understanding to predict the outcomes and the risks we are creating (Dickens 1996). Is global warming as a result of human practices really happening? Is the ozone layer really thinning as a result of human society's activities? Is the genetic engineering of food really damaging to humans and other animals? And, perhaps most importantly, do any of these processes, as they combine with one another and with local social and environmental circumstances, really matter in terms of risks to human and other life? Again, no one really seems to know. It is above all this uncertainty and lack of understanding that really constitutes today's 'life politics'. 'Life politics' is therefore not centrally about previously repressed existential questions being brought out into the open. It is also not simply about Soper's 'surface' understanding (one that is mainly visual and aesthetic) of something natural being replaced by something artificial.

In the case of the technologies discussed by Giddens, the picture so far is one of a continued suppression of the relatively powerless and their expertise. This is a process evident in the continuing and active separation of abstract science from the lay, tacit and local knowledges of the socially powerless. This is a characteristic feature of the environmental debate (Irwin 1995). As regards the genetic engineering of external nature, for example, attempts are indeed being made to explore how, and whether, the manipulation of seeds can be used not to increase the profits of multinational capital but to enhance and develop the traditional knowledges of farmers in South East Asia and East Africa (Bunders *et al*. 1996). In practice, however, they still offer little benefit over the practices (include such 'traditional biotechnology' as the fermentation of foodstuffs) already engaged in by local farmers. Furthermore, the new biotechnologies bring new unanticipated risks. These include damaging the environment through the release of genetically engineered organisms and, through the removal of the traditional knowledge often held by women, forcing females back into unpaid work in the home.

This discussion suggests that the distinction in Giddens' work between 'emancipatory' and 'life' politics is somewhat questionable. A consideration of the unequal relations existing between abstract and lay knowledges indicates that both emancipatory and life politics are centrally about knowledge and power.

Life politics and popular knowledge

To further appraise Giddens' theory of 'life politics' I carried out a preliminary and small-scale survey in the Mass-Observation Archive based at the University of Sussex. Giving special emphasis to the new reproductive technologies, I explored whether the so-called 'end of nature' in the form of the new reproductive technologies actually is spelling a new era of liberation for the population at large. Are the assertions made in the feminist literature correct? And how does 'the end of tradition' relate to perceptions of these technologies? Perhaps feminism has misunderstood the feelings of the population more generally. What evidence is there for Giddens' assertions about peoples' priorities in the modern age? What, anyway, do lay people conceive of as 'nature'?

The Mass-Observation Archive is a writing project started in 1937. From this year until the 1950s people from all over the United Kingdom reported on their everyday lives. In 1981 a new project was established with a similar aim and it now regularly issues a number of 'directives' eliciting the public's responses to a wide range of issues. The questions asked are open-ended, enabling people to write at the length they wish and in the ways they wish to respond. Two directives used in the following study contained an 'own choice' element; respondents were allowed, as an experiment, to name and discuss their own topics for writing. About 700 respondents, the majority of whom are women and older people, are on Mass-Observation's books, with the response rate varying around 55 per cent.

The responses outlined below were drawn from two other directives. One, dated Spring 1993, was concerned with 'birth' and with peoples' experiences surrounding birth. The other, from Spring 1985, was concerned with morals and religion. These directives were not directly commissioned to deal with surrogate motherhood and the new reproductive technologies but they enabled a preliminary exploration of popular responses to these new technologies. In addition, answers that did name reproductive technologies as their 'own choice' element in two other recent directives are covered below. There are 13 of these, all of them largely resulting from a widely publicised case in which a Scottish woman was impregnated with the sperm of an American man, with the child later being taken to the USA to be raised by the man and his wife.

What, then of the new reproductive technologies and 'the end of tradition' in these 13 popular responses? It would be wrong to suggest that these are at the centre of the great mass of lay people's concerns. Furthermore, those who did discuss these matters tended to locate them within the context of other, often more everyday, preoccupations. This particularly applied to women respondents. The value of examining the responses of the Mass-Observers is that they again show that peoples' reactions are far more complex and contradictory than Giddens would suggest. Typically they are not engaging in such abstract issues as 'the end of nature' or 'the end of tradition', 'choice' or large-scale existential questions. They are usually far more concerned with how such processes *combine*, both with one another and with the array of other practices and relationships involved in the creation and rearing of children. As feminist work mentioned above implies, their responses are above all situated. They are a result of a great range of processes and relationships, partly social, partly biological. It should therefore come as no surprise that peoples' responses are fragmented, uncertain and even contradictory. Certainly there is little evidence of a complete endorsement of these technologies as simply opening up new choices and emancipated ways of life. Similarly, there is no complete rejection of traditional and conventional morals. There remains, in other words, a complex and uneasy combination of the two, with no sign of a simple collapse of older, often religiously based, views.

The limited number of respondents to Mass-Observation for whom the new technologies could be available does suggest, however, a possible shift between age groups, with younger women being more open to the potential of the new technologies. In this sense, therefore, Giddens may be right about an emergent generation. I found just one woman, born in 1956, who took something close to what might be termed 'the Giddens view'. Here, then, is someone seeing the new technologies as potentially liberating:

> As for the possibility of birth where there was none before – I agree with it as long as there is no interference with the 'type' of child being produced – to produce a super human race would be wrong. Having a baby was the most wonderful satisfying experience of my life, an experience that I feel should not be denied to anyone. (P1219)

Against this, however, a man (a heavy goods vehicle driver) reports that reactions he was aware of 'seem to be a mixture of morality and legality'. He is referring to a recent case mentioned earlier of surrogate motherhood in which a Scottish woman had been impregnated with the sperm of an American man for £6,500. The child had been transferred to America to be brought up by the man in question and his wife:

> In particular, female reaction seems more based on feeling than reason. My wife thought it wrong but couldn't say why, I got the same answer from the two girls at work, one 23 – and married with no children, the other 17 and single. My married daughter thought it wrong because the child would always be illegitimate. (R470)

With this latter respondent we begin to see a notion of an 'end of nature' that is close to Elias' and Giddens' idea of emotions being civilised away by modernity. Note, however, that in practice it is producing tensions and problems within the individual. And with this man's distinctions between females' 'feeling rather than reason', we also begin to encounter the possibility of gender differences and the repression of feelings or supposedly irrational or emotional knowledge. This is an issue to which this chapter will return shortly.

A more typical response to the Scottish case (and one that seems to envisage a 'nature' previously untouched by humanity) comes from older women, for whom the opportunity to make use of these technologies has presumably passed. It is largely one of outright hostility. Here, for example, are three women born in the 1920s expressing their horror at the prospect of surrogate birthood:

> Personally, I find the whole thing repugnant – to quote from the lady in *Cold Comfort Farm* – 'tes flyin' in the face of nature'. (B1210)

> It is, I think, grossly immoral: why not end it, legally, by charging the mother as being a prostitute (which she is) and her husband for 'living on the immoral earnings'? Further, since the fertilisation took place, presumably within the building run by the American woman (who started it here in UK), that then becomes a brothel legally. (E178)

> Instinctively I find it repellent and unnatural. (S475)

So much for 'the end of tradition', at least amongst an older generation. For many such women the older, traditional, solution of adoption is preferable to surrogacy. Again, however, it must be admitted that these are not people who are likely to benefit from the new technologies. More central to Giddens' hypothesis are views amongst younger women who are still childless. One woman did directly raise the whole question of surrogate motherhood amongst the women she knew who were still childless. Again, the picture is distinctly 'messy', hardly one of imminent emancipation: 'None of my childless friends fancy it. One felt she would never feel the child was hers and would be jealous of the bond her husband had with the surrogate mother' (G1241).

Another woman, this time a 29 year old, had considered having a child but was rejecting it. 'I've never really wanted children,' she writes, 'though I sometimes think if financial circumstances were different, I might change my mind' (B2653). The point, here, is that conceiving a child, being pregnant, giving birth and raising a child is an immensely complex business involving power-relations and social practices as well as the 'choices' opened up by such techniques as IVF. The prospects offered by new reproductive technologies are just part of this much bigger picture. Again, so too are a host of other issues including family relations, health, money, changing forms of personal identity and the medicalisation of birth itself.

Returning to the precise question of surrogate births, the above brings us to some distinctive and possibly important differences between the reactions of men and women. These differences would again seem to confirm the more academic literature on the new reproductive technologies coming from the womens' movement. If women are more concerned to see the technologies in the broader context of social power, men seem to take a far more detached and rational view, one that centres on time and the cash nexus. It is above all here that we start getting closer to the view of the new reproductive technologies as being straightforwardly unproblematic and emancipatory. Here again, for example, is the heavy goods vehicle driver. He is referring to the same case involving the Scottish woman's surrogate birth:

> What Mrs Cotton and Mr and Mrs X did is to me just good sense, perhaps I have a strange sense of morality. Taking into consideration the actual physical effort involved in pregnancy through conception, morning sickness, backache, swollen legs and labour I think Mrs Cotton was underpaid at 96p an hour.

At the other end of the social spectrum, a director of a finance company living in an affluent area of Southern England, sees the whole issue in an extremely clinical and 'unemotional' way. It is not much more than a cash transaction in the context of a notional (and national) supply and demand curve. Wholly absent in this very dispassionate account is any notion that a child's birth might involve emotion, human engagement or complex social relations:

> An article in *The Economist* for 12–18 January 1985 gives some relevant figures. Up to 100,000 British couples at any one time would like to adopt babies but only a small fraction can now get them. For various obvious reasons, fewer children are available. Leaving aside 'step-parent adoptions' the rate of adoption of white, unhandicapped, healthy babies is about 1,200 a year. The demand is about 80 times as great. A.I.D. was condemned by various churches in the 50s but is now accepted. It is difficult to see why commercial surrogacy which would increase the supply of babies who want them, should be condemned. From what I read and comments heard there seems a general feeling that surrogacy in itself is acceptable but it is wrong for anyone to make money out of it. As there is effort and risk involved, why? It would be regrettable for the government to rush into an emotional decision on the subject. (C110)

Of course, quotations from a small number of individuals do not themselves 'prove' or 'disprove' Giddens' central ideas about the end of nature, the end of tradition, life politics and the supposed emancipatory choices opened up by the new technologies. Much detailed empirical research remains to be done, especially regarding the feelings and responses of younger people. Nevertheless, the comments above do illustrate the multiple and complex ways in which non-academic people understand the question of IVF and surrogate birth, seeming to confirm the much more problematic analyses offered by feminist writers. Statements such as those above surely do undermine any simple notion of a future composed of infinite choices and a sudden collapse of tradition. The women illustrated here are living through, and dealing with, collisions between the decline of tradition and morality, a notion that such interventions are somehow 'unnatural' and a host of other very complex and emotional issues about relationships between adults and between adults and children. All this is a million miles from a commercialised production-line view of human reproduction which, in the case of IVF and 'wombs for rent', clinically divides the process up into its component parts of sex, conception and pregnancy, pays all the people involved for their contributions and treats the child itself as a mere item to be bought or sold. It seems, however, likely that it is men (and maybe more affluent and powerful men at that) who feel most easily able to detach themselves from these issues and envisage, create, promote and celebrate such reductionist mass-production processes and the abstract 'freedoms' they supposedly make available to women. To that extent Giddens' analysis is in real danger of offering a parallel but intellectually more sophisticated version of that same male bias.

Conclusion. The end of nature or the end of sociology? Towards a realist reconstruction of 'life politics'

The contradictions and elisions within Giddens' analysis, the alternative forms of biological science outlined earlier in this chapter, as well as the responses in the Mass-Observation Archive, all suggest, therefore, that it is no longer possible to hold off or 'bracket' questions of epistemology. Realist philosophy, using Soper's second version of 'nature', helps to elucidate what is really at issue with so-called 'life politics'.

Realist philosophy or 'critical realism' offers ways of reorganising knowledge that help us understand not only the complexities underlying 'life politics' but, just as importantly, does so in an ordered and coherent fashion. Furthermore, it helps relate processes we associate with 'nature' with those in the human social world. Understanding such relations becomes increasingly important as human society steadily impinges on the mechanisms of internal and external nature.

Fig. 5.1 underpins and summarises many of the points in this chapter. As it illustrates, critical realism envisages knowledge as stratified between relatively abstract forms of understanding (to the left-hand side of the diagram) and more concrete forms (to the right). The top line, 'Philosophico-theoretical analysis', outlines a spectrum of forms of knowledge ranging from the relatively abstract to the more concrete. The bottom line, 'Theoretico-empirical assessment', shows these forms of knowledge applied to our particular problem: the relations between society and nature. Between these rows are 'Contingently related conditions.' These latter vary over space and time and affect how more general mechanisms and processes actually

116

Figure 5.1 The relations between abstract and concrete: a realist understanding of 'life politics'

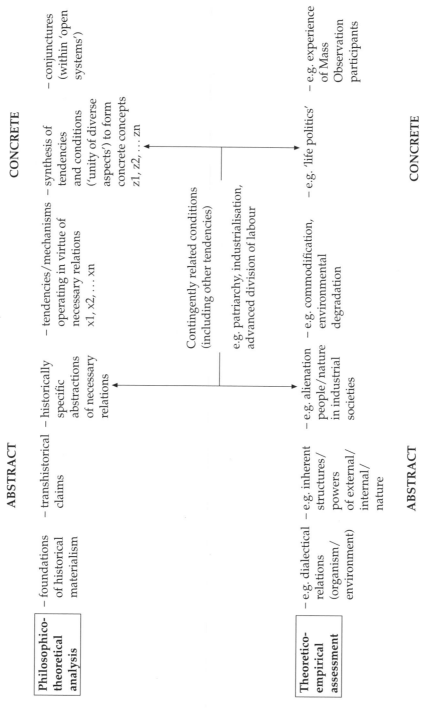

work out in concrete, experienced, terms. They also affect how a *range* of mechanisms combine with one another. Giddens' 'life politics' refers to people's engagement with highly complex combinations of such tendencies and mechanisms.

As we have seen Kate Soper suggesting, on the one hand there are relatively enduring generative structures and causal mechanisms in *both* the human social and natural worlds. Again, these are registered at the left-hand side of the diagram. Here are the more abstract and theoretical forms of understanding that are going to be of value in understanding concrete conditions. It is here, for example, where general claims are made about the necessary and internal relations between organisms and their environments and about the tendencies operating in virtue of such relations. These include, for example, the claims made by the life sciences regarding the relationships between organisms and their environment and the potential for organisms to grow and develop within such contexts.

Note, however, that entities such as human, as well as non-human organisms, are envisaged by a realist ontology as composed of only *latent* powers and ways of acting. Similarly, the internal relations within organisms and their relations with one another produce *tendencies*, but these are not necessarily expressed concretely 'on the ground'. As outlined above, and this is one of the core points about contemporary critical realism, these more general relations, potentials and tendencies combine with the contingent conditions referred to at the centre of Fig. 5.1. These latter are the particular circumstances in which these more general structures, potentials and tendencies actually operate. So understanding precisely *how* general processes actually work as concrete 'conjunctures' (again represented to the right of the diagram) is dependent not only on more general theories associated with science but on contingent factors and tendencies. Indeed, it may be that these contingencies will affect whether these causal powers work out *at all*. An organism such as a human being or a fish, for example, can in general terms be specified as tending to live and reproduce in certain ways as a combined result of its internal structures and its environment. But if particular social-cum-environmental conditions within which it is developing are contaminated it may cease to reproduce or even die.

Fig. 5.1, therefore, emphasises the contingent or specific circumstances affecting the growth and development of organisms. Abstract theories, developed mainly in the natural sciences, have much to tell us about the inherent structures, powers and tendencies within bodies or within the external environment. Social theory (particularly that deriving from feminism and Marxism) suggests, however, that contemporary industrial society alienates human beings from nature through its advanced division of labour, its fragmentation of knowledge into disciplines (such as sociology and the life sciences) while suppressing more tacit and lay understandings of such processes (for a full discussion see Dickens 1992, 1996). These latter, more 'emotional' understandings may not necessarily be correct, but one of their advantages is that they can start to over-ride the fragmentations introduced by the advanced division of labour and associated disciplinary thinking. Furthermore, the market (involving the selling and buying of information on a global scale) helps to promote *general* knowledge and expertise at the expense of the more emotional, non-expert, kind (Sohn-Rethel 1975, 1978, Dickens 1996). Prime examples are indeed the new reproductive technologies which turn a child into a commodity or what Phillips (1997) calls 'an object to be created or destroyed as an instrument of adult happiness'. Finally, and as we have seen from feminist work on the new reproductive technologies, separation of more scientific knowledge from lay and emotional understanding often marginalises self-understanding and alienates people from their own nature, their own bodies. The struggles between lay-people and the medical profession over the reproduction of children are a case in point.

Such are elements of a realist reconstruction of 'life politics', in admittedly brief outline. It should be pointed out here, however, that realism is not necessarily a royal route to understanding. Theoretical claims about organisms and the structures and causal mechanisms of which they are composed are not necessarily correct. An example of incorrect specification of underlying structures and mechanisms is sociobiology and its associated genetic reductionism. In short, while the theories at the higher levels of abstraction in Figure 5.1 are relatively reliable and robust, they are always subject to debate and revision in the light of the ongoing scientific discovery.

Assuming we adopt the interpretation of critical realism outlined above, the dualistic distinction between 'life' and 'emancipatory' politics again becomes a marginal one given that both forms of politics are an attempt by people to gain an understanding over their circumstances and power and control over their own lives. More research is needed on the complex relations and processes involved in producing the kinds of experience articulated by the Mass-Observers. And, while realism is certainly not a panacea (again, realists are as capable as anyone else of mis-specifying such structures and relationships), an ontology of this kind does at least begin to show that there are ways in which the creation of new knowledge can start to uncover and understand the necessarily complex relationships involved as human societies increasingly engage with and deeply affect the powers of nature. Realism is not therefore just a method of analysis. It can offer a route to understanding and thereby to human emancipation.

The conclusion from this critique is therefore that Giddens should now reconsider his views on realist philosophy as expressed some 14 years ago. He, and indeed most other sociologists concerned with the body and the environment, actively depend on realist views of underlying causal structures and mechanisms to accomplish what they are trying to achieve. The nature of these structures and mechanisms therefore needs making explicit. Sociology must nevertheless be careful not to make claims beyond its own expertise. In doing so it runs the risk of further confusing, and thereby further alienating, people's understanding of their circumstances. At the same time, the contemporary reconstruction of nature will necessarily entail the wholesale reconstruction of our *understanding* of society–nature relations.

How can sociology, and indeed other disciplines and knowledges, now combine with forms of understanding from which they have so long been separated? This question has to be central to any attempt at theorising modernity. A key first step, as indeed much feminist theory argues, is the overtly political one of raising the profile of lay, tacit and 'emotional' knowledge while seeing it in relation to the abstractions and power relations incorporated within Enlightenment science (Collier 1994). On the one hand scientific endeavour actively depends on lay, tacit and more concrete forms of knowledge to develop *as* science. On the other hand, non-scientific understandings often derive from the more abstract understandings of modern science (Collier 1994, 1997). There is a dialectical process at work here that needs properly explicating and understanding. And, in the end, this is a political process since it entails the democratisation of knowledge and the possibility of challenge to abstract science. Therefore in 'life politics', as in 'emancipatory politics', the central issue is power and knowledge. Once more, there is little important distinction between the 'new' and the 'old' forms of politics. Both are about subordinated people questioning dominant understandings and changing the world of which they are part.

CHAPTER 6

Criminality, social environments and late modernity

David Smith

Crime and criminality have not been central to Giddens' sociological concerns, though in his more recent work they do make some selective appearances, usually in relation to male violence against women or the sexual abuse of children. Equally, criminology has made little use of Giddens, a fact that will surprise only those who are not aware of the discipline's general isolation from the main strands of recent social theory. In this chapter I want to attend to the second of these points first, and note what limited uses criminologists have made of Giddens' work. I will then address the first point, examining the ways in which Giddens treats problems of crime, and suggesting that what is known empirically about the distribution of crime and victimisation, and the social problems associated with them, argues for a more thorough-going recognition than Giddens provides of the realities of inequality and social exclusion in the urban environment. Finally, I will suggest some lines of thinking which would allow criminological studies to make more productive use of Giddens' work, by connecting it with some of the themes in recent criminological theory and research that seem to me to offer the most hope for theoretical and practical progress. The focus in most of this will be on *Beyond Left and Right* (Giddens 1994a, hereinafter *BLAR*), since it is here that Giddens has addressed issues of crime and criminality most explicitly, though still tangentially, and has tried to develop the policy implications of his analysis of late modernity. In coming to terms with the arguments of *BLAR* I should say that I have moved from initial irritation and impatience to a position of greater sympathy and respect, a movement that is mirrored in the structure of this chapter.

Criminology and social theory

The great bulk of criminological writing (I mean writing in English, but my slender acquaintance with work from other European countries suggests that the same is true elsewhere) published over the past 20 years or so shows little interest in or influence from the main currents of social theory that have developed over the same period. This lack of connection between criminology and what most of those who profess it would still see as their mother discipline, sociology, is at first sight surprising, and for Anglophone criminology it certainly was not always so: Rock (1988, 1994) has written of the 'fortunate generation' of British criminologists, himself among them, who were recruited to universities in large numbers in the late 1960s and early 1970s. Their arrival was closely connected with the emergence of sociology as an undergraduate subject, and their main influences were a radically tinged symbolic interactionism, which gave birth to the labelling perspective (Becker 1963) and, later, a variety of humanist Marxism (Taylor *et al.* 1973). This was the generation that founded the National Deviancy Conference in 1968, that claimed to have definitively broken with positivism and the 'correctionalism' said to be entailed by it, and that established, as one of the most active growth-points of contemporary sociology, the 'sociology of deviance'; in the process, criminology was liberated from departments of law or social work and resettled in sociology (Matza 1969). The 'fortunate generation came to see themselves as the special creatures of a theoretical revolution' and 'the pivot about which criminology turned' (Rock 1994: 134–5); but by the late 1980s another revolution had occurred and another pivot was in operation. Rock (1988) wrote of the exhaustion of theory and a turn towards the empirical and practical, as the focus of criminological concern followed the interests of the funders of research, in government departments, notably the Home Office, and in an increasingly policy-oriented Economic and Social Research Council. At the time of Rock's second survey in 1992 (of all identifiable British criminologists, though using a rather restricted definition of who should count), 48 per cent were doing research on the criminal justice system rather than on crime, and only 10 per cent said that they working on 'theory' (Rock 1994: 146). The contents of the first edition of *The Oxford Handbook of Criminology* (Maguire *et al.* 1994) reflect this distribution of intellectual labour.

Of course, it would be nonsense to say that no recent criminology has been influenced by contemporary social theory: feminist theories have certainly influenced many, both in choice of research area and in conceptualisation of the issues, even though in some cases their effect has been to lead to a withdrawal from anything much resembling criminology (Smart 1990, Young 1996); and Foucault, horrified though he might have been at the thought, has clearly influenced much work on criminal justice systems, notably through *Discipline and Punish* (1977). Nevertheless, the editors of the new journal *Theoretical Criminology*, whose first issue appeared in early 1997, were surely right (from their perspective) to claim that 'far too much of the criminological enterprise has been reluctant to keep in touch with, or to display its connections to, the wider currents of thought in social and political theory, philosophy and political movements such as environmentalism, feminism, conservatism and socialism' (Beirne and Sumner 1997: 6).

Giddens has been as neglected by most criminology as any other social theorist, usually appearing, if at all, as a generic theorist of late modernity, risk or reflexivity – as a representative figure in a movement to be acknowledged in passing, rather than as a writer whose work could contribute specifically to the development of criminological theory. The occasional exceptions have focused not on risk, as one might expect given what is known of the very unequal distribution of victimisation risks, but on structuration theory (Giddens 1984). In particular, Bottoms (1994) suggests that the tradition of environmental criminology could be enriched by exploring the connections between 'routine activities theory' (Cohen and Felson 1979, Felson 1986) and the use Giddens makes of time-geography in developing his ideas on the contextuality of social action. But Giddens (1984: 116–7) was critical of what he saw as the theoretical weaknesses of time-geography (most relevantly here its naive conception of human agency), and would surely have been similarly critical of routine activities theory had he been aware of it. In fact, routine activities theory, rather than contributing to the development of theory in criminology, has been a powerful recent influence on the practice of crime control, notably the increased surveillance of vulnerable and attractive targets and the development of 'problem-orientated policing', based on the identification of spatial and temporal crime 'hot spots' and the concentration of police resources on them.

To date, the most ambitious and substantial attempt to explore the uses of recent social theory for criminology is that of Henry and Milovanovic (1996). This does make use of structuration theory, while also (despite the authors' concern to distance themselves from the irresponsible relativism – as they see it – of some post-modernist theory) having a distinctly post-modern air in its deliberate rejection of any interest in theoretical parsimony. Everything – autopoiesis, chaos theory, catastrophe theory, Gödel's theorem, quantum mechanics, fractal geometry and much else besides – is thrown into the pot. Structuration theory is, however, among the most consistent of the theoretical resources on which Henry and Milovanovic draw, in their general critique of 'modernist' (i.e. positivist) theories of the causes of crime and their particular attack on rational choice theories (of which Felson's work is usually taken as an example). Their use of structuration theory is thus very different from that proposed by Bottoms; Giddens is used (uncritically) to support their arguments about the 'mutually constitutive' relationship of agents and social structures. But, while much in sympathy with their political and policy stances, and with their attempt to produce a more theoretically informed criminology, I wish that Henry and Milovanovic had given a more sustained (and critical) demonstration of how structuration theory could be harnessed to the understanding of crime and its control; as it is, they do little more than indicate the kinds of understanding to which it might lead.

Some initial responses to the implications of BLAR for understanding crime and criminality

Thus far I have presented, selectively but I hope not unfairly, some of the hints – they are little more than that – which appear in the criminological literature about how Giddens' work might be used to inform criminological theory, and suggested some reasons for the criminological neglect of social theory. *BLAR* marks a break even with Giddens' immediately preceding work in that it is explicitly a political intervention in which broad ideas about the development of radical politics and policies are to be drawn from Giddens' own theoretical work and that of others concerned with the major questions of late modernity: globalisation, risk, reflexivity and so on. There is no need for puzzlement over what kind of text *BLAR* sets out to be, since Giddens tells us (p. 70) that he has in his sub-title echoed the title of Anthony Crosland's *The Future of Socialism*, once the 'bible' of reformists (old New Labour?) in the British Labour Party. One would expect, in such a text, to find more explicit references than in Giddens' previous work to social problems, including those associated with crime, and, up to a point, one does find them. I want first of all to record my reasons for an initial reaction of irritated scepticism to Giddens' arguments, considered in the light of what is known about crime and its effects (the subject of the following section). In summary, the reasons are Giddens' optimism and tendency to play down social problems, his voluntarism, and what might be called his 'Californianism' – his sunny sense that social difficulties can be largely solved by therapy and insight, and that everyone has access to the playful possibilities of reflexive identity construction available to 'clever people'.

An optimistic bias is to be expected in a work that is intended to show that there is a future for radical politics, but at times in *BLAR* Giddens' determination to look on the bright side of every social possibility leads to banality or sheer implausibility. Examples of the first are Giddens' repeated claim that rich and poor have common interests, notably in an ecologically sensitive anti-productivism, if only they would recognise them, and that 'male violence against women could be lessened if these developments [women's legal and occupational emancipation, male unemployment and the 'feminising' of some male careers] progress and at the same time new forms of sexual identity were pioneered' (p. 241). Examples of the second are the repeated claims, especially in Chapters 6 and 7, that poverty and social exclusion are not so bad really; indeed, they may be associated with increased opportunities for 'self-actualisation' (a suitably Californian concept). Giddens cites Latouche (1991) on the 'horrors and marvels' of the 'society of the excluded' (p. 166), but, like Latouche, he is more concerned with the marvels than the horrors, with the 'bursting variety of activities carried on by neo-artisans' than with 'the demoralised and dispossessed, often terrorised by crime and in hock to the drug dealers' (p. 167). The poor are celebrated as pioneers of a new life politics (e.g. pp. 91, 189), and 'reconstituted' families as the source of new possibilities for 'recapturing family solidarities' (p. 172). Even homelessness can provide opportunities for self-actualisation and the like (pp. 181–2), the example given being that of 'an Egyptian, who spends his nights in the parks of Milan' and 'describes his life as an odyssey' (though one without any homecoming). Giddens reports that the researchers who interviewed this man:

> found much evidence of Latouche's 'horrors': people who have given up hope, or turned to a life of violence, drugs and crime. But they were also astonished to see how many had been able to transform bleak conditions of life into a satisfying, even enriching set of experiences. (Giddens 1994a: 182)

Whether this accommodation to desperate circumstances is as much a source of hope as Giddens suggests is open to question. Compare this:

> It is not too much to say that in a country devastated by war, lying in ruins, poisoned, in a landscape blackened and charred under skies low with smoke, a Shikastan [human] was capable of making a shelter out of broken bricks and fragments of metal, cooking himself a rat and drinking water from a puddle that of course tasted of oil and thinking 'Well, this isn't too bad after all . . .' (Lessing 1981: 113)

The human capacity for resilience, for making do, making the best of intolerable conditions, is arguably not only a powerful support of inequitable economic relations but (as here) evidence of an alarming talent for self-delusion.

The criticisms that follow of Giddens' voluntarism and his rosy view of the possibilities of therapy are similar to those advanced by Hay *et al.* (1994) with reference to *Modernity and Self-Identity* and *The Transformation of Intimacy*, but they seem to apply with at least equal force to *BLAR*. Giddens consistently writes as if everyone is equally 'clever' and capable of informed, reflexive choices. Near the start of *BLAR* we are invited to 'take the decision to get married. Such a decision has to be made in relation to an awareness that marriage has changed in basic ways over the past few decades . . .' (pp. 6–7). *Has* to be made? And how much of a decision is it anyway, for a poor, ill-educated, lonely pregnant teenager? (Come to that, how much of a decision is pregnancy or having children, one of the 'happenings' said to have 'become subject to independent decision-making'?) Similarly, Giddens' discussion of anorexia (pp. 82–3) as an example of the negative consequences of reflexivity as it is applied to the self and the body suggests that everyone can both decide what to eat and therefore 'how to be' in respect of the body; and, discussing responses to health problems, he writes that 'a host of alternative treatments and therapies vie for attention' (p. 96). One wants to ask: 'What kind of choices about what to eat are available to someone who is constrained by income and lack of access to transport to shop at the local corner store? For whose attention do the varieties of therapy compete?' The answers do not need to be spelt out (on health and lifestyle variations see Blaxter 1990, OPCS 1996); we (or Giddens) are already in a virtual California (from which South Central Los Angeles has magically disappeared).

In *BLAR*, as in *The Transformation of Intimacy*, Giddens takes an uncritically positive view of the socially transformative possibilities of therapy, which he usually seems to conceive as some form of vaguely humanistic individual or group psychotherapy (e.g. the approving reference to Maslow's conception of a hierarchy of needs with self-actualisation at its apex on p. 166), but which includes Alcoholics Anonymous, treated (pp. 120–21) as a model of anti-hierarchical and liberating practice rather than the quasi-religious exclusive club that many professionals and problem drinkers have judged it to be (Saunders 1982). No doubt consciously, Giddens' enthusiasm for therapy is in marked opposition to the traditional leftist suspicion of therapeutic approaches as a means of individualising and depoliticising social problems (Mills 1943 being the classic statement of this position; see also Bailey and Brake 1975). Of course, an either/or polarisation of politics and therapy is crude and unrealistic (Pearson 1975); the point is that once again, in a field in which there is at least room for debate and scepticism, Giddens chooses the optimistic alternative as if it were unproblematic.

Criminological research

I now want to set these criticisms of *BLAR* in a more specifically criminological context, to suggest something of the reality of crime problems in contemporary Britain that Giddens' optimism and voluntarism obscure, despite his frequent off-hand recognition that the processes he discusses can and do have negative and disruptive consequences. To take statistical evidence first, it has been clear ever since a geographical breakdown of national crime survey data was undertaken that the risks of victimisation are very unevenly distributed, and that in general people living in the areas of poorest housing, and with the lowest disposable incomes, are at higher risk than the more affluent. For example, the latest British Crime Survey (BCS) findings (Mirrlees-Black *et al.* 1996) show that the risk of domestic burglary was highest for people living in inner-city areas, in rented accommodation, in flats rather than houses, with lower levels of disposable income, in households headed by a single (and young) adult, and without household insurance. A similar, though not identical, pattern of differential risks emerged for offences of violence and car crime (poorer as well as better-off households were at lower risk for car crime). Analysis of British Crime Survey data (Pease 1993) has suggested that the variations in risk between areas increased between 1982 and 1988, as a result of an increase in multiple victimisation (in the 1996 results, 28 per cent of car crime victims had been victimised more than once in the previous year (Mirrlees-Black *et al.* 1996)). The areas most vulnerable to burglary are generally also those which contain the highest number of known burglars (Maguire and Bennett 1982, Hope and Hough 1988). While the same does not hold for offences of violence, many of which are committed in and around city centre pubs and clubs, there is no doubt that areas with high crime rates tend also to be areas with a high rate of offender residence, and this is true by definition of offences on which the British Crime Survey has little to say – violence and sexual abuse in the domestic sphere.

The division of victimisation risks is thus social as well as spatial, and there are further important distinctions to be made along lines of gender, age and ethnicity in analysing the impact of crime on people's social lives and experiences (Mirrlees-Black *et al.* 1996). Women consistently worry more about crime than men (the one apparent exception, worry about car crime, disappears when only car owners are counted), and are much more likely to report feelings of insecurity on the streets, a particular worry for older women (and older men worry more than younger men). According to analysis of 1988 and 1992 British Crime Survey data, 'all minority [ethnic] groups are at greater risk than whites for both household and personal offences' (Fitzgerald and Hale 1996: 10), most of the difference being explicable by demographic and socio-economic factors, and their greater risk is reflected in higher levels of anxiety about crime, particularly serious crime, than among whites (Fitzgerald and Hale 1996: 40–44). Mirrlees-Black *et al.* (1996: 55–6) comment that, while 'BCS results have sometimes been used to argue that fear of crime is excessive', in fact: 'The consistent message of BCS results is that fear is highest in areas where the chances of victimisation are greatest, and among those with the most direct and indirect experience of crime. In other words, those who worry most generally have more grounds for doing so.'

High crime and offender rates can be both cause and effect of neighbourhood deterioration, in a 'spiral of decay' (Skogan 1990), as perceived disorder (symbolised for Wilson and Kelling (1982) as 'broken windows' which no one bothers to repair) undermines informal processes of local community control, engenders anxiety about neighbourhood safety, and undermines the local housing market. Bottoms *et al.* (1989) and Foster *et al.* (1993) provide further evidence in a British context that neighbourhoods can 'tip' rapidly into the kind of neglect and disorder in which nobody with any choice in the matter would choose to live, and that in these circumstances a violent and predatory sub-culture can quickly develop, in which young men, often the deprived and abused products of unhappy or violent families and of the official systems of care and punishment, fight among themselves and harass and exploit those most vulnerable to victimisation – the often isolated and ill-supported recipients of community care. In other words, the effects of high crime rates and the concentration of serious offenders in particular areas have consequences beyond the immediate distress and anxiety of victims, in an overall deterioration of the quality of life in the neighbourhood. Evidence of a less statistical and more ethnographic kind comes from, for example, Robins (1992) and Campbell (1993), leading Nellis (1995: 188) to note that the 'glossy brochures which herald and explain crime prevention policy to the public rarely acknowledge just how desolate life in high crime localities has become . . . and how difficult it is to reduce crime, let alone restore a sense of community, in such places'. Campbell (1993) in particular stresses the threatening presence of young, unskilled males facing the prospect of permanent unemployment in areas deprived by sometimes sudden changes in the labour market of the traditional industries of modernity, and of the social support and solidarities which they helped – however imperfectly and partially – to maintain.

There is a good deal of evidence, too, that those who typically commit the bulk of the crime in such areas tend to have suffered from various forms of social exclusion. All recent surveys of the social circumstances of known offenders have found that, as a whole, they are a group who have experienced a range of deprivations and difficulties which make their lives very different from those of Giddens' playfully reflexive choosers of their own identities from the limitless possibilities presented by globalisation. Of course, by definition known offenders are among those who have not found in poverty and exclusion an opportunity to pioneer new ways of living and of consumption, and Giddens does not deny their existence; but he certainly plays it down. Far from developing or acting out new values and new ways of relating to themselves and their environments, the aspirations of the marginalised and vulnerable young people who appear in such surveys as those of Stewart and Stewart (1993) and in Carlen's work on youthful homelessness (Carlen 1996) emerge as traditional and conservative ones (see also Heath 1992, Gallie *et al*. 1994). These young people want the conventional goods of a modern developed economy, and are painfully conscious of how their own histories and their current experiences of exclusion and deprivation act as barriers to their achievement.

The survey by Stewart and Stewart (1993) covered almost 1,400 people under the age of 24 and known to the probation service in England and Wales in January 1991. Supplemented by material from subsequent interviews (Smith and Stewart 1997), the report of the survey provides a few examples of the kind of creative and co-operative responses to poverty that Giddens would like to believe are common, but these are overwhelmingly outnumbered by cases in which poverty and exclusion seem to have produced little but strain, insecurity, unhappiness, crime, and victimisation (since known young offenders are among the groups most liable themselves to be victims (Peelo *et al*. 1992)). There was also strong evidence that compared with the survey conducted in the mid-1960s by Davies (1969), the likelihood of unemployment and poverty had greatly increased: the 1993 survey found that 21 per cent of the sample were in employment, against 59 per cent in Davies' sample. Davies concluded that material stress was not generally a plausible explanation for his sample's offending: on the contrary, 'probationers and their families were for the most part well in the mainstream of Britain's economic affluence' (1969: 31). In the later sample, poverty, usually associated with unemployment, was the most obvious source of exclusion in the lives of the young people, including those who had family responsibilities, but it was far from being the only one. As well as the stigma associated with the status of 'offender', they were far more likely than the general population to have left school with no qualifications at all (often after some experience of exclusion from school or of truancy), and far more likely to have had some experience of local authority care (a finding also true of the prison population, according to Dodd and Hunter (1992)). They were often insecurely housed, reflecting in many cases conflict with their parents, and, perhaps most strikingly of all for a population of young people (aged 17, 20 and 23), over a fifth were assessed as suffering from some chronically incapacitating disability, illness or addiction.

In this section, then, I have tried to show that recent criminological research suggests that Giddens' emphasis in *BLAR* on an alternative view of the 'underclass' to those associated with traditional left/liberal or right-wing positions in previous debates (Giddens' representative figures being Galbraith, 1992 and Murray, 1990) is at best debatable, at worst simply implausible. The experiences of victims and offenders, who are often enough the same people, in the areas of Britain's cities that are most blighted by crime, and associated problems such as drug and alcohol abuse, seem far removed from Giddens' stress on the positive potentiality of poverty and exclusion. Far from experiencing an embarrassment of choices, offenders especially but in many cases victims too are so preoccupied with problems of everyday survival, of avoiding disaster, that they have few choices to make about how (or where) to live, what to eat, what clothes to wear, or what therapy to select for their late modern identity-related ailments. There is no evidence that things are very different in the larger countries of Western Europe (Van Dijk *et al.* 1990), some evidence that things are worse in North America (Currie 1996), and strong evidence that violent crime especially has increased rapidly in post-Communist countries (Currie 1997). Everywhere crime is a far more apparent product of structural poverty and social exclusion than the creative and positive responses that Giddens wishes to use as a basis for his hopes for a 'generative politics' and 'positive welfare'.

Having recorded my irritations with *BLAR*'s blandness and tried to show how the criminological literature makes it suspect, I will now identify some aspects of Giddens' position which seem to me to be capable of fruitful linkage with the strands in recent criminological theory with which I am most in sympathy. Having overcome my initial resistance to Giddens' sunny, late hippie all-you-need-is-love optimism (with a bit of therapy where needed to get your head together) – resistance which Giddens would see as typical of liberal or leftist defenders of traditional concepts of state welfare and social reform – I will now risk incurring the same kind of criticism from the same kinds of source. In reviewing the ways in which the ideas in *BLAR* might be useful in criminology, I will first suggest the potential value of Giddens' concept of fundamentalism(s), and then explore the links between his thinking and a number of inter-related themes in recent criminology: the importance of insight and self-knowledge, relationalism, masculinities and feminisation, reintegration and social cohesion, and communitarianism. The over-arching theme of this final section is peacemaking, in the sense of the term developed in a criminological context by Pepinsky (1991): an alternative to the 'warmaking' and exclusionary approaches to crime control that have dominated recent penal policy and practice in Britain and North America, and that Christie (1993) argues are increasingly influential even in western European countries with traditionally more liberal penal policies.

Fundamentalisms and crime

In several places in *BLAR* Giddens writes of 'fundamentalisms' not only of religion but of ethnicity, the family and gender. For Giddens, fundamentalism is the defence of tradition in traditional ways, and is associated with violence and the refusal of dialogue. The concept seems a potentially fruitful one in criminology for understanding, for example, male violence against women (attributed by Giddens to gender fundamentalism), and can be connected with existing criminological work on the development of defensive sub-cultures, representing a fundamentalist attempt to re-create an imagined community. For example, Cohen (1972) described the emergence of the skinhead sub-culture in East London in terms of a defensive reaction formation in response to rapid and dislocating changes in housing, the labour market, family life (stressing the decline rather than, like Giddens, the growth of multi-generational kinship networks), and patterns of leisure; the skinheads' exaggerated representation of traditional working-class masculinity represented the 'downward', traditionalist option, while the mod subculture embraced an imaginary upwardly mobile consumerism.

'Fundamentalism' could thus be a useful concept in developing a more theoretically complete account than is currently available of the nature of the motives behind racist attacks and abuse; as Bowling (1998) points out, most recent work on this, at least in Britain, has concentrated on protecting victims rather than on the motives and meanings that perpetrators of attacks ascribe to their actions, but one can hypothesise that a fundamentalist conception of 'community' (cf. Anderson 1983) may be a cultural resource in discourses about inclusion and exclusion (Back 1996). A perceived threat to an imagined community could produce a fundamentalist response, involving the revival of cultural stereotypes and the exaggeration of available cultural identities (Cohen 1988), which could establish the conditions for high levels of racist violence, justified in terms of a struggle for resources and the translation of anxieties about identity into racial hatred. A process of this kind could explain the findings of one of the few empirical studies of this issue (Webster 1997), that those who commit racist attacks often regard themselves as victims with a justified grievance, and that such attacks are often condoned if not actively supported within the imagined dominant community.

Such an approach would also predict that racist violence will be associated with a strong reassertion of stereotypical masculinity, a suggestion which is supported by Campbell (1993), and with male bonding, more or less organised gangs, and a keen sense of territoriality. The concept of fundamentalism could underpin a more critical perspective than has been usual in criminology on the associations between 'community' and crime, recognising that in particular circumstances a strong sense of community may be actively criminogenic, at least in the case of racist violence, rather than, as has been commonly supposed, automatically protective against crime and disorder (the assumption behind such 'community-building' efforts as Neighbourhood Watch). Aye Maung and Mirrlees-Black (1994: 14) estimate that in England and Wales in 1991 there were 130,000 incidents of crime and threats against Asians and Afro-Caribbeans which their victims interpreted as racially motivated, so the problem is far from being solely of theoretical interest. A critical use of Giddens' sense of 'fundamentalism' could provide a rare example of the deployment in criminology of a concept from wider social theory that could not only increase theoretical understanding but contribute practically to the reduction of crime and fear; and criminologists have long argued that penal and social policies which stigmatise and exclude will tend to increase the cohesion and solidarity of criminal sub-cultures (Braithwaite 1989).

Elements of peacemaking

Recent criminology, in its collective efforts to acquire a respectable sociological pedigree and to distance itself from the supposedly conservative and correctionalist psychologism of its origins (Taylor *et al.* 1973), has tended to prefer social and structural explanations of crime and to be suspicious of the more personalist approach of, for example, social work. Any mainstream criminologists happening across *BLAR* are therefore likely to have been irritated by Giddens' stress on the need for 'a democracy of the emotions' (p. 16) and the links between the quality of immediate personal relationships and the potential for more authentic democracy. It is true that Giddens sometimes sounds alarmingly like an earnest marriage guidance counsellor: 'Individuals who have a good understanding of their own emotional makeup, and who are able to communicate effectively with others on a personal basis, are more likely to be well prepared for the wider tasks and responsibilities of citizenship' (p. 16).

It is also true, as noted above, that he takes a surprisingly uncritical view of the value of therapy, including 'marital and sexual therapy' (p. 117). And yet, would anyone except a sociologist anxious to preserve the purity of the discipline against psychological encroachment seriously dispute the truth of the passage quoted? There are signs that some criminologists are becoming less anxious about talk of the personal dimensions of their own practice. Pepinsky (1991), for example (and still more in his 'Peacemaking Primer' on the World Wide Web, Pepinsky 1995), stresses the need for insight into oneself and one's motives if one is to intervene effectively in situations of conflict. Christie (1997), a venerable if maverick figure in the field, has recently complained that too much criminology is tedious, repetitive and trivial, and suggested that one of the reasons is loss of access to oneself: '. . . in the process of giving room to the authorised perceptions, a depreciation of the importance of one's own personal experiences will take place'. This, one result of the over-socialisation of social scientists, may be particularly limiting for criminology:

> We have sinned and been sinned against, we have acted as law-breakers, as police, as prosecutors, as defenders, as judges, as prison guards. . . . We have also all used alcohol, abused it, or not used it at all and by that very reason had our struggles. We eat and overeat, or maybe just the opposite, and strive to control ourselves or others or to protect ourselves or others from still other people's attempt to control us. We are all continuously torn between lust and loyalties, confronted with dilemmas, often ending up with regrets for our failures. There is so little in the field of criminology we have not yet experienced. The problem is access to ourselves. Access, and respect for what we find. (Christie 1997: 14–15)

The importance of feeling and of insight into oneself and one's relations with others has also been stressed in recent criminological theory (for instance, Braithwaite's (1989) insistence on the centrality of shame, of which more later) and research. For example, Leibrich (1993) found that among the most common reasons people gave for desisting from crime were a sense of shame, a newly acquired sense of self-respect, and a reassessment of what mattered most in their lives, and that these changes in their perception of themselves were often associated with changes in their immediate social environment that created a new pattern of relationships and personal obligations, such as finding a partner and having a baby.

In *BLAR* Giddens consistently stresses the importance of the quality of relationships and of 'dialogic communication', at the personal level of marriage, family life and friendship networks, and for the development of the democratic processes, which he detects and wishes to see develop further in social movements and organisational life. Fundamentalism is conceived 'exactly as a refusal of dialogue' (p. 124) both in personal life and at the level of the global order, and while dialogue cannot be guaranteed to produce non-violent outcomes, it is often the only alternative to 'coercion and violence' (p. 244). This is true, according to Giddens, both for the gender fundamentalist perpetrators of violence against women and in the context of conflict between cultural and sub-national groups; in both cases (and Giddens argues for a 'direct line of connection' between the two), dialogic democracy becomes a prime means for the containment or dissolution of violence' (p. 244).

This line of argument has interesting and persuasive resonances with the movement for 'relational justice' (Burnside and Baker 1994), which seeks to substitute open dialogue between parties in conflict for the coercive responses to crime characteristic of formal criminal justice systems, of which incarceration is the most obvious example. Drawing on a variety of sources, including 'small society' critiques of formal, bureaucratic systems (e.g. Christie 1977) and Quaker and related thought on the value of forgiveness and reconciliation (e.g. Zehr 1980), this approach has recently gained more convincing theoretical support from the work of John Braithwaite (1989, Braithwaite and Mugford 1994). Braithwaite's concept of 'reintegrative shaming' represents a creative development of earlier versions of control theory (e.g. Hirschi 1969), which likewise stressed the importance of strong emotional attachments to others whose good opinion we would be loath to lose, but goes beyond them both in its attempt to link criminological thought with 'republican' political theory (Braithwaite and Pettit 1990), and in its capacity to suggest practical alternatives to traditional criminal justice processes. Relational justice generally takes the form of victim–offender mediation intended to achieve a mutually satisfactory settlement of the conflict represented by the offence, or, increasingly, the more public and communitarian form of family group conferencing, in which the participants are enabled to explore and express the damage done to their relationships with each other by the offence, offenders are encouraged to acknowledge and take responsibility for the harm they have caused, and they and their supporters enter into commitments designed to promote the offenders' future good behaviour. The shift, compared with traditional practice, is from stigmatisation and outcasting to reintegration, or from judging and condemning to the practical expression of care and concern. The scope of this approach, its transferability across cultures, and the range of cases in which it is likely to be feasible are still uncertain (most, though not all, of current practice is with juvenile offenders), but relational (or restorative) justice is now a significant social movement in Australasia, North America and Europe, and is a model of the kind of movement in which Giddens invests much of his hope for political change and renewal.

Feminist criminologists and those influenced by feminist thought have justifiably complained of the neglect of gender issues in most mainstream criminology (e.g. Heidensohn 1988), and have sought to remind the discipline, among other things, that the best single predictor of criminality is masculinity. In *BLAR*, Giddens several times suggests connections between traditional masculinity, violence and war (notably pp. 235–40), connections which have been more fully developed in some recent criminology (e.g.

Newburn and Stanko 1994). Nobody in the field would now dispute that explanations of crime need to take account both of the aggressive, individualistic and competitive elements in the socialisation of boys and of the apparent success of the socialisation of girls in producing (generally) more conforming and considerate behaviour. Graham and Bowling (1995) provide evidence of the continuation of marked differences between males and females in offending – and especially in serious and persistent offending – whilst Campbell (1993) makes a strong claim that the co-operative work of women is – empirically – the only constructive response to the aggressive and predatory behaviour of young men in economically deprived neighbourhoods. Giddens, following among others Gilligan (1982), argues not only that masculinity as we have inherited it in western societies is associated with aggression and violence, but that in the conditions of modernity, 'a concern with the emotions, care and responsibility tends to become devolved on women. Women become the keepers, so to speak, of the moral fabric of social life . . .' (p. 176); and elsewhere he asks: 'will femininity, with its greater emphasis on interdependence, emotional understanding and care, increasingly be transferred to the public sphere?' (p. 190).

The relational justice movement described above can be seen as an example of just such a transfer of 'feminine' values and practices to the public sphere. Braithwaite's theory of reintegrative shaming argues that inter-dependence and 'embeddedness' in networks of relationships of mutual support and care are strongly protective against crime, and therefore has a built-in explanation for male–female differences in offending; and the practices that have developed from the theory exemplify the feminine virtues of empathy, care and relationalism – Gilligan's (1982) 'ethic of care' as opposed to the ethic of justice, based on a conception of universal, decontextualised rights and values. As such, they represent a partial fulfilment of Heidensohn's (1986) hope that responses to offending might be 'feminised' by finding ways of giving greater scope to the ethic of care (Masters and Smith 1997).

Braithwaite's (1989) stress on the importance for crime reduction of the reintegration (as opposed to the exclusion and stigmatisation) of offenders has affinities with Giddens' concerns in *BLAR* with social cohesion and exclusion, and with repairing 'damaged solidarities' (p. 12). Repair or reparation of a damaged social fabric (a 'feminine' imagery of weaving and mending is almost inescapable here) has been one of the consistent aims of relational justice and, beyond the level of responding in a reintegrative way to individual offenders, a commitment to integrative and inclusive (rather than exclusionary) social practices has implications for broader crime prevention strategies.

The prevention of social harm, including that which results from crime, is a recurring concern in *BLAR*, expressed by Giddens as the need for a 'generative' politics. Reintegrative strategies for individual offenders have the potential to promote social cohesion by reclaiming offenders for membership of some caring network, rather than rendering them vulnerable to the appeal of criminal subcultures by outcasting and stigmatisation. In crime prevention strategies, an exclusionary approach could be exemplified by the 'deeply offensive image of young criminals as hyenas' (Arnold and Jordan 1996: 41) presented in Home Office television advertising: they are no longer even human, but predatory scavengers prowling round the camp-fires of the respectable citizenry. An alternative approach (Currie 1988) starts by recognising that offenders are also citizens and members of (some) com-munity, and, while not ignoring 'situational' measures such as increased physical security and means of surveillance such as CCTV, seeks to supple-ment these with 'social' measures which aim to give offenders access to the social goods of education, training and health services, and to improve their chances of participation in the labour market (Smith and Stewart 1997). It has long since been argued (Cohen 1985, Blagg *et al.* 1988) that purely situ-ational measures are likely to be socially divisive, and are liable to increase fear of crime in vulnerable social groups, notably older people in urban envir-onments, as well as contributing nothing to the reintegration of offenders. A 'generative' approach to crime prevention would also incorporate pre-school programmes and targeted support for parents, whose potential is attested by empirical research (Farrington 1996), and efforts in schools to reduce bullying and violence and to promote a sense of social responsibility, for example by peer mediation (there are accounts of this and other relational strategies in Pisapia and Antonucci 1997).

The potential value of Giddens' account of fundamentalisms in enabling criminology to develop a more sophisticated concept of community was noted above. Throughout *BLAR*, Giddens is wary of the negative possibil-ities entailed by a successful 'call for a revival of community' (p. 124), par-ticularly that of a return to an exclusionary 'cultural segmentalism' and the renewed tension and violence this would bring. Braithwaite, too, firmly rejects the feasibility as well as the desirability of a nostalgic recovery of *Gemeinschaft*, and while his work has been criticised for its communit-arian implications (neither shaming nor reintegration are possible without some accessible and influential moral consensus), he has argued that shame retains its force in conditions of modernity (Braithwaite 1993). His examples of communitarianism in effective action (Braithwaite 1995) are social move-ment politics – in the fields of domestic violence, drunk driving, and envir-onmental pollution – and the 'micro' communitarianism of 'community accountability conferences' (a somewhat extended version of family group conferences). These are opposed to the 'utopian yearning for a lost geograph-ical community that is not to be found in the contemporary metropolis' that lies behind many efforts at community policing and programmes such as Neighbourhood Watch (Braithwaite 1995: 199–200). Although some might feel that this represents a rather last-ditch effort to save the idea of 'com-munity' for criminological (and 'republican') use, it at any rate indicates Braithwaite's distance from the communitarianism of, for example, Etzioni (1993) and his followers, 'those American communitarians for whom it seems to mean beating up your neighbours if you catch them smoking on the street' (Eagleton 1997: 23).

Braithwaite can also claim that empirically both his versions of communitarianism have shown that they can produce desirable results: social movements in Australia have reduced the acceptability of violence against women in the home and of drunk driving, both associated with fundamentalist masculinity, and used shame, or the threat of it, against the corporate crime of industrial pollution (Braithwaite 1995); and there is evidence of the success of community accountability conferences and similar relational approaches to offence resolution in producing outcomes that the participants regard as fair and helpful, and in reducing subsequent offending (Umbreit 1994). Braithwaite (1995: 201–2) argues that the relative positive effect of a micro-communitarian response to offending should be greater 'in a multicultural metropolis suffering high unemployment than in a homogeneous white town with little unemployment', because the negative effects of the traditional criminal justice process – stigmatisation, exclusion and heightened resentment – weigh more heavily on oppressed minority groups. Thus, a relational, peace-making strategy is feasible and potentially effective, according to Braithwaite, even, or perhaps especially, in neighbourhoods with high rates of criminality and victimisation, and among the most oppressed and excluded social groups.

I have suggested that the concept which unites the various strands in recent criminology discussed above is peacemaking, though not all the authors cited would accept all the arguments of the explicit movement for 'criminology as peacemaking' (Pepinsky and Quinney 1991). The language, concepts and interests of this movement are very close to those of the parts of *BLAR* to which I have given most attention, and incorporate (with variations of emphasis among individual authors) all of the strands of thinking and practice in criminology outlined above. The clearest example is Pepinsky's (1995) *Peacemaking Primer*. This stresses the need for personal insight and self-awareness ('First step to peacemaking: pause to survey what you know and feel . . .'; 'Peacemaking requires self-possession'); the importance of 'honest trust' in relationships (compare Giddens' 'active trust'); and the centrality of dialogic communication:

> People cannot talk and listen together and fight one another at the same time. Peacemaking is a matter of injecting quanta of conversation into our social space – conversation which embraces the greatest victims and most powerful oppressors of the moment. The sooner the conversation begins, the less explosive violent reactions have a chance to grow to be, the sooner power imbalances will be mediated, the sooner peace will be made. (Pepinsky 1995)

Pepinsky, like Giddens, in effect, tells us that 'peacemaking is women's work', and he constantly uses the metaphor of the 'social fabric': 'social security lies in the strength of the empathic social fabrics we weave'; or

'Peacemaking is the art and science of weaving and reweaving oneself with others into a social fabric of mutual love, respect and concern. . . . The other attitude is that of . . . warmaking. We are all familiar with the art and science of warmaking. We all well know what deterrence is, for example'.

The parallels with many of Giddens' concerns are evident, and before the talk of peacemaking is dismissed as superannuated hippie wishful thinking it is worth mentioning that while Pepinsky can show that peacemaking is sustained by an active and international social movement he is if anything pessimistic about the harm inflicted by acts of violence and abuse, and assumes that large-scale social transformation is necessarily a project that will span several generations.

The 'Primer' is deliberately written in unadorned English, with a minimum of theoretical elaboration, but even Pepinsky and Quinney's (1991) more academic collection of (very diverse) essays could benefit from more coherent theoretical development. Henry and Milovanovic (1996) might begin to provide this within a criminological context; Giddens, in BLAR and elsewhere, might do the same in the broader context of social and political theory. In particular, Giddens could provide a useful reminder that peacemaking or 'pacification' (Giddens 1985) need not be (and usually is not) the non-coercive, participatory, reintegrative process described above; and this applies to crime reduction as well as to conflicts between nation-states or sub-national cultural or ethnic groups. From the point of view of advocates of 'zero tolerance' policing, those who call for a 'war against drugs', and those who encourage us to see young offenders as hyenas, 'peace' can only, or preferably, be made through the exercise of superior force. From this perspective, which is undoubtedly the dominant one in contemporary western penal policies (and to some extent also in social policies on housing and social security), peace is to be achieved by further exclusion, segregation, incarceration and coercive control; and, as in the 1994 Criminal Justice and Public Order Act, this may entail the stigmatisation and criminalisation of entire minorities. The tendencies in recent criminology outlined above seem to me to represent the most promising alternative to further coercion and repression, but it should be said that they face a daunting task, and that the process of translating criminological theory into sustainable policy has only just begun. As it progresses, the limits as well as the potential of reintegration and peacemaking as means of repairing damaged solidarities will become clearer.

Conclusion

In this chapter I have tried to summarise the (under-) use of Giddens' earlier work by criminologists, before concentrating on some of the arguments and positions of *Beyond Left and Right* that seem to have criminological relevance. I have recorded an initial reaction of irritated scepticism to the blandness and optimism of Giddens' arguments, suggesting that recent research on crime, offenders and victimisation, and the effects of crime and associated problems on economically dispossessed neighbourhoods, presents a considerably harsher picture. Some of the arguments of *BLAR*, notably its optimism about the potential for poverty and social exclusion to provide a seed-bed for pioneering ways of life appropriate to a post-productivist society, and its uncritical acceptance of a variety of therapies, still seem to merit such a reaction. Nevertheless, a more reflective response allows for some fruitful connections to be identified between Giddens' work and some important developments in criminological theory and in practical attempts to find alternatives to the coercive processes of formal criminal justice systems which, like Giddens, I regard as a demonstrable failure. *BLAR* provides an accessible route for criminologists into some of the leading ideas of recent social and political theory, and criminology can only benefit from further (critical) engagement with them.

CHAPTER 7

Modernity and the politics of identity

Martin O'Brien and Jenny Harris

Introduction

> To analyse the institutional forms through which signification is organised is to analyse symbol orders and modes of discourse; such an analysis must, however, also consider how symbol orders and modes of discourse interconnect with forms of domination and legitimation. (Giddens 1995 [1981]: 47)

In this chapter we pose a number of challenges to and offer alternative formulations of the concept of identity within the framework of structuration theory. Our intention is to develop a positive critique of the concepts of reflexivity and interaction through an assessment of the theoretical role of language use in Giddens' ontology of modern social systems. Our aim, in part, is to take up the assessment of structuration theory where other critics have left off (notably Thompson 1989, Bauman 1989) and to analyse inter-action as an 'ethnopolitical' as much as an ethnomethodological phenom-enon. We suggest that Giddens' treatment of language, interaction and social practice is both innovative and perplexing at the same time. It is innovative in shifting sociology's approach to social reproduction from (Habermasian) system pragmatics to a concern with practice and in theorising the connec-tions between agents' routine actions and institutional patterns as dynamic rather than systemic. It is perplexing because the traditions of natural lan-guage philosophy on which Giddens draws do not provide the necessary sociological bridges between agents' and institutional knowledges, resources and practices. Our discussion of language, identity and institutions will take this claim as its starting point because it is in the terms of these traditions that Giddens' ontology of recursive social systems is formulated. Respond-ing to Thompson's critical questioning of this philosophical dependence, Giddens writes:

> I do quite often seek to illustrate the recursive qualities of social systems by reference to the syntagmatic and paradigmatic aspects of language use. I feel

unrepentant about doing this, so long as one remembers that language use is not only an 'exemplar' of the enactment of social practices, but is incorporated within and expresses aspects of what those practices are. We run into problems only if we try to push the comparison beyond helping us understand how the recursive character of social systems should be understood. I would point out, though, that the term 'language' often sounds overly formal for what I want to convey. The term favoured by ethnomethodological authors, 'talk', in some ways provides a more apt parallel. (Giddens 1989: 259)

In rejecting the formalism of the 'language' comparison, Giddens restates the centrality of an ethnomethodological approach to *language use* or 'talk' in his account of social systems. Although the qualifier 'in some ways' is introduced here, 'talk' or spoken language-in-use has always been the model of social practice in structuration theory, as we explain below. This qualifier is a further elaboration of his defence of the language metaphor in *The Constitution of Society* where Giddens (1984) acknowledges that people share rules of language in ways that they do not share rules of social action. We suggest, however, that the spirit of Thompson's critique remains important and that language-use, conceived as ethnomethodological 'talk', is less helpful in theorising the relationships between interaction, identity and institutions than structuration theory implies.

In order to introduce some of the problems to which the ethnomethodological focus on language-use gives rise when used as an exemplar of the recursive character of social systems we draw on research by one of the authors with people attending a Deaf Centre (see Harris 1995a, 1995b, 1996). Our presentation of these issues is not intended to single out Deafness as a unique Other of what sociological theory takes for worldly normality. There are specific features of Deafness as a sensory reality that should alert sociologists (and natural language philosophers) to the partiality of contemporary theoretical frameworks and to the taken-for-grantedness of sociology's exclusive models of sensory experience and interactional management. As Corker (1993) explains:

Deafness is unique among disabilities in that it is the clearest example we have of the way a different experience of the world can forge a completely different approach to life, which is expressed through a *separate and unique language and culture*. The sensory world is a very *different world* without audition, and sign language is possibly the only way of fully expressing the meaning that the world has, for it is a gestural-visual-spatial language. (Corker 1993: 150, our emphasis; see also Corker 1996: 53)

We are also not suggesting that sign language is a special form of communicative deviance whose uniqueness is the exception that proves the recursive rule. Rather, we want to point to some ways that paying attention to the intersecting worlds of Deaf and Hearing cultures leads to critical questions about the concepts of common-sense, mutual knowledge and practical consciousness that underpin Giddens' (and many another's) sociology

of modern life. In presenting this discussion we focus on the political disjunctions and social differences that characterise Deaf–Hearing encounters.
We acknowledge that Deafness is constructed and experienced in many different ways and that the politics of Deafness is not reducible simply to a
binary distinction between audition and non-audition. The complex politics
of Deafness and the ways that Deafness is politicised routinely in hearing
interactions and institutions are features to which we wish to draw sociology's
attention. Our aim is not to castigate sociology for failing to treat Deafness
sociologically, however accurate this state of affairs may be. Instead, we
wish to suggest that the relationships between Deaf and Hearing experiences should encourage sociology to examine more closely the assumptions
and presuppositions on which contemporary theories of the 'modernity' of
the world are constructed. The issue that underpins our discussion of such
constructions is not *whether* actions and systems are recursive, nor *whether*
they are linked recursively, but why the social systemic recursiveness of
everyday interaction should take *this* or *that* form: why, in Giddens' (1989:
258) formulation, the institutionalisation of practices in the reproduction
of given social settings should engender *this* or *that* structural constraint
rather than a *different* structural constraint. In answer to this question ethnomethodological 'talk' is 'blah, blah' (see below) or, in other words, silence.
In the remainder of this chapter, unless otherwise stated, the words 'Deaf'
and 'Deafness' refer to what Hearing cultures commonly call prelingually
profound deafness. In this chapter we capitalise 'Deaf' and 'Deafness' to
remind readers that Deaf–Hearing encounters expose political, not merely
communicative, differences.

Reflexivity and competence

Giddens' sociological synthesis of action and structure draws on a wide
range of theoretical resources. The theory of structuration arises out of a
detailed encounter with classical sociology, which Giddens seeks to mod-
ernise. In reformulating the analytical tasks of a specifically modern sociology, Giddens has emphasised the importance of interaction and language
in his elaboration of the structuring and authorising properties of social
institutions:

> A classification of institutions applicable to all types of society must be derived, in
> my opinion, from an analysis of the structural characteristics universally implic-
> ated in human interaction. . . . All human interaction involves the communication
> of meaning, the operation of power, and modes of normative sanctioning. These
> are constitutive of interaction. In the production of interaction actors draw upon
> and reproduce corresponding structural properties of social systems: *signification,*
> *domination* and *legitimation.* (1995[1981]: 46–7)

In common with much contemporary sociology, Giddens' perspective has been influenced strongly by the 'linguistic turn' in social and cultural theory. The 'linguistic turn' itself is not a unified body of intellectual work. Rather than being a single new direction it is more a spaghetti junction of social scientific debate from which several different lines of investigation and conceptualisation may be followed. One such line, for example (itself comprising a number of branches), leads to post-structuralist perspectives on the materiality of discourse and its deconstruction; another leads to the semiotics of representation and its analysis; a third leads, via speech act theory, to Habermas' universal pragmatics. Giddens rejects each of these directions and develops the interpretive sociologies of European hermeneutics and natural language philosophy and incorporates elements of American ethnomethodology into a social theory of modern life. It is on the basis of these traditions that Giddens posits the 'centrality of language as the organizing medium of the "lived in world"' (1977: 173) and defines language as a medium of social practice (1979: 40, 1976: 103 *et passim*). Language, conceived as such a medium – a medium with structuring and authorising properties – supplies the necessary theoretical link that enables Giddens to extend the concept of reflexivity from interactional to institutional processes or, in other words, to expose the 'duality of structure':

> The notion of the *duality of structure*, which I have accentuated as a leading theme of this book, involves recognising that the reflexive monitoring of action both draws upon and reconstitutes the institutional organisation of society. The recognition that to be a ('competent') member of society, every individual must know a great deal about the workings of that society, is precisely the main basis of the concept of duality of structure. (Giddens 1979: 255)

The importance of this quote lies in the terms in which the duality of structure itself is defined. For example, in the quote above (and elsewhere, see Giddens 1979: 71, 73 *et passim*), Giddens argues that the concept of the duality of structure is based on the recognition of members' competent knowledgeability in the everyday world. The claim to competence, as Giddens' argument acknowledges, can be taken in more than one sense. On the one hand, competence may be understood as an *a priori* of interaction – in the same way that Habermas understands the possibility of agreement as an *a priori* of communication. Here, competence might comprise a foundational concept in the theory of structuration: to engage in everyday interactional and institutional settings is, by definition, to be competent in them at least to some degree. On the other hand, competence might be understood as an empirical feature of interaction: as the manifest, publicly warrantable ability to carry out actions. Here, competence is equivalent to normatively sanctioned behaviour, subject to various kinds of regulation and training by differently competent institutions and individuals.

For structuration theory, this statement of the problem comprises a conflation of questions relating to practical and discursive consciousness. Practical consciousness is a subtle 'know-how' that underpins engagement *in* interactional and institutional settings. Discursive consciousness is an accountable 'know-what' *about* interactional and institutional settings. Giddens' point is that people are both competent in the taken-for-granted, common-sense routines of social life *and* can provide reasons and justifications for their actions when called upon to do so: 'virtually all of the time', he suggests (1991a: 35), people know what they are doing and why. Practical consciousness and discursive consciousness consist in a duality that underpins engagement with the institutional and everyday realities of the modern world. Although it is not clear how, it seems evident, for Giddens, that discursive consciousness can alter the contents or operations of practical consciousness – as when people incorporate into their everyday routines new norms or tacit stocks of knowledge made available via global migration and media, for example. In turn, the subtleties of know-how by which new (e.g., 'global') interactions and institutions are co-ordinated can alter the discourses through which the latter are made socially accountable. Logically, then, movement between or across forms of practical and discursive consciousness is also something that members of society competently do. Indeed, on this basis, the reflexive monitoring of action expresses the competence of individuals to negotiate a world of intersecting practical and discursive knowledges.

An interesting lacuna in the analysis of reflexivity is that Giddens does not provide a counterfactual: an action, a knowledge, a co-ordination that would comprise 'incompetence' and/or the absence of skilled knowledgeability in everyday and institutional contexts. Extending the analysis, the counterfactual case might suggest that incompetence is as chronic (or more so) a feature of institutions and individuals as is competence. In other words, modernity may be the reproduction of chronic incompetence on the part of all humanity. Stated in this way, the thesis seems somehow more extreme than its reverse: that modernity is reproduced through the skilled and knowledgeable actions of its competent institutional and individual constituents. Yet the two statements have the same propositional form, their only difference being that one proposes the origin of the modern world to lie in competent action and the other in incompetent action.

The significance of this counterfactual view may seem obscure but there are important instances, we claim, which disrupt the relationships between agency, reflexivity and the institutional organisation of society comprising the terms of reference of structuration theory. By drawing on such instances it is possible to formulate a counter-perspective on identity and its relationship to institutional contexts. We should note, before proceeding, that it might be argued that Giddens' double-bracketing of '('competent')' in our selected extract is intended to marginalise, or place in doubt, its importance in the theory. This is not plausible, however, both because it is used without brackets in many important parts of Giddens' discussion and because it refers to the skilled and knowledgeable agents whose reflexivity is at the heart of Giddens' account of late modernity. To reflect on the competence of agents, therefore, is to reflect on the status of reflexivity as the sociological foundation of late modernity.

The incompetent agent?

We began our discussion by acknowledging the importance of language in Giddens' social theory. Language is central to both the sociological and historical dimensions of structuration theory: it is the basis of interaction, a model for understanding incremental societal change and the keeper of meaning through change:

> The mutual intelligibility of acts and of discourse, achieved in and through language, is perhaps the most basic condition of sustained interaction. (Giddens 1979: 218)

> Perhaps the prototypical instance of this [incremental change] is change in language. Every instance of the use of language is a potential modification of that language at the same time as it acts to reproduce it. (1979: 220)

> For human life, language is the prime and original means of time–space distanciation, elevating human activity beyond the immediacy of the experience of animals. . . . The spoken word is a medium, a trace, whose evanescence in time and space is compatible with the preservation of meaning across time–space distances because of human mastery over language's structural characteristics. Orality and tradition are inevitably closely related to one another. (1991a: 23–4)

Giddens introduces language into the discussion of structuration theory in many different ways, each of which is illuminating in its own right. The reference to 'orality' in the above extract is of particular note and we will return to it below. For reasons of brevity and focus, we will concentrate our discussion on 'ordinary language and common sense' because it is here, according to Giddens, that the sociologist may discover the significance of 'mutual knowledge' to both the conduct of everyday life and sociological research (1979: 252): 'Mutual knowledge is a necessary medium of access in the mediation of frames of meaning, and brackets the factual status of the tacit and discursive understandings shared by an observer with those whose conduct he or she wishes to characterise' (1979: 251).

It is not clear whether the bracketing applies to all tacit and discursive understandings or only those that the observer shares with the observed. The former would seem an implausible strategy because it would eventuate in bracketing the factual status of every understanding of every kind. In consequence, the second interpretation is more reasonable but it also brings analytical problems. For if the observer shares only *some* tacit and discursive understandings with the observed, how is the observer to know which ones are factually shared and thus bracketed? Similarly, if only some understandings are shared between observer and observed, does this not imply that similar situation may hold amongst the observed themselves? In this case, does mutual knowledge bracket all of the understandings shared between observer and *any* of the observed, or only those shared with *all* of the observed?

These methodological questions about mutual knowledges expose a theoretical issue about the relationships between knowledge, discourse and interaction in structuration theory and disturb the status of shared or mutual knowledge in ordinary language in Giddens' theory of modernity. Pursuing the counterfactual case introduced earlier, it can be argued that ordinary language and common sense display not the mutuality of (tacit or discursive) knowledge but interactional and institutional patterns of divided and dominated (tacit and discursive) knowledges. If shown to be plausible, this view of ordinary language and common sense suggests an alternative approach to the sociological problem of interactional and institutional identity formation. In order to make this case we begin with an example of everyday interaction before returning to theoretical questions about agency and language.

When is a competent agent not a competent agent?

'A competent agent is one routinely seen to be so by other agents' (Giddens 1991a: 56).

The concept of competence is not one that Giddens has addressed in any detail. Yet it is crucial to the claim that the modern world is populated by skilled, knowledgeable, clever people. However, in theoretical terms, the ethnomethodological view of competence is a problematic means of linking agency, structure and practical knowledge. We illustrate this claim by reference to ethnographic research carried out by one of the authors (Harris 1995a). Below are two versions of a field note from that research. The first version of the note is deliberately abridged because we want to draw attention to shared layers of practical or tacit knowledges in interactions:

> The hotel receptionist had accosted Edna and was asking her very slowly whether she had handed in her room key. Edna looked at her blankly. . . . The receptionist repeated the request, even slower and exhibiting keys. Still no joy. I stifled my inclination to go over and help. . . .

This field note (which we fill out below) gives rise to a number of different lines of inquiry. Here, we want to focus on the 'tacit knowledge' shared (or otherwise) among the participants. There are some features of this description of events that supply interpretive resources for competent readers of the English language. Contextual information about the scene of events, handing in a key, the slowness and repetition of speech and the inclination to assist suggest that there may be a communication difficulty. Some readers of this text may recognise similar kinds of experience on holiday or at gatherings where language differences have appeared as the stimulus to such behaviour. However, to propose that competent *readers* may share in the common sense of this description is not equivalent to proposing that *speakers* or interactional *participants* share in the knowledges or conventions of the events described. We suggest below that what is tacit knowledge for some is discursive knowledge for others in the same interactional and institutional frame. In consequence, it can be suggested that the mediation of meaning frames is not a characteristic of *mutual* knowledge as such but is importantly achieved through the *disconnections* between tacitly and discursively constructed knowledges. These observations become clearer when we fill in the gaps of the field note:

> Signing with Alastair in a secluded part of the Conference Lobby when Edna approached me. She interrupted us and *said* to me very loudly 'Is it OK to do the interview tomorrow instead of today?' I replied, 'Yes, but it will be in the Sun Lounge, not in the room allocated'. I was rather affronted by her brusque manner. Alastair was then called away on business. As I watched a curious scene began to develop in the lobby. The hotel receptionist had accosted Edna and was asking her very slowly whether she had handed in her room key. Edna looked at her blankly. [*Observer comment: I was sure that Edna understood her*] The receptionist repeated the request, even slower and exhibiting keys. Still no joy. I stifled my inclination to go over and help. Just then, one of the Conference Interpreters drifted through and Edna called her over. Edna then proceeded to insist on a BSL [British Sign Language] interpretation of the request, duly found the key and the matter was resolved. (Harris 1995a: 151)

Once the substance of the apparent 'communication difficulty' is revealed, the extended text discloses more levels of tacitly and discursively constructed knowledges. For example, it discloses normative assumptions about interactional conduct – the affront at brusqueness or the stifling of communicative inclinations; interpretive glosses on the social event – the 'curiosity' of the lobby scene and the 'accosting' of Edna; and factual claims about shared understandings and communicative contexts. But it also points to social divisions in the very tacitness or discursiveness of mutual knowledge. For what is discursive knowledge for Edna – in interactional and institutional settings I can/do participate in oral English culture – exhibits the form of a practical knowledge for the Receptionist – speak slowly with object orientation to make a Deaf person understand oral English culture. Similarly, the observer's discursive knowledge of Edna's membership of oral English culture is informed by tacit understandings of that culture (the loudness of speech) shared with the receptionist but not with Edna. The point is that, in this case, the mutual knowledge – what it brackets and what it does not – of ordinary language and common sense is anything but mutual.

The mutuality of knowledge in ordinary language and everyday interaction is, in important respects, a political as much as a social phenomenon: it is about doing the sharing, as much as it is about sharing in the doing. In relation to Deaf culture, the process of sharing and the construction of mutual knowledgeability is not a two-way political traffic. Deaf people share Hearing constructions of Deafness (HCDs) in ways that hearing people do not share Deaf constructions of Deafness (DCDs). At the same time, the background, shared knowledges and assumptions together with the contextual markers and rhythms of Deaf and Hearing interaction differ in fundamental ways. The background noise to Hearing interaction – traffic noise, conversational babble, radios, dog-barks or computer-hums – is constituted as a contextual feature of that interaction: it is drawn upon tacitly to co-ordinate interaction and is discursively accountable in interaction. Similarly, what Hearing people tacitly understand as the process of discursive accounting – the oral expression of reflexivity and indexicality – often represents background visualisation – discursive 'blah, blah' or 'jabber' (Harris 1995a: 63, 117) – to Deaf people.

What we aim to draw attention to here is the *incompetence* of participants to negotiate specific intersections of practical and discursive knowledges. This is not to assert that there can be no communication between Hearing and Deaf cultures; nor is it to pass normative judgments on the skills or behaviours of others. It is to suggest that there are differences between the mutual knowledges involved in Hearing and Deaf interaction that are irreducible to their basic or distinctive features *qua* interaction. Our argument, in summary, is that neither ordinary language nor common sense necessarily or sufficiently underpin the mutual knowledge of interacting participants. By extension, the differences between, in this case, Deaf and Hearing interaction are not consequences of problems of translation or of contrasting communicative conventions. They are, rather, power differentials: features of the location of mutual knowledges in hierarchical and dominating institutions that exhibit struggles over the ordinariness and the taken-for-grantedness of language and interaction. To borrow a phrase from Giddens, power is always exercised *over* someone (1977: 341). Locating power, rather than competence, at the centre of the construction of mutual knowledge leads to a revision in the role of reflexivity in the sociological account of modern society and a consequent reconceptualisation of the relationships between identities and institutions.

A different modernity

Deaf communication is both oral (but not aural) and visual. In the history of language training for Deaf people there has been a division between the advocacy of oralist methods (primarily training in forms of lip-reading and speech skills) and the advocacy of manualist methods (sign language). The strategic division between these two forms of language training marks a political division in processes of identity-formation and institutional development. The division is remarked upon by the British Deaf Association (BDA) in their observations on the oralist tradition of Deaf language training in the

UK. At an international congress on the future of educational policy for Deaf children in Milan in 1880 it was resolved that 'in teaching the deaf, the pure oral method ought to be preferred' (BDA 1987: 5). According to the BDA, the consequence of the resolution was the suppression of sign language: schools taught oralist methods, Deaf teachers were forced out of post and British Sign Language (BSL) was effectively outlawed. At a single stroke, a disjunction between and disconnection of visualist and oralist languages and an institutional politics of 'pure oralism' were introduced. The restructuring of the education of Deaf children in this way meant that many Deaf people were denied official access in educational settings to forms of communication through which other Deaf people interact richly (see Harris 1995b, Baynton 1997). It has been claimed that generations of Deaf people have been exposed to diminished forms of communication and inappropriate interactional assumptions and expectations at the hands of the oralist tradition. We will discuss below some broader issues in the relationships between language, reflexivity and identity. Here, we want to point to some special features of the Deaf/Hearing case that draw attention to the need to rethink the concepts of reflexivity and identity in modern social theory.

First, we should note that Deafness in the UK or anywhere else is not a consequence of modernity. It did not arrive in the UK through processes of migration, it is not a consequence of time–space compression, nor of globalisation or the spread of mass media. There is no territory whose cultural traditions, communicative conventions or state forms are Deaf and it is therefore difficult to understand how Deafness may have become 'detraditionalised'. There is no originary 'place' from which to trace the temporal and spatial elaboration (or compression) of Deafness or the signs of Deafness, so it is questionable whether the separation of space from place has affected Deaf cultures in the manner described by Giddens for dominant Hearing cultures. Participating in Deaf culture is not the same order of interaction as participating in, for example, German culture. To participate in German culture you might learn the German language and through that the assumptions and norms of ordinary German conduct, but Deaf culture is characterised by different sign language forms relating to different dominant Hearing languages.

Second, the day-to-day routines of the lived-in-world of modernity that are reproduced by 'practical consciousness' do not provide modes of orientation that answer existential questions (Giddens 1991a: 37) of Deafness. The conventions and routines of hearing interaction may supply theoretical answers to the 'Hearing' question: 'Am I (is s/he) Deaf?' but they provide no philosophical solution to the 'Deaf' question: 'why do people keep moving their lips around like that?' Or, 'what is "sound"'? A Deaf person orients to hearing language in the manner that a physicist orients to a quark. The 'sound' of hearing language – that people are in fact communicating through a hypothetical medium – is a theoretical construct whose realisation in the lived-in-world requires conscious and discursive engagement.

Third, for Deaf people, bodily control does not comprise what cannot be stated in words (1991a: 56): it is not a background condition to successful interaction. Bodily control, movement, posture and spatialisation are important discursive forms, lived-in realities of the same order as what can be spoken 'in words'. In this case, it is difficult to sustain the idea that a Deaf child's early experiences (of gestures, movements, touches) predate the acquisition of language (1991a: 56). The temporal distinction between early experience and language acquisition is viable only so long as the contents and form of the language acquired do indeed differ from the contents and forms of early experiences. Such a view of experience and language development is contentious in relation to the acquisition of spoken languages, and even more contentious in relation to sign languages.

There are senses in which Deafness has been 'modernised'. For example, cross-fertilisation between British Sign Language and American Sign Language represents the political and economic spread of Anglo-American institutions and media. Some research has been undertaken, for example, into the 'standardisation' of BSL since the introduction of programmes in sign language (Woll 1990). Similarly, some forms of acquired hearing loss – due to industrial noise, for example – are importantly tied to modern social processes. However, this is not the same as construing Deafness or specific sign languages or forms of interaction as being consequent upon or rooted in processes of global modernisation. An important conceptual issue here is whether to treat Hearing languages and cultures as the *containers* of Deaf languages and cultures and thereby to apply the same interactional and institutional analyses to Deaf and hearing cultures. Ultimately, this raises the question of whether, sociologically, it is productive to theorise inter-action in the primordial terms of a public 'talk' whose properties exemplify the practical consciousness underpinning the reflexive monitoring of action and contribute to the maintenance of a (biographic) project of the self across social situations.

Rather than theorising inter-action (oral or otherwise) as the mutual vehicle of identity-maintenance and biographic coherence, it is more useful to theorise interaction as a contested vehicle of identity-stripping and biographic incoherence or, at least, identity-channelling and biographic disarticulation, issues to which we return below. Here, we would propose that modern interactions reveal not necessarily the 'opening' of the world to existential questions of life and identity but, instead, its closure to these questions. The routines and habits of both everyday and institutional life are media for the division and disconnection of mutual knowledges, practical and discursive consciousnesses. The following quote, from a Deaf respondent, illustrates well the mundane, worldly disjunction between such knowledges:

> I know hearing people but they're not friends. My husband has his friends and I have acquaintances but they're his friends really, not mine. I've got my Deaf friends, they're mine, my friends because we share a lot of things. . . . We have a

lot of things in common, share a lot of things, talk, sign and I feel it's natural – my natural language and I can feel really relaxed in that. So the Deaf world's different. If I'm in the hearing world I feel lost, alone, it's quiet and people just jabber all the time, they talk and that's nothing really, it's empty, it's not for me. It's too cold for me. It's warm in the deaf community. (Harris 1995a: 117)

From this perspective, the modern world of talk (of spoken interaction) is a cold, empty and isolating world: a world of acquaintances but not friends, a world of unnatural nothingness whose time is filled with 'jabber'. Deafness, in this perspective, rather than being construed as a medicalised or pathologised incapacity, comprises a 'way of being' (Lane 1991: 7) that is different from the taken-for-granted knowledges and identities embedded in Hearing cultures. Deaf–Hearing interaction is not intrinsically an encounter between *differently skilled individuals* – people who are more or less competent or more or less artful in the communicative conventions of commonly available languages. It is an encounter between *differently constituted individualities* – people whose practical and discursive knowledges are refracted by disjunctions in normative expectations and assumptions and divisions of political access to resources and statuses.

It may seem that we have taken a very circuitous route to reach the proposition that modern individualities are not simply the mutual products of taken-for-granted forms of interactional mediation. After all, throughout Giddens' writings on reflexivity and identity, issues of power and norms are referred to regularly. However, our discussion has suggested that the focus on the competent knowledgeability of interactional participants reproduces normative assumptions about the structuring of the lived-in-world (as a world of mutual knowledge that provides answers to existential questions in which orality *per se* – rather than any specific oral tradition – is the primary medium of inter-action management). Such assumptions should be treated as theoretically problematic rather than as theoretically unproblematic. Rendering competence as an ethnopolitical problem rather than as an ethnomethodological solution leads to new questions about the relationships between identities, institutions and interactions. We turn to these questions next.

The uncertainty of membership

'Membership' of any everyday or institutional situation, we want to suggest, is invariably uncertain, not because of the *existential ambiguity* of modern social systems but because of their *political unevenness*. Membership is never only an achievement. It is always-already an ascriptive status in the context of which individuals struggle to realise *this or that* specific interactional and political outcome. Struggles and disjunctures characteristic of Deaf encounters with Hearing cultures reveal important uncertainties about the status of competent membership in those cultures. We address two connected aspects of these uncertainties. The first aspect relates to the adoption or rejection of membership status by individuals and groups. The second relates to the (un)acknowledged conditions of action that characterise Deaf–Hearing interactions.

Membership of Hearing cultures is not a pre-paid possession: a member of a Hearing culture does not carry an identity card that guarantees access to the facilities and sites of the culture. Instead, 'competent membership' is an intricate social and political process involving the location and dislocation of multiple identities in both everyday and institutional orders. In inter-actional terms, membership involves both the *passing* and *submerging* of iden-tities, as well as the acknowledgement and achievement of identities. The action of 'passing' identities, according to Garfinkel (1967) and others (Denzin 1990, 1991, see also West and Zimmerman 1987), is a mutual accomplish-ment of social actors operating by reference to publicly available normative frameworks (Heritage 1987: 245–6). 'Passing' means pulling off or achieving a social identity *through* the normative expectations that define the social basis of the identity. Garfinkel illustrates the process by reference to an 'intersexed person' ('Agnes') who passes as a woman, observing that 'being' a woman socially consists in 'doing' aspects of gender publicly. Giddens (1991a: 63) picks up on this work as an example of 'the details of bodily display and management by means of which gender is "done"'. Whereas Garfinkel and Agnes were eager, yet differently motivated, conspirators to the bi-partisan passing of gendered identities, there are many instances in which passing disrupts the public basis of the normative frameworks through which identity work is accountable in common-sense terms. Indeed, Rogers (1992a, 1992b) unpacks the Agnes case to reveal some of the background assumptions through which Garfinkel's ethnomethodological conclusions were reached (see also Zimmerman 1992, Bologh 1992). 'Passing' is a phenomenon of richer signific-ance than Garfinkel, or Giddens, has allowed, as we illustrate below.

Above, we commented on the divisions in tacit and discursive knowledges that characterise Deaf–Hearing social encounters. Our example of the lobby scene illustrated the social disruptions that ensue when a Deaf person passes as a non-member of a Hearing culture: a normative framework is instigated that authorises repetition, exaggeration and gesturalisation as the basis on which a hearing person may share information and knowledge with a Deaf person. The framework applies also where a Deaf person passes as a mem-ber of a Hearing culture. In the extract below, an interviewee is describing her experiences of hearing situations:

I would go in (to a hearing pub) yes, with my husband for a meal or a drink or something, not a proper drink but (after) I say 'Oh, let's go to the deaf club, I'd rather go to the deaf club'. (But) if we stay and talk, he can hear, but *I'm bored, I'm bored*. I want to get out because I'm so bored. There's all the people there, and they all talk, talk, and they never talk to me. Sometimes they say (we'd better) talk to your wife and they say 'HALLO' [*Researcher comment: very exaggerated mouth movement*] and I get really frustrated because of the way they treat me. . . . I pretend I'm enjoying it, but I'm not. (Harris 1995a: 115)

In both of the examples the person who is *doing the passing* is Deaf: passing is an ethnopolitical feature of Deaf–Hearing interactions. Although a Hearing interactant would not be aware of it, in the first instance Deafness is publicly upheld and Hearing is politically challenged; in the second instance Deafness is publicly submerged and Hearing is politically validated. In both instances the Hearing response to Deafness is the same because hearing people are routinely not competent in the reflexive monitoring of Deaf–Hearing interactions. In each case, passing and submerging comprise the public–political location of Deafness in relation to hearing cultures but *practically* hearing cultures are unaware of the difference. *Discursively*, whilst individuals may be able to provide reasons for what they are doing socially, these reasons may have no connection whatsoever with what they are doing politically. It follows that, for a Deaf person, membership of the Hearing world is practically and discursively politicised: the Hearing world silences the politics of Deafness, even going so far as openly to denigrate 'gesture politics'.

Our discussion has suggested that there are instances in which the reflexive monitoring of action does not express the competence of individuals to negotiate a world of intersecting practical and discursive knowledges. If incompetence is as chronic as, or more so than, competence, then it is difficult to claim that the social relations between Deaf and Hearing cultures are 'reflexively organised' in the manner of spoken interaction or 'talk'. Instead, we propose that hearing individuals and institutions mediate Deaf–Hearing interactions through the unacknowledged politicisation of Deafness. Whether a Deaf identity is asserted in interaction or not, whether Deaf people's biographies enable them to realise a coherent identity in the everyday world or not, whether Deaf people know what they are doing and why or not, the political location of Deafness in everyday and institutional orders remains an *unacknowledged* condition of hearing action. For Deaf people, on the other hand, the politicisation of Deafness is a (discursively) conscious process characterised by struggles, alliances, competing agenda, philosophical reflection and diverse disagreements. The politics of BSL, the classification of Deafness in institutional orders, the normative assumptions of hearing interactions are all *acknowledged* conditions of action. Deaf politics is characterised by divisions between pre-lingually profound deaf persons and persons with (partial and total) acquired hearing loss amongst many others (Lee 1992, Kyle 1991, see Harris 1995a: 154–5). Indeed, Deaf people hardly ever use the terms of reference by which the hearing world defines Deafness as a disability or deviant condition. Concourse across Deaf and Hearing cultures is always-already culturally mediated by definitional and identificatory differences that are 'discursively', not 'tacitly', exposed in Deaf cultures (Erting 1987: 148–9).

The difference of Deafness confronts the theoretical premises of structuration theory and its elaboration into a social theory suitable for modern times. The dependence of structuration theory on ethnomethodological notions of talk – the way that social encounters are described and explained as if they exhibited the practical consciousness rooted in hearing interaction management – represents a problematic political basis for the development of social theory. Indeed, one can observe that the 'linguistic turn' in social theory more generally has failed signally to consider the experience and the politics of Deafness: it is an exclusive theoretical direction that takes an apparent common denominator of dominant forms of interaction as the basis for descriptions of global social phenomena. Deafness alerts sociology to the danger of so easily accepting something that is *politically dominant* – a specific medium of oral/aural communication – as if it were *socially normative* – a framework for social life as such. The basis of Deaf–Hearing interactions is not the mutual knowledge embedded in spoken interaction. As we have seen, the expression and management of such mutual knowledge for Deaf people is often cold, uncommunicative, exclusive 'blah, blah'. Yet, whilst Deafness brings a specific inflection to the experience of interaction, the coldness, exclusion and uncommunicativity is not only experienced by Deaf people. Contemporary social interactions of many kinds are marked by these features: by the policing and denial of mutual, practical knowledges and by the erection of barriers to, and boundaries around, 'competent' social membership. The political critique posed by Deaf cultures simultaneously articulates counter-perspectives on how the 'normal' world of everyday and institutional interactions is constructed.

The passing of modernity

The ethnopolitics of Deaf–Hearing interaction reveals the extent to which the social world is criss-crossed by political differences that destabilise the fixities of identity categories and problematise the 'normal' social functioning of both everyday and institutional contexts. Identities are not realised in and through the normative conventions of social 'talk'. Instead, they are (at least as often) suppressed, hidden or denied through those very conventions because identities are relational: any particular identity persists in relation to others that are socially differentiated and politically irregular. The work of identity passing and submerging, on which we commented above, exposes the fact that the irregularity of membership is an implicit and irreducible dimension of social interaction: passing is at one and the same time a personal display of socially sanctioned membership criteria and a public suppression of the political differences in which social identities are rooted. Passing, in this regard, may disclose a 'tragic' socio-logic (Butler 1993: 185) through which the 'normal' operations of the social world are maintained at the cost of denial, domination, secrecy and subterfuge.

Whilst it may be the case that social 'talk' frames the realisation of some identity or another in everyday and institutional contexts, it does not follow that this applies to any and every identity at all, nor does it follow that the model of talk provides the 'degree zero' of identity validation. We have addressed this problem by focusing on the relationships between Deaf and Hearing cultures but similar issues invariably arise whenever power is located at the centre of interactional and institutional processes. The work of identity passing has been explored in feminist sociological and cultural studies (Ahmed 1999, Tyler 1994) in the context of racialised and sexualised social relations. Ahmed's discussion of passing (1999), for example, notes that identities are inherently political and that there are structural constraints on their realisation in all social encounters that exceed the structuring properties of interactional conventions – an issue to which we return briefly below. Ahmed's work is important for many reasons but for the purposes of our discussion we would note that her analysis of passing reveals much about the limitations to which identities are subjected in modern social life. In particular, Ahmed's discussion draws attention to processes of *identification* rather than to categories of identity as such. Here, Ahmed observes that the mobility of the subject – the movement of subjective identifications across social locations – comprises a persistent 're-staging' or 're-opening' of the fractured histories of identity politics. That such histories are fractured is made apparent by the *difference* that passing introduces into the mundanity of social life. Passing, she argues, is not an 'ability' or skilled accomplishment available to everyone by virtue of their being already human. Rather, passing is an exclusive technique which 'depends on the relation between subjects and structures of identification where the subject sees itself – or is seen by others – as not quite fitting' (1999).

To acknowledge the fractured and relational character of identifications is to acknowledge that the status of competent membership in both the lived-in world of everyday encounters and the institutional world of structured social orders is simultaneously an achievement and an ascription. The status of competent membership in one setting does not guarantee competence in all settings: competence must be worked at discursively, socially and politically and is denied in the same measure as it is bestowed. It is not something that can be taken for granted on the basis of interactional skill. To pass for a competent member – to be 'routinely seen' to be competent by others – comprises a *denial* of identifications, their histories, their referents and their differences. Passing reveals the extent to which specific political differentiations are inscribed in the very heart of 'normal' social transactions. Such transactions – whether interactional or institutional – do not routinely provide resources for realising the coherence of biographically co-ordinated identifications. Instead, they provide for the routinisation of 'not quite fitting' into socially ordered patterns of conduct and control. Modern identitifications comprise routine identity passes by individual and collective agents who *never quite fit* the normative conventions of social 'talk'.

Concluding comments

The basic proposition of structuration theory is that social structures are both media and outcomes of situated social activity. We would suggest, on the basis of our discussion, that neither the situatedness nor the structured-ness of activity comprises a mutual condition for the development, realisa-tion or achievement of competent membership in modern social orders. Social membership in the modern world is relational and hierarchical, exclusive and fully politicised. Our discussion has suggested that the ethno-methodological notion of 'talk' is a problematic basis for the development of a social theory of modernity. We have indicated that the social routines, the mutual knowledges and the shared common sense of 'talk' do not provide the resources necessary to realise identities in, or competent membership of, modern social orders. Our aim has been to draw sociology's attention to the intersections between Deaf and Hearing cultures in order to problematise taken-for-granted assumptions about the management and co-ordination of both everyday and institutional contexts. Sociology has ignored Deafness – except in the terms of a social 'problem' – and in doing so has failed to reflect critically on the validity and applicability of important concepts in its theoretical frameworks. We have suggested, in relation to the structuration-theoretical perspective developed by Giddens, that such frameworks are based on assumptions about the normative universality of politically dom-inant forms of interaction that do not stand up to critical scrutiny.

A sociological assessment of Deaf–Hearing interaction shows that it is char-acterised by a dualism of the self that rests on the politicisation of Deafness and not on the routine reflexivity of the everyday world. For a Hearing person the 'I' of the Deaf person's identity and the 'I' of the Deaf person's interaction are the same: inside the Deaf interactant is a Hearing person's identity that can be socially realised by the invocation of specific codes of behavioural conduct. As we have argued, however, this code expresses precisely the *incompetence* of hearing people to negotiate the intersection of the practical and discursive knowledges involved in Deaf–Hearing encoun-ters. For a Deaf person, on the other hand, the 'I' of interaction in the Hearing world and the 'I' of identity are distinct: a Deaf person is subject to the 'jabber' of hearing interaction in ways that a Hearing person is not. Inside the Deaf person is not a Hearing identity that can be socially realised through 'jabber'. A Deaf person passes as a competent member of a hearing world into which, politically, Deafness does not quite fit. Sociology needs must pay attention to the conditioning of such differences – to the fractured identifications through which interactional and institutional encounters are routinely seen to be competently done by agents – in order to retain a crit-ical focus on the irregularities and inequalities of social membership. To coin a phrase: the 'I and I' of modern interactions is not the 'we' of the modern world: modern interactions routinely expose an ethnopolitics of difference in the everyday and institutional settings of contemporary life.

CHAPTER 8

Theorising identity, difference and social divisions

Floya Anthias

This chapter explores contemporary approaches to late modernity, identity and globalisation and assesses their potential for developing new understandings of difference and identity. In particular, I will focus on the differentiations and inequalities relating to ethnicity and racialisation. The aim is to go beyond Giddens' structure–agency framework and to explore alternative views found, especially, in debates about cultural hybridity and diaspora. The chapter develops a framework for theorising social divisions and identities that points to the existence of socially constructed ontological spaces (of gender, ethnicity and class) on the one hand, and locates the understanding of social relations of difference and inequality in their intersections, on the other.

In much of his recent work Giddens deploys a universalising notion of 'we', related to modernity. However, western modernity, with its universalising and hegemonic discourses, has been a product of the exploitation of 'subaltern' peoples and cultures and therefore the term modernity needs to be used with caution. Giddens constructs a notion of the self as a collective agent who is historicised through the globalising tendencies of modernity. For Giddens, late modernity is characterised by global as opposed to national forms of capital and the globalisation of culture. The self is presented as unitary within these processes, thus downplaying issues of power and subordination within globalisation and modernity. The person becomes reduced to the essentialised figure or self of high modernity, which is identified with western social forms.

Yet, it could be argued that the self in high modernity is constituted in the different existential or ontological places of class location, sexual difference and collective or ethnic belongingness at the global as well as national levels. These do not take any necessary social forms but are intertwined in complex new ways that produce contradictory social locations, arising from the differential positioning of persons within the hierarchical orders of each existential location. The self is thus constructed in terms of multiplicity and contextuality rather than as a unitary process. The ideas of hybridity and double consciousness, it will be argued later on in this chapter, have attempted to pay attention to this but fail in as much as the hybrid or diasporic self is constructed as a unity. Although such contradictory locations have always existed they have been made more acute by the increasing differentiation and fragmentation of social life in the post-modern period or, using Giddens' term, the period of late modernity.

It is the effects of the latter, for Giddens, that give rise to the self's orientation towards 'pure relationships'. For Giddens, such orientations no longer depend on consonance with given social roles: the self is oriented to others in terms of his or her own personal growth and in a self-reflexive way – for example, through a process of individuation. Giddens thus shares with Weber the link between individual orientations and the 'spirit of the age', in this case modernity rather than capitalism. It has been argued (Scott 1995, Ellison 1997) that this view places too much emphasis on voluntarism. However, it could also be argued that Giddens retains a notion of selfhood that is uniformly constituted through objective social processes, on the one hand, but that fits and contributes in a self-regulating way with those processes on the other.

The chapter will address recent debates on hybridity and diaspora in order to explore alternative visions of identity (as synthetic, dynamic and historicised) to that proposed by Giddens. Through a critical engagement with these debates the chapter argues for the importance of abandoning the spectacles of 'identity' and focusing instead on social practices, processes and outcomes relating to the prime existential spaces of gender, ethnicity and class. However, there is no doubt that the differential positioning and identifications of racialised, diasporic and minority ethnic groups, as well as the growth of hybridised forms of identity, have put into question the universalising 'we' of modernity.

The self-reflexive self

Much of Giddens' work is dedicated to describing the major distinguishing characteristics of modernity from traditional societies and to linking modernity to globalisation. The 'bendability' of social structures in modernity, according to Giddens (1991a), is a product of ever-present reflexivity, understood in the Weberian tradition – which sees the key to modernity as the growth of rationalisation and rationality in the orientation of actors – but now in its post-traditional form, produced by the range of knowledge and information present in a global system.

The characteristic forms of identity linked to modernity are seen as reflexive projects of the self that depend on trust relations and foster the growth of the 'pure relationship'; relationships seen as ends in themselves rather than bounded by roles and group interests. In post-traditional society this is linked to the breakdown of solid social bonds such as kinship, property and place, which also relate to the minimisation of stable stages of life progression, such as childhood, marriage, children, and the traditional life cycle. The strong link between place and identity is dismantled for, with globalisation, reflexivity and information flows via communication media, there occurs a disembedding of social relations from fixed localities: a unitary framework for action appears through the spread of universal symbols and cultural products via electronic, printed and visual media. The separation of space from place leads to the growth of choice by individuals about how to live their lives, which in turn gives rise to a concern with life politics, as opposed to emancipatory politics.

Giddens rejects the binaries of agency and structure found in most sociological theory approaches. Such a problematic constructs the individual as either potentially free of social constraints or as totally determined by them, which ties either with methodological individualism stressing voluntarism or social holism stressing structural determinism. At the end of the day a form of reductionism or reification lies within this problematic. Giddens asks us to take seriously the ways in which will or agency and structural constraints are intertwined. Structuration treats the modern order as a process: as an evolving equilibrium rather than a series of picture frames, focusing on the 'plasticity' of social order.

It could be argued at this point that Giddens fails to acknowledge the importance of positionality and differentiation in the constitution of knowledge claims. A sociality which is not only differentiated, but hierarchical and conflictual cannot be adequately conceptualised through a focus on the self-reflexive self of high modernity, nor through the notion of the 'pure relationship'. Moreover, it could be argued that the issues debated within the structure–agency problematic (retained through the notion of structuration but in a non-binary way) are of a philosophical rather than sociological nature and cannot be resolved. Since this area of debate is essentially philosophical or meta-theoretical it might be more useful to elicit from it the general principle that individuals make choices (they clearly do for they do not behave like automatons), and that their choices are related to their personal experience which takes place within a set of interactions with others that themselves have organisational and representational components that cannot be reduced to individuals themselves.

The point is then not to debate the structure–agency issue, however important and interesting at the philosophical level, but to depict the processual levels involved that lead to particular social outcomes for individuals and groups. These outcomes can be seen in terms of the construction of places and positions for individuals and groups according to social evaluation and the allocation of resources of different kinds (economic, political, territorial and cultural) that the groups can then deploy in a dynamic attempt to reproduce, usurp or exclude others – in terms of positionalities broadly conceived.

This approach reaffirms the central role of 'struggle around resource allocation', which involves a range of social processes within different kinds of arenas: those of class, those of ethnicity and those of gender. This leads us to the acknowledgement of the importance of differentiation and stratification in the modern social order.

'Difference' and modernity

Classical sociology has been pre-occupied with the question of differentiation, often predicting the demise of differentiated identities. Marx refers to 'the long march of the productive forces' reducing human beings to quantities of labour power, thus stripping them of all forms of social and personal identity. Durkheim suggests 'a situation where the members of the same social group will share nothing in common save their quality of humanness (*leur qualité d'homme*)' (Giddens 1977: 240). Weber sees the increasing rationalisation of social life leading to powerlessness and the domination of rational economic behaviour: economic man (sic) reigns supreme. Modern debates however, have been more centrally concerned with difference and division, although this is not adequately taken up by some modern social theorists, particularly those, like Giddens, who attempt to rethink some of the fundamental aspects of social relations around the binaries of structure and agency, modernity and tradition and objectivity and subjectivity.

The recognition of difference and diversity, both at the theoretical and political levels is not equivalent, however, to the concern with inequality, disadvantage and exclusion – key features of social divisions in society. Recent debates in sociology on post-modern theory, concerning issues of difference, have already begun to give social divisions 'their place in the sun'. As Avtar Brah (1991: 53) has put it: 'Difference, diversity, pluralism, hybridity – these are some of the catch-phrases of our time'. Our world, as the post-modernists constantly remind us, has seen both the proliferation of difference and its increasing celebration (Rattansi and Westwood 1994). Political movements around class, social movement theory tells us, have been displaced by movements around identity, around the environment, around lifestyle. There has been a growth of ethnic nationalisms, and a growth of feminisms of different varieties, including Black and Third World feminisms.

Other features of the modern world include the development of the transnational state form (for example, the European Union), the demise of the Eastern Bloc and the Soviet Union accompanied by a rise of ethnic conflict and ethnic cleansing (a new term in our vocabularies although not such a new phenomenon historically), recession at a world level and struggles over material resources using a language of locality and domesticity. The 'end of ideology', manifested in the demise of Marxism and the end of the

Cold War, has been accompanied by the growth of claims to authenticity and community. At the same time we have seen the growth of consensus politics and claims about the end of 'the working class' in academic and political arguments. New Labour has discarded its cloth cap and red flag. Only the red rose remains and in its last guise looked suspiciously pink!

These various developments form the substance of several strands of post-modern theory, which has tended to focus on the issue of social diversity as a corrective to homogenising and essentialising notions found in earlier sociological work. This theoretical concern is reflected in the discourse and practice of multi-culturalisms, which focus on cultural difference and promote policies that will enable the cultural differences of groups to be validated and reproduced within a multi-ethnic and multi-cultural society. In many ways this has been seen to be a way of countering the social and economic disadvantages of ethnic minority groups and is part of the fight against racism and exclusion (Anthias 1990, 1994). The attempt to deconstruct the categories of gender, 'race' and ethnicity is a characteristic feature of contemporary debates on these issues. A pluralist and multiplex analysis is no longer an accusation to be levelled against theory but a form of praise. By the end of the 1980s deconstructing categories became an essential part of the new post-modern discourse that swept the social sciences. There is a danger, however, that deconstruction may lead to its own form of essentialism, an essentialising of the difference. Does too much emphasis on specificity and diversity not also reify the places of difference it locates? It may correct the tendency of First World feminists to treat women from the 'Third World' as 'others' – or as Spivak's (1987) 'narcissistic self-consolidating other' – but as Robert Young (1990) points out, Spivak has to homogenise First World women in order to unpack the heterogeneity of Third World women. Can, or indeed should, all be always unpacked?

A major criticism of deconstructionism has been that it appears to debilitate the possibility of talking in terms of categories at all, particularly as major axes of differentiation, exclusion, disadvantage and inequality. The organisation of difference and identity is never merely relational and neutral, but serves as nodes for practices and discourses of inferiorisation and inequality. These take place at the level of intersubjectivity, discursive practice and structural effects. However, individuals will be placed in this system of hierarchical production and organisation differently according to different grids. This produces a complex interweaving of forms of advantage and disadvantage (Anthias 1998a).

A number of other problems beset post-modern theory. It does not elaborate adequately enough its own theoretical foundations from within which the critique of others derives. The mere recognition of difference does not help us rethink the categories we use. Post-modernism does not provide sufficient help to produce theories that are particular and local and that look at interrelations. The epistemological agnosticism, as Boyne and Rattansi

(1990) argue, may be politically disabling. Once the notion of sisterhood or a racialised divide is rejected, then there may be no obvious basis for a feminist or anti-racist position. Indeed the post-modern critique of the unitary conception of 'woman' and the fractured and contradictory nature of subjectivity do not lend themselves easily to *any* political action. A provisional and contextual closure around the terms Black or feminist may be necessary to engage in particular political projects. The recognition of diversity need not dispense with provisional and contextual commonalities – as oppositional consciousness, multiple otherness – rather than as Spivak's 'strategic essentialism' (1987).

The recognition and celebration of difference, in all its guises, may lead to political and moral relativism, found in arguments and policies around those multi-culturalisms that ratify and celebrate difference (see Anthias and Yuval Davis 1992, Anthias 1994). Difference is not static nor politically neutral. It may be the case that challenging dominant ethnic, gender and class-based cultural constructs is part of the struggle towards fighting inequality and subordination, but the right to difference can also be turned on its head. If there are differences of culture and differences of need and each group may legitimately make claims to resources in terms of those differences, then the dominant group may also legitimise its greater claims to resources in these same terms (Anthias 1998a).

Difference may be constructed therefore as an ideological weapon; it should never be treated as a mere empirical fact. It is true that the recognition of diversity, fragmentation and multi-faceted and emergent identities leads to the abandonment of a view of the fixed and essential nature of identities. The post-modernist critique which began with this insight, however, assumed that this must lead to the abandonment of generally accepted tools of analysis. It is possible to make a distinction between identities seen as outcomes (of variable and specific social forces that are contextual and situational) and as explanations. In order to be able to understand the production of these outcomes we require carefully refined conceptual tools. In the next section I will suggest that understanding the multiplicity of identities and inequalities in society requires developing an approach that can move beyond difference and take seriously both the commonalities and differences between parameters of differentiation and inequality (see also Anthias 1996 and 1998a).

Post-modernism puts at the centre of analysis a decentred subject with the result that there is no collective actor, be it a class, an ethnic group or a gender. The insight is that social identities are multiplex and the result of practices in different social spheres. However, there is no way in which these social spheres can be specified within the analysis for they cannot be read off from the practices. The negation of collective action debilitates the possibility of understanding social movements and processes as a more than ad hoc coalition of social forces.

Social divisions

A nod in the direction of the panoply of gender, ethnicity and 'race', as ongoing and important social constructions, has now become the *sine qua non* of being a good sociologist. Laurie Taylor's weekly column in the Times Higher Education Supplement sums it up nicely in a parody of an undergraduate answer to a Sociological Theory exam question on Anthony Giddens: '. . . Giddens does not say anything at all about women or for that matter ethnic minorities. It is also important to consider whether or not what Giddens has to say might only be true for some societies but not for others. This would be an important criticism if it were found to be the case . . .'

Unlike Giddens' focus on the unitary self of high modernity, whose political project is self-actualisation, I argue that social divisions must be at the heart of social theory, that there are common parameters to the social divisions of gender, ethnicity, 'race' and class, and that the study of these divisions must be undertaken in local and specific contexts paying attention to their articulation. The social divisions of gender, ethnicity 'race' and class *must be pivotal concerns in Sociology because they lie at the very heart of the social order and of culture. They are central in terms of the constructions of identity and otherness and in terms of producing differentiated and complex social outcomes for individuals and groups* (Anthias 1998a).

Different modes for the classification of populations, differential treatment on the basis of labelling, or attributions of capacities and needs, and modes of exclusion that operate on this basis (the core features of what may be called social divisions), are characteristic of modern social formations. Such social divisions (like ethnic and 'race' categorisation and gender categorisation and the socially produced inequalities that surround them) permeate societies in different ways, although they are by no means universal in the forms they take or in the meanings that underlie the entities constructed. In the modern period they lie at the very heart of discursive, symbolic, psychic, economic and political practices. The very fabric of our social structure is therefore endemically gendered, ethnicised and indeed racialised (Goldberg 1993).

These social divisions may be considered in two separate but related ways. The first is in terms of constructing categories of difference and identity involving *other-* and *self-*attributions, or labelling and self-identity, entailing the formation of social categories of the population and boundaries of differentiation. The other is in terms of constructing social relations in terms of differential positioning, and the allocation of power and other resources, an issue that relates to social relations of stratification or inequality. Social categorisation is an essential part of the classifying principles found in human societies, although there are no uniform ways in which societies categorise individuals. Kinship systems (Durkheim and Mauss 1963, Levi

Strauss 1969 [1949]) have a central role in charting the entry point to culture: it certainly appears that most societies will categorise according to familial role. This does not *always* give rise to a clear differentiation on the basis of a discourse about biological sex, although it usually does. In some societies biological sex role and social role may not be the same thing. Biological women may be honorary men and vice versa. Biological fathers may not be regarded as social fathers; this is another example of the distinction between biological role and social role. Once individuals are placed into categories (although they are not mutually exclusive) across different dimensions, the relational terms of otherness and sameness are constructed. In the process notions of self and other, identity, identification and division come into play. Usually the categories are constructed in a binary way and as mutually exclusive. They endow individuals with attributions of difference which are then seen to have necessary social effects.

Such constructions are rarely neutral or value-free. They organise possessive properties and attributions of individuals whilst allocating differential value and producing hierarchies. They are also implicated in the development of particular types of social relationships. These range from forms of closure where the group has resources it wishes to protect, to exploitation, which is a form of subordinated inclusion (although this also entails closure in terms of the denial of access to the resources of the exploiting group). Relations of avoidance are found as in the case of the caste system and certain forms of racism (such as apartheid), in the case of class stigmatisation and in the case of women in some cultures at certain times of the month and in certain contexts (during the menstrual cycle, for example). The logic of extermination may be applied where the threat of the 'Other' is seen as too great and/or complete dehumanisation of the group has taken place (as in the Holocaust). We can see, therefore, that the discussion of social divisions entails considering social categorisation and social identification. It also entails looking at differentiated social interactions and the formation of collective or solidary bonds as well as forms of closure.

In my understanding of social divisions the specification of essential unities of identity and difference is abandoned in favour of the identification of ontological spaces or domains that are contingent and variable in their specificities. *A relational ontological* space or social domain constitutes the framework for investigating the social relations of difference and inequality. The ontological spaces are not essentialist but social, in as much as they have experiential, intersubjective, organisational and representational forms. The concepts relating to the ontological spaces are merely signposts. *Ethnos*, for example, is a concept that can be an heuristic device enabling the delineation and specification of those experiential, intersubjective, organisational and representational processes related to the ontological space of *collectivity*. It need not emerge in any specific form. It enables the investigation of patterned social relations and their outcomes at a number of different levels both with regard to the process of differentiation (and identification) and the process of positionality, constructing places in the order of things (Anthias, 1998a).

Levels of analysis

There has been a great deal of debate on the structure–agency problematic that has motivated Giddens' construction of the self-reflexive self (for example, see Scott 1995, Layder 1996, Mouzelis 1995), and this chapter has merely touched on some of the problems that have been identified with it as well as the generally flawed attempts to resolve them (see Mouzelis 1995 for a useful discussion). In this chapter I will not draw on such a binary but instead focus on the idea of different levels of analysis that can be operationalised in substantive work. I want to argue that crosscutting the two problematics of *differentiation* and *positionality* are the *experiential, intersubjective, organisational and representational factors* that enable a focus at different levels: the personal (experience), the action (interaction/practice, intersubjectivity), the institution/structure (the organisational), the symbolic, discursive (representational). Each one may act as a context or habitus and field (Bourdieu 1990) for the others and enable an exploration of how they interlink with each other. The distinctions here are heuristic rather than actual and enable different sets of questions to be investigated. Giddens' autonomous self-reflexive self does not encourage a focus on both unique and shared contexts of identification. The analytical levels involve the following:

the experiential: this focuses on the experiences of persons (within specific locatable contexts, say in the school, in the workplace, in the neighbourhood) of being defined as different, identifying as a particular category.

the intersubjective: this arises from the level of intersubjective relations: the actions and practices that take place in relation to others (including nonperson actors such as the police, the social security system and so on).

the organisational: this focuses on the institutional and other organisational ways in which the ontological spaces are played out: for example, family structures and networks, educational systems, political and legal systems, the state apparatus and the system of policing and surveillance. For example, how are sexuality, biological reproduction or population categories organised within institutional frameworks and in terms of the allocation of resources?

the representational: What are the symbolic and representational means, the images and texts, the documents and information flows around the ontological spaces?

In the following section I will provide a schematic outline of some of these ideas in the context of the social divisions of gender and ethnos.

Categories and social outcomes/relations

Ethnicised, racialised and gendered discourses and outcomes often take the form of a set of exclusionary mechanisms that may be conceptualised through three principles of *social relations* that relate to categories of differentiation and stratification (for an extended analysis see Anthias 1996 and 1998a):

1. The principle of hierarchisation
2. The principle of unequal resource allocation
3. The principle of inferiorisation

The principle of hierarchisation

Earlier, I noted that the difference postulated by the categories was not value-free. Indeed the construction of difference is usually accompanied not only by a relative value, on a pole of negative to positive; the categories construct *places* or *positions* in the social order of things. Sometimes this involves the allocation of specific social roles, such as occupational (caste and class) or familial (gender) but more often than not these are accompanied by a pecking order of roles and places.

This may be seen in terms of the constitution of gender, race and class as systems of domination (Spivak 1987). However, none function in a coherent manner and neither are they mutually exclusive. All individuals occupy places in each one of them. But how they are attributed, the claims that they themselves make and their own psychic identifications may vary greatly. Indeed, some of the claims and identifications may be seen as forms of resistance as well as external constructions and social attributions. To be proud to be woman/feminine, Black/minority ethnic (or, say, disabled (Oliver 1995)) is to refuse the attribution of a hierarchical otherness. Also people's identities are multiplex, contextual and situational.

Therefore, in terms of social relations that are hierarchical, it is not purely a question of a hierarchy of individuals within a category. For example, in the category of race, where the distinction between, say, white and Black is constructed, the white is dominant over the Black. The white is able to reproduce advantages and privileges and reproduce the evaluative components of whiteness. However, within this construct, there exist class differences and gender differences also, which interplay with those of race to produce various hierarchical outcomes for individuals. These may lead to complex forms of ranking across a range of different dimensions. If the constructs are read as 'grids' their salience will not only vary in different contexts but the interplay of the different grids needs to be always considered in any analysis of social outcomes or effects.

The principle of unequal resource allocation

Resource allocation has often been conceived in terms of economic resources, which have generally been theorised in terms of class. The empirical evidence

165

that 'race' attributions and gender attributions are correlated with economic position in general terms has meant that many of the explanations concerning the dynamics of 'race' and gender have reduced them to some form of economic category. Instances of this are found within Marxist, Marxist feminist and radical feminist theory. Much of the debate on 'race' and class (Anthias 1990) takes as a starting point the economic position of Black people, and explains this with reference to economic processes and their link to racism. In much of the analysis that links 'race' and economic processes it is racism as an ideology that connects racialised groups with a specific economic positioning. However, it is not so easy to show that economic disadvantage is the effect of racism, or that racism itself is constructed as the medium by which capital benefits from an underclass that can act either as cheap labour or a reserve army of labour (Castles and Kosack 1973, Castells 1975). As Miles (1989) points out, there is a range of exclusionary practices in society that is not merely coterminous with racism but is integral to the configuration of disadvantage derived from class location.

However, despite the problems of the class analogy, the principle of unequal resource allocation, in general, stands. This is not only because of the wealth of empirical evidence that shows that women and ethnic minorities suffer disadvantages in the labour market (see Anthias 1993): these are well known. It is also because unequal resource allocation involves the issue of power at the political, cultural and representational levels. Gender, ethnicity and 'race' are structured in terms of unequal social relations. Regarding cultural resources, for example, such as language, education and religious values, there is no doubt that the dominant ethnic, 'race' and gender groups within the state have privileges in terms of cultural production and reproduction: this despite the growth of equal opportunities policies at various levels and the growth of multi-culturalism (for a critique of these see Anthias and Yuval Davis 1992, Anthias 1994).

The principle of inferiorisation: 'otherness', normality and pathology

One side of the binary divide in each case is seen as the standard, as the norm, and also as expressive of the ideal. The yardstick for the individual where gender is concerned becomes male capacities or achievements, male needs or interests. This is one example of the assumptions that underlie the specification of binary social categories. These assumptions are often reproduced in struggles against the disadvantage conferred on the 'wrong' side of the binary divide. This is found in feminist struggles that argue for equality of capacities and needs taking as given that those expressed in the masculine are the yardstick, leading to forms of theory and practice that are concerned with redressing disadvantage relative to the 'normal/right' side. It may lead theoretically to treating the 'normal/right' side as the explanatory field for the 'other/wrong' side. This is expressed in those arguments within feminism, for example, that treat men as the cause of women's oppression, or those arguments by anti-racists that treat whites or racist individuals as the problem that needs to be countered, rather than locating the sources of racism within broader social relations. In many discussions, the Other is contrasted to Self (for example, in symbolic interactionism): the Self cannot also be Other. Yet the work of Fanon (1986) shows us how within the experience of colonialism the Black assumes a white mask, how in other words the Self is considered as the Other.

At the same time, and as a corollary, normality and pathology become ascribed to individuals within these categories in two ways. One is that the 'Other' becomes pathologised. The second is that individuals who do not perform the ascribed roles in a satisfactory way also become pathologised. In the first way pathology is seen as endemic to particular categories (Blacks, ethnic outsiders, women). In the second way, pathology is derived from failing to perform adequately the appropriate roles imputed to a particular positionality.

Theorising heterogeneity

The three principles of social relations outlined above relate to the ways in which 'difference' on its own may not be able to redress the collective 'we' found in Giddens' work: rather, serious attention must be paid to organised social divisions both in terms of categories and in terms of outcomes. Such an approach may be investigated with reference to debates on multi-culturalism and debates on hybridity and diaspora. First, I will look briefly at multi-culturalism.

Multi-culturalism and ethnicity

One of the ways in which social divisions in terms of difference and disadvantage have been addressed is through the ideology and practice of multi-culturalism. However, one of the difficulties here is that ethnicity tends to be treated as merely a question of culture and identity, thus disassociating the *practices* of ethnicity and racism, the one being a case to be celebrated and the other to be abhorred. Another feature is the failure to look at class and gender differentiations. Within multi-culturalism, difference is simply recognised and is a cause for celebration. This stems from the view that ethnicity is not related to racism, leaving racism and disadvantage to be fought by the celebration and provision of, and for, ethnic difference. There is in fact an assumption that to allow and foster ethnic difference and culture is coterminous with fighting racism. However, although ethnic diversity is a necessary prerequisite of a truly egalitarian and multi-cultural society, the fight against racism cannot focus primarily on culturalist concerns (Gilroy

1987), as racisms are ideologies and practices that produce political and economic subordination. In addition, the concern with ethnic pluralism has tended to treat ethnicity in terms of static cultural attributes rather than as dynamic and contextual. It has also tended to ignore the role of gender.

Thus, there are many difficulties in culturalist versions of ethnicity found in multi-culturalist discourses. Ethnic difference is considered chiefly as pertaining to the question of culture and identity by many of the most dominant formulations in the literature on ethnic and race relations also (for a review see Miles 1982 and Omi and Winant 1986). Such a culturalist perspective is unable to attend to the political dynamics of ethnic difference (Cohen 1974, Hechter 1987, Anthias 1982), such that the links between ethnicity, nationalism, race and racism in terms of processes of group formation, and the political pursuits of collectivities so formulated or proclaimed, may never be made. The political projects attendant on the pursuit of cultural difference may fail to get addressed, and no assessment can be made concerning how they might link to anti-racism. Treating categories of the population as unitary and static fails to note the dynamic and heterogeneous nature of ethnic groups and their responses and adaptation. It also has effects on ethnicising and producing modes of struggle that focus on culture and identity, repeating for themselves the static and ahistorical nature of the racialised definitions that they are subjected to. It serves furthermore to promote forms of politics that can be divisive.

Hybridity

An alternative focus to that on multi-culturalism is one that hails the formation of hybrid and diasporic identities in the post-modern world. We are all becoming global, diasporic and hybrid! Yet diasporic hybridity, although denoting important developments and challenges to static and essentialist notions of ethnicity, migration, culture and identity, also presents important conceptual and substantive difficulties. The key problems relate to the location of culture as the core element for defining identity and community. The forms of ethnicity hailed by the notion of hybridity therefore require delineating: to what extent does hybridity signal the end of ethnicity on the one hand, and to what extent does it tie in with the notion of 'new ethnicities' (Hall 1992) on the other? What, if any, is the new and transgressive potential to be found within hybridisation processes in purportedly globalising contexts?

Globalisation processes have been characterised as political, economic and cultural. It is the last that is most relevant to the arguments found in current formulations of diaspora and hybridity (although diaspora has been used to denote political economy and political processes) in the work of Cohen (1997), Segal (1995), Said (1979), from both a traditional sociological and political economy framework. Globalisation has been seen as a challenge to the nation state, although also seen as generating ethnic and cultural parochialisms and localisms or 'glocalisation' in Roland Robertson's own 'hybrid' term (Robertson 1995). It has been argued that the boundary of the nation state is traversed in multiple ways, identified with: the movement of capital and the growing penetration over the globe of transnational financial capital; with the growth and penetration of new technologies; with the export and movement of communication modes, including media forms and images; with the growth of transnational political and juridical groups (for example, the European Union and its potential); with growing international resistance and action groups (for example, the Beijing Conference of Women); with penetration of ideologies producing a 'world system' (Wallerstein 1980, 1990) or Global Village (McLuhan 1964). Diasporic and hybridisation processes have been related to all of these processes.

One key element of globalisation theory is the identification of cultural globalisation as a core contemporary process. Diaspora groups or communities are seen to embody the transnational principle, moving ethnic and solidaristic organisation from the confines of the nation state to the global arena. The nation-building project of nationalism (never fully successful anywhere), of marrying the boundary of ethnicity, the boundaries of the state and the boundaries of the nation, becomes challenged. In addition, diaspora groups, it has been claimed (Gilroy 1993, Brah 1996, Clifford 1994), are characterised by the growth of synthetic or mixed cultural elements, taken selectively by succeeding generations from a range of cultural resources. It has been proposed that the global culture is constituted in and through hybridisation (Pieterse 1995). Whilst the issue of ethnic and other fundamentalisms appears either to result from a spread (time–space compression) through communication or as a reaction/contradiction to globalisation, the issue of diasporic hybridity is seen as a substantive consequence of increasing cultural interpenetration allied to self-reflexive or 'open to the other' cultures, and epitomised by cosmopolitanism (as found in Bhabha's counter-narrative (1994) or in Hannerz (1992) and Friedman's (1997) cosmopolitans). In these respects, Giddens' emphasis on the global cosmopolitanism of the modern world and the self-reflexivity of its individual and institutional actors reverberates with some of the themes of post-colonial cultural studies.

However, there are senses in which hybridity and diaspora have become fashionable terms, commonly hailed. They constitute a kind of 'mantra' within what may be loosely called, in Ali Rattansi's words (Rattansi and Westwood 1994), 'the post-modern frame'. I am sympathetic to the opening up of spaces hitherto foreclosed by traditional approaches to ethnicity and migration, and welcome the deployment of these concepts as anti-essentialist projects and as critiques of static notions of ethnicity and culture. I am not convinced, however, that hybridity and diaspora concepts have been able to redress fully some key problems. I want to point to some conceptual and substantive difficulties raised by these debates that cut across both Giddens' effort to reconstruct modern sociology, and the post-modern positions against which he constructs his own concepts of self, subjectivity and identity. In

169

particular I want to raise some questions about the concept of culture and its positioning in contemporary theories of hybrid and diaporic identities.

Hybridity and the notion of culture

There are three main ways in which the term 'culture' has been used. First, it is used as a set of attributes or contents of a locality or a particular group, denoting its symbols and practices in their general and external manifestations (in Durkheim's sense of social facts). Here there may be a distinction between high culture (music, literature, art, poetry expressing the production of universalisable meanings in local form) and low culture (that of the masses).

The second way in which the term may be used is that of culture as a world view – an orientation to the world-ways of being and doing or what Banuri (1990: 77) calls 'software'. A culture is the pool of components from which forms of cultural products and resources is drawn. The third way views culture as patterned ways of knowing and doing, institutionalised within hegemonic processes and structures, where transgression of the central core elements leads to forms of social regulation, prohibition, exclusion, or banishment.

These three senses are regularly confused in contemporary social theory. Culture, I argue, needs to be deconstructed, to coin a phrase. The object of reference in debates on global culture needs differentiating and specifying. I would suggest that the use of culture within debates on hybridity is confined (in a rather incoherent and unclear fashion however) to the first definition above – it is seen in terms of cultural products or attributes. I would also suggest that hybridity functions on an assumption of an essential unity to the two or more cultural forms from which it is composed. Moreover, it does not attend to the uses given to the cultural elements and to the combination of elements. From this point of view, cultural artifacts *or* practices do not have singular or fixed meanings. Moreover, the concept of hybridity assumes a free-floating person who can voluntarily choose (as in Mannheim's (1972) free-floating intellectual). It is important to recognise the role of agency, but it is important also to explore how it is exercised within a system of social constraints linked to the positionality of actors (both individual and collective) within specific social contexts. Hybridity is often examined in terms of the intermingling of cultural components without considering the question of how they are used and in what contexts. For example, the hybrid nature of much pop music is discussed, divorced from the question of agency. Such hybridities cannot be judged as either transgressive nor progressive without paying attention to their deployment.

Some aspects of culture may be incommensurable and not all aspects of culture have been equally malleable to globalisation (if that, as it often does, implies homogenisation particularly around western values and actions).

This is particularly the case with regard to family organisation and gender relationships on the one hand and religion on the other. The mixed cultural patterns of second and third generation diasporic actors underplays the ways in which gender and religion, for example, serve different ends in different contexts (for example, see Afshar 1994). In other words the bringing together of different cultural elements syncretically transforms their meaning, but need not mean that dialogue between cultural givens is necessarily taking place.

It is also important to distinguish between the problematic of culture and that of identity and the formation of solidary projects. For example, young white adolescents have been seen as synthesising the culture of their white English backgrounds with the new cultures of minorities. New cultural forms are forged in music and interracial friendship networks and movements (Hewitt 1986, Back 1996). The pick and mix of cultural elements does not necessarily signify, however, a shift in identity or indeed the demise of identity politics of the racist or anti-racist kind. The whole area of the link between culture in terms of patterns and products, and the issue of identity and boundaries of belongingness, requires much more systematic analysis. Moreover, it could be argued that the acid test of hybridity lies in the response of culturally dominant groups, not only in terms of incorporating (or co-opting) cultural products of marginal or subordinate groups, but in being open to transforming and abandoning some of their own central cultural symbols and practices of hegemony. Until there is evidence of this, it seems somewhat over-enthusiastic to denote contemporary cultural forms as hybrid. This is particularly the case when the dimension of power over the deployment of different cultural symbols is rendered visible. Apart from the realm of music and fashion, there is very little evidence of dominant white culture seceding its role in defining the cultural domain.

Gilroy (1993) uses W.E.B. Du Bois' notion of 'double consciousness' to denote the hybrid and diasporic condition. He contrasts it to prevailing ethnic absolutism as the theorisation of 'creolisation, métissage, mestizaje and hybridity' (1993: 2). Bhabha (1994) too sees the transgression of national or ethnic borders as the key to the condition of hybridity – a double perspective becomes possible and signals the migrant artist/poet/intellectual as the voice that speaks from two places at once and inhabits neither. This is the space of liminality, of 'no place' or of the buffer zone of 'no man's land'. For Bhabha (1994: 38) the space of the 'inter' is 'the cutting edge of translation and negotiation, the *in between* space'. This always produces a counternarrative or 'third space' to 'elude the politics of polarity and emerge as others of ourselves'. Bhabha therefore sees hybrids as cultural brokers. But this assumes that cosmopolitans and others lack a central cultural narrative of their own. Is this third space not also boundary making? And are identities not multiple, not like cloaks we can don and discard but like different coloured layers, some on top, some below at different times and diaphanous so the colours blend (see Anthias 1996)?

I do not have the space to address these problems in detail but I want to summarise some central problems of the debate on cultural hybridisation here:

- It privileges the domain of the cultural, but meant in terms of a set of objects.
- It homogenises the group in not attending to differentiated hybridisation.
- It deploys culture in a particular way to mean lifestyle, cultural beliefs in terms of particularity of contents/objects rather than culture as a tool, a set of resources or 'software', as dynamic, relational and contextual, or as a process.
- It signals the bringing together of two or more pure types or essences of culture and therefore still works within the framework of a culturally essentialist model of social relations.
- It depoliticises culture in as much as it does not link it to the differential projects of diaspora groups or the divisions within them.
- It does not pay attention to majority hybridities.
- It focuses too much on the transgressive element; for example, fascism is a reactionary version of hybridity. Hybrids are not always the 'new world of bricoloeurs' that Cornel West (1992: 36) talks about.
- It underplays the alienating and damaging features: for instance, hybridity as alienation and violence, hybridity as fundamentalism.
- It does not explore the links with exclusion and violence.
- It loses sight of cultural domination-power as embodied in culture disappears (see Tomlinson (1991) for a development of the idea of cultural imperialism).
- Hybridisation as 'the ways in which forms become separated from existing practices and recombine with new forms of new practices' (Rowe and Schelling 1991: 231) may be seen as a depiction of all culture and therefore neither new nor essentially related to diasporic experience or diasporic space (Brah 1996).

Cultures may be more open or closed to different ways of doing, and some may be more permeable than others. Indeed through migration and diasporisation the opposite to hybridisation may occur: a ghettoisation and enclavisation, where groups may live in a 'time warp', a mythologising of tradition, which Hall, following Robins, sees as the alternative adaptation to that of translation (where new more transgressive forms emerge) and a concern with homeland and its national project, or the long-distance nationalism found in the political projects of the Irish, the Jews and the Greeks (Anderson 1995).

Diaspora

Recent debates on the configuration of ethnic and 'race' boundaries in an era of global transformations have re-focused academic attention on the concept of 'diaspora' (Anthias, 1998b). 'Diaspora' denotes transnational movement and ties in with arguments around globalisation and the growth of non-nation based solidarities (Robertson 1992, Appadurai 1990) in the contemporary period. As we have seen, debates on globalisation have identified the economic and political dismantling of national borders, as well as the growth of transnational cultural formations (Featherstone 1990, Robertson 1995), with new notions of diaspora identities and experiences emerging (for example, Hall 1990, Gilroy 1993, Bhabha 1990, Cohen 1997, Clifford 1994, Brah 1996). This also follows a wider tendency to insert and promote a less essentialised, and more historically and analytically informed, vocabulary into the traditional concerns of 'race and ethnic relations', which have dominated the field (for example, Miles 1982, Anthias 1990, Anthias and Yuval Davis 1992, Hall 1990, Gilroy 1993, Mason 1994, Brah 1996).

I want now to draw attention to the disjunction between what the term 'diaspora' purports to do and what in fact it often fails to do. My argument is primarily that the concept of diaspora, whilst focusing on transnational processes and commonalities, does so by deploying a notion of ethnicity which privileges the point of 'origin' in constructing identity and solidarity. In the process it also fails to examine trans-ethnic commonalities and processes and does not adequately pay attention to differences of gender and class. This failure seriously hinders the use of the concept 'diaspora' as an enabling device for understanding differentiated and highly diverse forms of transnational movement and settlement. The issue of gender is particularly important given the increasing recognition of the ways in which gender, ethnicity and class intersect in social relations.

There is no doubt that the impetus for the contemporary revival of the term comes from the enterprise of 'diasporic' Black writers like Stuart Hall (1990) and Paul Gilroy (1993, 1997), and the chapter will proceed by considering their contributions. These two approaches are central, although there are others that stress political economy processes (Segal 1995), the condition of 'exile' (Said 1979), 'diaspora' as a descriptive *typological* tool for understanding migration and settlement in the global era (Cohen 1997) and diaspora as a social *condition* and as a societal process (Clifford 1994). 'Diaspora' refers to a connection between groups across different nation states whose commonality derives from an original but maybe removed homeland; a new identity becomes constructed on a world scale that crosses national borders and boundaries. Although the term is often limited to population categories that have experienced 'forceful or violent expulsion' processes (classically used about Jewish peoples), it may also denote a *social condition* entailing a particular form of 'consciousness' that is particularly compatible with postmodernity and globalisation. It is seen by some to embody the globalising principle of transnationalism (for example, Waters 1995). Stuart Hall has played an influential role in the recent popularity of the term 'diaspora'. His concern, over the years, has been to reconstruct an approach to cultural identity and 'race' that avoids the pitfalls of essentialism and reductionism.

The concept of diaspora emerges as a way of rethinking the issue of black cultural identity and representation away from the notion of the essential black subject (Hall 1990). Hall (1990: 226) wishes to focus on positionings; for 'histories have their real, material and symbolic effects', and:

> The diaspora experience as I intend it here, is defined, not by essence or purity, but by the recognition of a necessary heterogeneity and diversity; by a conception of 'identity' which lives with and through, not despite, difference; by hybridity. Diaspora identities are those which are constantly producing and reproducing themselves anew, through transformation and difference. (Hall 1990: 235)

Hall's work is useful in historicising ethnic and cultural identity, but in the process reinserts a Black subject, constructed historically, whose body is reinscribed with different societal effects: the sameness here wins over the difference that Hall so clearly wants to affirm, and this is largely because of the centrality of racialisation. This to some extent undermines a de-essentialised notion of cultural identity and does not adequately deal with the importance of interethnic, class and gender difference. However, the very strength of this position lies in the analysis of the interplay between historicised and differentiated cultural identities and the structural and systemic forms of subordination (and their resistance) that are at the heart of the experiences of Black subjectivities.

Gilroy's book *The Black Atlantic* (1993) probably presents the most sustained theoretical defence of the concept of diaspora, and has been hugely influential in encouraging writers on transnational migration and settlement to deploy the term as a heuristic device (see Vertovec 1996). Gilroy's concern is to reconstruct the history of the West through the work of Black intellectuals like Du Bois and Richard Wright, whom he sees as inhabiting 'contested "contact zones" between cultures and histories' (1993: 6). Intermediate concepts like diaspora 'break the dogmatic focus on discrete national dynamics' that has characterised modern Euro-American cultural thought and reinstate the role of 'intercultural positionality'. Like Hall, Gilroy rejects the notion of an essential Black subject and the unifying dynamic of Black culture. Instead he relies on the concept of diaspora as an heuristic means to focus on the difference and sameness of the connective culture across different national Black groups. The connective tissue is seen to lie in a discourse of racial emancipation on the one hand and the conflictual representation of sexuality on the other, constructing communities that are 'both similar and different', or 'the changing same', to use Leroi Jones' (1967) term. Relying for much of the argument on the hybrid but distinctive forms of music and performance, he roots the diasporic consciousness (or 'double consciousness' in Du Bois' famous phrase) in a relatively privileged knowledge space. Despite, however, referring to the centrality of gender and the representation of sexuality in constituting 'the changing same', Gilroy fails to give women any agency within the Black diaspora and is more interested in the male gaze (see also Helmreich 1992). Gilroy's insightful analysis of the 'Black Atlantic' constitutes a highly original and historicised account of the continuities and discontinuities of the Black cultural domain within the space of racial subordination, although it is essentially androcentric. This has been used to fuel a vast array of different conceptual uses of the term, often made to substitute for theoretical work in substantive analysis. What may succeed for the Black diaspora in its specificities, may not necessarily be translatable into a general theoretical tool.

I have argued elsewhere (Anthias 1998b), that the concept of diaspora fails to pay adequate attention to transethnic (as opposed to transnational) processes because it assumes a unitary community of actors whose commonality derives from an original 'seed' or fatherland. I have also argued that it forecloses issues of differences of gender, class and generation within diasporic groups. However, these writings are important because, whilst globalisation may indeed mean the dissemination of different ways of being and doing, this does not mean that all will adopt one form. Interpenetration is a feature of social relations but the combination of different elements produces new yet highly heterogeneous effects. This does not only mean that a homogeneous culture doesn't exist (as Pieterse 1995 rightly claims), it mean that hybridisation (in the sense of interpenetration) cannot be read into processes of cultural spread without paying attention to the array of social places, political projects and social divisions that will encounter them and imbue them with local and particular meanings. Also if, as Pieterse says, the one distinguishing feature of the present phase of globalisation is that no single mode has overall priority, this could deny the forms of cultural and ideological hegemony structured in and through capitalist penetration and other forms of the dominance of the West.

These perspectives provide a more fragmented and discontinuous picture of 'cultural globalisation' (Featherstone 1990, Featherstone *et al.* 1995), than that presented within some versions of globalisation theory. They also present a much more discontinuous notion of the self and identity in high modernity than the one proposed by Giddens. For example, a large number of the diaspora is not exposed to the self-reflexivity of Giddens work, or alternatively the hybridisation which is seen to characterise the globalisation process by other writers. This applies particularly to working-class women, ethnic niches or economies, older migrants and transnationals – but not cosmopolitans (Hannerz 1992) – who may be ethnic chauvinists. We may have global imagery but these global images are read through local eyes. Not all those eyes are self-reflexive or would recognise the risk society! On the other hand, global images of women as represented by a recent issue of *Cosmopolitan* magazine on its twentieth anniversary, showing covers of worldwide Cosmopolitan issues – including those from India, Russia, Japan and Greece – display how homogenous the images of women have been, despite subtle changes in nuance. Woman as sex-goddess is clearly a globalised image purveyed to the select few – reminding us that we need to distinguish between the existence of the global image and its differential transmission, availability and relevance in a world dominated by illiteracy, poverty and disease. This in addition to the fact that images may be purveyed and may be common, but the local eyes with which they are seen endow them with different meanings. Finally, one of the substantive historical problems with the idea of transnationalism (translated often as hybrid heterogeneity) is that religion, ideology, capitalism, as well as 'communities', have existed in the transnational sphere prior to the identification of new forms of globalisation.

Sideways to modernity

As a counter to Giddens' notion of the global 'we' identity and the 'pure relationship', I would like to suggest the importance of 'othering', on the one hand, and resource struggles on the other. These may take particular forms in the period of 'high modernity'. These forms yield reflexivity in recognising multiple selves and others (hybrid/diasporic), but at the same time involve using a highly contradictory process in maintaining resource advantages to persons along the lines of the relations of gender, 'race' and class. These interconnect in specific contexts and it is important to focus on these rather than trying to build a totalising theory. This does not mean the abandonment of theory, however, for some analytical framework is always necessary. Understanding the placement of collective subjects who stand in the camps of gender, ethnicity, 'race' and class and at their crossroads is a complex issue. In this chapter I have argued that this understanding lies at the heart of social theory. I have also argued that such an understanding requires not merely the recognition of a proliferation of identities (found in the post-modern frame), nor a conception of the 'self' as befitting high modernity (found in Giddens), nor a notion of hybridised identities and diasporic consciousness, but an analysis that can indicate their connections in producing specific social outcomes.

I have maintained that the problematic of the self in high modernity is inadequate in addressing the issue of the multifarious nature of identifications and social divisions as parameters of social inequality and exclusion. Such an approach requires specific and local analyses of differentiated social outcomes looked at through the complex interweaving of social relations. Gender, ethnicity, 'race' and class are pivotal forms of differentiation and stratification of human populations in the modern era. They may be seen as crosscutting and mutually interacting discourses, practices and intersubjectivities that coalesce and articulate at particular conjunctures to produce differentiated and stratified social outcomes. The analogy of a grid may be useful, and can be overlaid onto individuals. The different grids are experienced contextually and situationally as sets of simultaneous and mutually effective discursive instances and social practices.

The discussion of connecting threads pinpoints two ways in which social divisions may be seen to articulate. The first way is in terms of crosscutting and mutually reinforcing systems of domination and subordination, particularly in terms of processes and relations of hierarchisation, unequal resource allocation and inferiorisation, which I discussed earlier as fundamental principles of social divisions. For example, racialised or minority working-class women may be seen to inhabit the worst social spaces in a range of contexts, from the economic to the political and cultural. In this case social divisions articulate to produce a coherent set of practices of subordination. The second way in which the articulations may be seen is in terms of the construction of multiple and uneven social patterns of domination and subordination. This is where human subjects are positioned differentially within these social divisions, for example, where white working-class men may be seen to be in a relation of dominance over racialised groups and over women but are themselves in a relation of subordination in class terms. This leads to highly contradictory processes in terms of positionality and identity.

The exploration of reinforcing aspects of the divisions and their contradictory articulations also opens up fundamental political questions. In other words the discussion of connecting social divisions is not purely theoretical. It has a direct relevance in terms of how inequalities, identities and political strategies are conceptualised and assessed. First, whether mutually reinforcing or contradictory outcomes are produced, the articulation of social divisions makes a conception of individuals as having singular identities problematic. To identify, say, as a woman without considering one's ethnic or class location produces problems of being able to understand the relationship one has to women and men in terms of the other dimensions. This is one reason why western feminism, organising around the category 'woman', was unable to address issues of racism and economic subordination.

Secondly, this also makes a politics of identity problematic, for such a politics assumes a unitary subject whose identity and political struggle is given by a position, say as a woman or as a member of a class or a member of a racialised group. Such a politics of identity seeks to make the self (defined in a unitary way) as the main protagonist in striving against subordination. This position, albeit differently conceptualised, is found in Giddens' approach to dialogical democracy in *Beyond Left and Right*: to what extent does this help to rethink the identity politics found in multi-culturalisms? To what extent can this pay attention to social divisions in the way I suggested above as parameters of difference and of inequality, as categories and outcomes?

Giddens posits a need for radical politics but not socialist thought, one that may preserve some of the core values of socialist thought (1994a: 12) but that focuses on the conditions for trust relationships and the repair of damaged solidarities. For Giddens this may imply selective preservation or re-invention of tradition, not civil society revival, but reordered conditions for individual and collective life. This reconciles autonomy and interdependence, creating a growth of active trust and personal and social responsibility to others. Such a politics takes the form of life politics, an emancipatory politics about lifestyle but generative in as much as it allows individuals to make things happen (1994a: 15) in the public domain. Dialogic democracy requires a space for resolving differences. Greater transparency of government, discussion and an interchange of views, enable the development of active trust, a democracy of the emotions. Self-help groups and social movements are seen as important in opening up a space for public dialogue.

One of the central problems in this position is the failure to think through issues of citizenship, in terms of people belonging to different and multiple groupings and having a range of different, contextual allegiances. Instead the focus is on the politics of self. Moreover, it assumes that there are no ordered or relevant inequalities of power and position that need to be addressed politically and through engagement in forms of contestation and struggle within the state. Like identity politics, a direct relationship is assumed between politics and experience. The self is so concerned with fighting its own battles and subordinations that it fails to see that the battles of others may be as fundamentally legitimate and important. A more emancipatory approach may be found in a politics of multiple identifications (rather than identities), a politics of identification with subordinated others/selves. This opens up the possibility of more reflexive forms of political struggle and avenues to greater dialogue and collaboration between groups organising around particular kinds of *struggles* rather than particular kinds of *identities*. It is the former particularly that I have been concerned to theorise in this chapter.

Concluding remarks

I have suggested a shift in the level of analysis away from the debate around structure and agency. I suggest the development of a framework that looks at social processes at the experiential, intersubjective, organisational and representational level: in this way neither reifying structures nor reducing social relations to agency. The framework asks us to devise investigatory tools for exploring sets of relations around particular kinds of realms of social existence (the social ontologies around sexuality, collectivity and production), and focuses on the different levels entailed in their practice. In such a schema, the collective 'we' of modernity and the problematic of the self in modernity as a unitary phenomenon becomes replaced with the investigation of sets of articulations and narratives relating to realms of existence, and identified through investigating their place in personal experience and its depiction, in practices between social agents, some of whom will be persons, the organisational arrangements implicated and the representational forms that are produced.

CHAPTER 9

A world of differences: What if it's so? How will we know?

Charles Lemert

I remember very well the response of my sociological acquaintances when Tony Giddens first began to dawn across the sociological seas in the early 1970s. Among academics, response to young phenoms generally obeys a fixed three-step ritual. (1) First, one must rush to the library to find who this is everyone is suddenly talking about. (2) Then, as soon thereafter as possible, it is expected that one think to oneself (at the least) – and, in some all too sad cases, even say in public – 'Oh, is that it? We've known that for a long, long while.' (3) Thereafter, when the one dawning is of a true light, one of two kinds of behaviour may ensue: (3a) some will return the borrowed books from whence they came, thus to keep faith with the doctrine that this is not new light; (3b) others (usually those who had the good sense at step 2 to keep their envy to themselves) may keep the books in hand, or purchase the others as they appear year after year, trying as best one can to read them and learn.

On the occasion of the kind invitation to participate in this symposium on the work of Tony Giddens, I went to my shelves there to find some 19 of his books. By contrast, I found only 12 by Bourdieu, which is unforgivable inasmuch as I was once generously acquainted with him. (Only Foucault, whom I never knew but on whom I once wrote a book, was better represented than Giddens, if only because I felt obliged to own both the French and English editions.) I doubt very much that there is any writer alive (and only Talcott Parsons among the dead) from whom I have learned more in indirect but powerful correspondence to the earnestness of my disagreements. Yet, to this day – and notwithstanding Tony Giddens' astonishing influence among academic people in many different disciplines and, now, even among political people and the literate public – there are hundreds of sociologists, too embarrassed perhaps by envy, who continue to dismiss Giddens more or less out of hand.

Back in the 1970s, when Giddens was just dawning, the knee-jerk complaint was that his work was, at best (or worst) mere exegesis and (worse yet) it was devoid of empirical grounding. Though there is less excuse for such a silly objection today, then there was good, if not sufficient, reason. Upon the appearance, in 1976, of *New Rules of Sociological Method* (Giddens' first memorable and, in my opinion, successful stab at what became his structuration theory), the hegemony felt to have been exercised over sociological work by Talcott Parsons was still very widely felt. In the United States, especially, this was a time when the older generation of people trained in the Parsonsian style still were forced to do battle on two fronts at once: against the empiricists who had been held somewhat in check during Parsons' more or less free reign through the 1940s and 1950s; and against the rising generation of radicals who were attempting to refashion sociology after their experience in politics in the 1960s. It hardly need be said that, since many of the new radicals had to get their degrees with older people, many of them empiricists who hated the Parsons' method for their own reasons, more than a few sociologists of my (and Giddens') generation cut their eye-teeth by finding ways to distance themselves from Parsons or, more to the present subject, from anyone whose work looked like Parsons'. This made for quite a mess that has yet to be entirely cleaned up. The untidiness of this unhappy coincidence of sociological temperaments was that something called 'theory' came to be widely taken as the kind of thing Parsons did and, thus, hopelessly worthless because of its lack of empirical content. Not many of those who thus believed bothered to consider Parsons' own defence of his method as analytic realism. Parsons himself considered his theoretical work rigorously empirical in its frames of reference, if not in its display of the hard-won numbers themselves.[1]

Giddens dawned on us just when this mess was most foul. Thus, because his best early books were indeed critical rethinkings of classic social theorists in the *apparent* style of Parsons, Giddens' early reputation was fixed negatively in the minds of many. That, in the years hence, he has done so brilliantly well in the minds of so many others is tribute indeed to the seductive quality of the thinking and writing. But it is tribute as well to a feature of his thinking that is all too easy to miss if one thinks of his method as 'mere theory', namely, the breathtaking inventiveness of Giddens' method of social thought, an invention so important, if not always successful, that one can hardly estimate the value of his ideas without taking prior account of the method from which they issue.

One measure of the originality of Giddens' theoretical method is that it is so utterly daring as to have exceeded even the ideas and proposals it has spawned. This condition, if I am right, is of substantial importance in light of Giddens' current role as, simultaneously, the administrative principal of one of the world's most distinguished and sometimes radical schools of social thinking and as spiritual brother and intellectual resource to a prime minister of the United Kingdom. *Beyond Left and Right: The Future of Radical Politics* (1994a), the book to which the latter of these important posts may reasonably be attributed, is, thus, both a wonderful summing up of his thinking over the previous decade and a courageous coming out of the underlying caution such thinking can encourage. On this, more later. For the present, I wish only to isolate, to begin, one important claim with respect to the assessment of Giddens' way of rethinking the social world.

When a theorist who works as Giddens does is challenged for what is taken to be a lack of sufficient empirical grounding, the right question is often being asked even when the one asking fails to appreciate a hard-to-swallow limiting condition upon empirical social research. In respect to certain times and conditions of the human social order, empirical grounding, in the usual sense, is both impossible and probably undesirable.

It is right, therefore, to ask the questions that must always be first in mind: *'What if it is so? How will we know?'*. But it may be foolish to insist on certain kinds of answers, however strong the desire to have them. Some questions simply do not allow for verification, much less falsification, in search for their scientific truth. Some questions, indeed, can barely be asked if the only proper answer to them must be put in the language of proof and the grammar of empirical data. Though he was doing something entirely different from Giddens, that was at least the problem with which Talcott Parsons sought to contend in his attempt to define and work within the protocols of an analytic realism.

Wittingly or not, Tony Giddens, though not by any means an analytic realist, has done something homologous, if not analogous, to Parsons (for which he gave ill-formed justification to his early detractors). Giddens has, at least, taken seriously the idea that theoretical method entails its own, and powerful, empirical capacity and that, whatever the value of the direct empirical study of social things, there are certain large objects of sociological investigation that can only be studied theoretically – for which a distinctive method is required. One need only reflect on Giddens' writings over the last two decades, and most especially those including and since his 1984 masterwork, *The Constitution of Society*, to see just how bold and inventive his method has become. By inquiry, first, in 1976, into the most fundamental rules of sociological method, then into the very foundations of society as such, Giddens has laid the groundwork for his important studies since 1984 which can be summarised, at some risk, as an attempt to establish the conceptual basis for thinking about the social world as such – a world that some consider post-modern, while others, Giddens most especially, consider merely transformed but still, somehow, like normally constituted modern social worlds. By daring to enter this controversy, Giddens has taken the risk of being misunderstood in spite of his numerous cautions to fix his position at worst on the near side of what he calls 'radicalised modernity' (a phrase that should not be lost on attempts to appreciate the politics that have been assigned to him – those of a 'radical centre'). Yet, risk or not, no serious social theorist today ought to beg the question of the supposed end of the modern era, if only because *if it is so, then we must know it!* If there is any reason to believe that the world and its culture has changed, or is changing, in a degree that threatens a transformation in kind of the social world, then no self-respecting social thinker can refuse to consider the prospect.

While it is regrettably true that all manner of foolishness is done in the name and for the sake of what people call post-modernism, this alone does not mean that the post-modernism question must not be asked and, where possible, answered. The trouble with the post-modernism question is, however, two-fold.[2] Giddens seems to honour, at least, one of the two, and though it is evident that Giddens has gotten the one, it is far from clear that he has caught up with the second.

The first of the two troubles is this. If there is *any* reasonable prospect that the world has changed such that all of the cultural assumptions to which we who are above, say, 40 years have grown accustomed may be suspect, then the language we use to ask our questions must be remade. If, otherwise put, there is any possibility that the world has changed, even to the degree that radical modernists like Giddens believe it has, then we can hardly investigate it with languages and methods from the prior, now possibly out-of-date, culture. In still other words, the *'What if it is so? How will we know?'* question of the post-modern world requires at least a modification, perhaps a complete revision, of the languages of social thought. This, the first trouble with the post-modernism question, Giddens understands with striking clarity, which may itself be the reason he has, over the last decade plus, set about the task of reinventing the vocabulary of social thought.

Unfortunately, as I said, there are two troubles at hand. The second can be put this way: if the world has in fact changed in some truly radical way (or, even, if it is still changing), we are unlikely to be able to know, under any empirical or conceptual circumstances, that this is so. When the *'What if it is so? How will we know?'* question is applied to the near prospect of world transformations that might, under ideal conditions, be subject to empirical verification, verification may not in fact be possible. We may be too close in time and space to be able to answer so big a question. Since it took anywhere from two to five centuries for it to dawn that a modern world had somehow evolved out of a traditional one, it is reasonable to suppose that it may take more than the one or two decades since the prospect has begun to be taken seriously before there is any real hope of an answer actually (as opposed to, ideally) susceptible of some kind of rhetorically plausible empirical verifications (and much longer, one supposes, before a higher order of falsifiable proof – if by then this is considered worth the while).

Though Giddens clearly appreciates the first trouble attendant to the questions he himself has insisted upon asking, it is less evident that he is willing and able to take in the second of these troubles. Even, and especially, in his last book he writes, as he has before, as though he were perfectly sure that what he says is so. This may be why he irritates the empiricists and their fellow travellers who, as a general rule, merit less attention than in some quarters they are still, for some reason, given. In the social sciences, empiricism is nothing more than a distortion of the reasonable scientific desire to find evidence where evidence can be found. The precise nature of the distortion takes the form of dismissing all questions that are insusceptible of empirically well-meant answers. Just the same, some questions must be asked, even by social scientists, even if they can not be answered. Not in the life-time of many of us, have there been so many unanswerable questions of this sort. Still, *'What if it is so? How will we know?'* is a question that always needs to be put. The trick is to know when one must put up with indefinite answers. Empiricists, by and large, refuse to enter such a fray, and at their worst they revile those who do. Others, and Giddens may be one, will enter the fray so conceptually well-prepared for the battle that they do not realise that the answers they give, however worthy of intellectual and political consideration, are beyond knowing.

In the present situation near the end of the twentieth century, which some take as the last modern century, the one question, above all others, that is clearly both urgent and beyond knowing is the question of the true nature and depth of social differences. If, at some point in the future, it turns out that the modernism ideal of a universal humanity – one, true, and in essential respects singular in nature – turns out to be implausible, then it hardly need be said that modernity will in fact have come to an end far more portentous than even the radical transformation on which Giddens has placed his bets. No one can say what that truth will be, but the question is put necessarily. If differences of race and gender, of sexualities, of ethnicity and social class, turn out to be unbridgeable, then we shall indeed be beyond the usefulness of modern culture. It need not be that these differences are found to be essential or, to use an old word, ontological in nature for them to have the practical effect of destroying the ideals of modernist culture. The urgency of the question explains why it has provoked so many cultural (and real political) wars, and why Giddens takes it as the central theme of *Beyond Left and Right*, the book of his political coming to power. I believe that the stand he takes in this book on the question of social differences is an entailment of the very inventiveness with which he has attempted to restate the *'What if it is so? How will we know?'* question – an inventiveness the brilliance of which may have actually prevented him from answering this unanswerable inquiry when it is applied to the prospect of a post-modern world.

Thus, to test the theme I have set, I want to examine Giddens' most fundamental theoretical method, against which, at the end, I propose to reconsider the political conclusions he takes from it.

Though there are a good many outside sociology who have tried to do what Giddens has done, he may well be the sociological social theorist who has most radically, and successfully, revised the language of social science. In respect to this ambition, Giddens' key concept is, of course, *structuration*, a concept that evolved, directly and unambiguously, from his understanding of the nature of sociological analysis. As he put it in 1976 in the closing words of *New Rules*, 'In sum, the primary tasks of sociological analysis are the following: (1) The hermeneutic explication and mediation of divergent forms of life within descriptive metalanguages of social science; (2) Explication of the production and reproduction of society as the accomplished outcome of human agency' (Giddens 1976: 162).

Behind the clumsiness of the language (a defect that fell away over the years) lie the indivisible principles of Giddens' thinking as it would evolve, which can be summed up as: how we talk about the world in order to understand it obeys the same recursive rules that also govern how we act in the world.

To the end of developing these, at first, plain-spoken principles, Giddens developed a distinctive literary style that has permitted him to obey them. Quite in contrast to the painfully formal construction just quoted, Giddens seems to have taught himself what few other social scientists of his stature have – to engage his readers more directly. This is not to suggest that Giddens' language is, even today, plain, only that he aims somehow to make himself understood in terms that are, in principle, shared between himself and his reader. The effect is that of drawing the reader outside the passive role of reading into an odd, but palpable, contact with the world being read. It is as if Giddens is in continuous pursuit, in spite of a series of literary and conceptual obstacles, of the very modern society he aims to describe. The effect is that, the difficulty of the language aside, Giddens' reader senses that somehow she is in the very presence of the thing itself, the world itself.

This appealing, even heroic, quality of Giddens' writing and thinking is evident in what may be his most unsettling and thus memorable interpretation of the concept *structure*, from *Constitution* in 1984:

> Structure thus refers, in social analysis, to the structuring properties allowing the 'binding' of time–space in social systems, the properties which make it possible for discernible similar social practices to exist across varying spans of time and space and which lend them 'systemic' form. To say that structure is a 'virtual order' of transformative relations means that social systems, as reproduced social practices, do not have 'structures' but rather exhibit 'structural properties' and that structure exists, as time–space presence, only in its instantiations in such practices and as memory traces orienting the conduct of knowledgeable human agents. (Giddens 1984: 17)

Some of this is quite opaque, but just the same the reader encounters a tone of voice closer than anything in *New Rules*, and books of that era, to the startling intimacy of Giddens' speaking style. In fact, this quality of being 'spoken to' is exactly what the attentive reader begins to sense behind, even, such mind-numbing words as 'instantiation'. In this passage that quality appears disarmingly in the operative verbs in the two main sentences. 'Structure thus refers . . .' is a phrase in which the 'thus' serves to carry the reader along through a thicket of definitions, just as the 'to say' locution beginning the second sentence has the effect of embracing the reader by opening the possibility that she already understands and is well cared for in the conceptual journey under way.

This remarkable sense of being spoken to, even when (as is often the case) one can hardly be sure what is being spoken, is not, I think, merely a stylistic trick. It is much more an entailment of the social theoretical method, the foundational principle which is that everything – both thought and action – is recursive. Everything, that is, is being constituted as it is being understood, just as the understanding itself is part of the constituting process. Giddens aims, clearly, to redefine the terms of social thought, but this cannot be accomplished without, at the very same time, redefining the social world itself. Hence the literary effect and the reason why paying some attention to it is more, much more, than an exercise in literary criticism. Thus, in the passage just quoted, the series of qualified neologisms by and in relation to which Giddens aims to define the concept *structure*, are the building blocks (a phrase he has used on numerous occasions) for the new concept he is introducing, namely *structuration*. But note also the odd manner in which he obliges himself to offer his newly defined terms: the 'binding' of time–space, the 'virtual order' of transformative relations, not 'structures' but 'structural properties'. There is something a little off in the flurry of quotation marks (all his) that qualify an otherwise supremely confident prose, as if to signal the approach of something that could be its undoing. For those who making a habit of reading social theory, Giddens' language has the effect of creating a degree of drama.

What Giddens is signalling in these literary apologies may be the most distinctive feature of his theory of structures. He is writing about structures as though he were writing of them in more or less the same terms in which they are normally thought of. But, in fact, he does not think of structures as others do. Structures, for Giddens, are not so much things in themselves as, to use his phrase, 'virtual order' properties that exhibit themselves only in concrete instances of social practice, as 'memory traces orienting the conduct of knowledgeable agents'! This turns out to be a big and courageous theoretical step.

To say that structures are virtual order properties is, in effect, to say that structures are not real social things, which, if one stops to think about it, is most disconcertingly obvious. And Giddens is one of the first to admit and announce this shocking truth. Others chose to avoid it. Durkheim, for one example, was consumed with interest in the reality of social things, yet in all his writings he avoided ever engaging in a positive description of the structure of modern society. Perhaps, in some reflexive way, Durkheim knew that the structures of the modern division of labour and the ethical crises that gave occasion to this founding of sociology, were not as real as, at least, his own rules required them to be. In like manner, to take a more current instance of someone who ought to have done otherwise, Pierre

Bourdieu, who clearly agrees with Giddens on the virtuality of structures, avoids saying so in so many words. Bourdieu, who wants most of all to be known as an empirical sociologist, sets up the inscrutable black hole of the *habitus* in order that he might explain the agential aspect of structures with having to consider it in so many words.[3]

Giddens, by contrast both to Durkheim and Bourdieu (not to mention virtually everyone else who has written about structures), wants nothing so much as to say, in so many words, the complete theory of modern societies. Hence the heroism behind his enterprise. Structuration theory is a theory of structures that grants the irreality of social structures in order to define 'structural properties' in the only places they can be observed, which are, as he says at the very end of the passage, practical actions and memory traces.

A cynic might argue that the reason Giddens remains entirely within the discourse of social theory, never writing what others consider empirical studies, is that it is impossible actually to describe a virtual structure, thus to prove his theory. This, I think, would be a cheap shot. Giddens is among those who believe that the discursive activity of writing, and saying, the social theory of things in modern societies is a nearly sufficient, certainly necessary, hence good-enough, way to do sociology. But, to maintain this position Giddens must make a move with which he is not, in the end, completely satisfied. Giddens' theoretical intention to say everything that can be said about radically modern societies requires him to account for the virtual *unconscious* as corollary to his virtual structures. This, however, is not an immediately apparent leap because, first, Giddens must pass from his idea of structure as virtual properties to their practical status in the reflexive nature of mundane action in the world.

There is another, less technical way to see this alarming and alluring feature of Giddens' social theory. When he actually speaks about sociology for a general audience, as in his 1986 inaugural address at Cambridge ('What Do Sociologists Do?'), Giddens (1987) writes of sociology as though it were a social science among other social sciences differing only in its greater capacity for reflexivity. He thus assumes a narrative position within sociology, the professionalised field of study, looking out on the social world that he believes sociologists see better for reason of their better polished reflexive gifts. As a consequence, when Giddens makes 'empirical references' in books like *The Nation-State and Violence* (1985) and *Beyond Left and Right*, he makes them *ex officio*, from the office of the reflexive sociologist. Though Giddens seems to be providing the exhaustive representation of structures in the text, he is ever aware of his public, of the reader whom he addresses, the one who bears the prior responsibility for the reflexive attitude in daily life. For Giddens, the virtual reality of structures is, thus, always outside, even over against, the natural reflexive capacity of the most ordinary human subject. Though a society's structures are virtual, they are necessarily a redoublement of a primary, if inaccessible, reality of social life.

Hence, on the one hand, their necessity in Giddens' recursive theory of structures and, on the other, a theory of their necessary duality. The central notion of structuration theory is that if structures build as they are being built then they, obviously, must be double. This necessary duplicity of structures is what accounts for and requires their status as virtual properties which, in turn, is required by the rules of Giddens' own sociological method, if he is to speak the social world to those who, in his view, build it.

Giddens thus seeks to transcend the notorious dualism of subjects and objects by recourse to the double nature of structures themselves. 'According to the notion of the duality of structure, the structural properties of social systems are both *medium and outcome* of the practices they recursively organise' (1984: 25, emphasis added). The statement is amazing. Having defined structures as properties of practical actions (and the memory traces that may orient those actions), Giddens still speaks of them as though they had real effects. Structures, being resources as well as rules, do 'recursively *organise*' social realities. They are, thus, real players, perhaps actors. This is a coherent view, perfectly defensible given its own logic. But it comes onto shaky ground soon enough.

It is very difficult to describe the recursive properties of structures, as is evident in the figure of speech to which Giddens resorts when attempting to simplify: 'We should understand human societies to be *like buildings that are at every moment being reconstructed by the very bricks that compose them*' (1987: 12).[4] He is trying (now with atypical clumsiness) to describe the most subtle of human processes with reference to the long, laborious construction of a building. This is already a slight clue to the difficulty of the task he has set for himself. Here, in a word, is the problem: within the language of theory it may not be possible to say what Giddens wants to say. Could this be the point at which the *'What if it's so? How will we know?'* question arises, against his expectations, even for a sociologist of radicalised modernity? It would seem likely given what now begins to pass in the development of the theory.

The duality of virtual structures means that knowledgeable agents, being the only real actors in society, act partly under the direction of structured rules and partly in reliance on structured resources made available by those social structures. But structures are never observed in themselves, only as reflected in the practical actions of individuals which are observable. The structured inequalities of the class system of modern urban societies is not, for example, ever in itself observable, except *through* the obvious instances of actions in which real people defer or condescend, starve or stuff themselves. Virtual realities are nonetheless real but without their own specificity. Giddens does not say it in exactly this way (and might well resist such a characterisation), but they are observed only in their being said.

This is why Giddens takes so seriously the idea of sociology as an extended conceptual discourse on and in the nature of modern societies. More specifically, this is why discourse (the ability to say things in so many words) is the key to consciousness which in turn is the theoretical key to virtual reality. It is plain to see that, if there is no literal, positive reality to structures, the only place one can observe them is in what people say about their actions. Observing actions themselves is insufficient. A poorly clad young person, with unkempt hair, begging for food might appear to be hungry and thus an instance of the structural property of the system's virtual inequality. Yet the same individual could also be a middle-class person of means who, for their own political or personal purposes, assumes the appearance of poverty – an act they would have been able to execute over time not *in spite of* their relative wealth but *because* of it. One could only determine such a character's place in the scheme of virtual structures by talking to and with, or about them and their kind. Even then, the results would be uncertain, because the reliability of such a conversation would depend utterly on the state and mode of their, and the observer's, consciousness. Discourse always bears some relation to consciousness, even if the relation is perverse.

This is the insight that brings Giddens to the unconscious aspect of social life. He distinguishes practical and discursive consciousness, without which there could be no reflexivity and thus no recursivity in society. Practical consciousness is that awareness of structured reality one holds in the head without necessarily being aware of it at any given moment (if ever), even though it is the resource by which one goes on and gets by.[5] We speak a language grammatically without being able to list the grammatical rules we use. We may, depending on our social background, defer to others of presumably greater status without knowing exactly why. Discursive consciousness is the capacity to talk coherently about our very own social actions even on those occasions when, without fully knowing why, we scrape and bow before those of superior status.[6] Discursive consciousness, thereby, encompasses the ability to understand and, if called upon, to recite the grammar of the actions, even of the actions we resent having to take.

Here is where the sociologist enters as the crucial actor in society. 'Human actors are not only able to monitor their activities and those of others in the regularity of day-to-day conduct; they are also able to "monitor that monitoring" in discursive consciousness' (Giddens 1984: 29); even when, under the conditions of practical consciousness, all human actors (in principle) and professional sociologists (by definition) are capable of acting competently in society, and talking about those actions and the actions of others (and talking about that talk). Otherwise, there is no way to know structures, thus, there are no structures. The ability of persons to put into words what they, and others, are doing is the only reliable way one has to know the virtual reality of structures. But (and Giddens refrains from putting it quite this radically), it would *also* seem to be that the ordinary, untutored capacity of individuals to put into words what they think of their own social actions is the principal (perhaps sole) access they have (*we* have) to the knowledge of virtual reality. If so, then discursive consciousness *is* the sole basis for that virtuality. Virtuality of structures in social life must mean 'mediated for all sufficient purposes by talk' – by discourse about structures.

Even if Giddens might not go quite as far as I have in interpreting him, his theory would seem to entail some central elements of this characterisation. Certainly, for a salient example, the virtual reality of his structures has not in the least prevented him from engaging in exceptional, and convincing, discursive practices with respect to social structures: nation-states, capitalism, the modern state and the class system, modernity itself. Theoretical seriousness has little of necessity to do with the hardness of one's theory of reality. Giddens' refusal to allow his theory of virtual structures to inhibit his theories of real structures is one of his most generous contributions to sociology.

Here, that turn one supposes Giddens would have preferred to avoid presents itself. Discursive consciousness requires some sort of theory of the unconscious life. In the few places where Giddens discusses the Freudian theory directly, he takes a simple, popular interpretation of the psychoanalytic view. In effect, if discursive consciousness is that which is available to be put into words, then practical consciousness is that aspect of the not-necessarily-conscious life available for use in practical life. Though Giddens grants that there is a deep unconsciousness that resists practical life, he is, quite understandably, very much more interested in the unconscious play between practical and discursive consciousnesses. When he sets about to discuss the unconscious,[7] his interest turn much more directly to memory than to Freud's notion of the perverse, resisting unconsciousness. The unconscious aspects of social (or does he mean mental?) life come, therefore, to the fore of his argument only because some version of the unconscious life is required to account for what he considers the fundamental dilemma of modern life. If for some, like Weber and Habermas, that dilemma was 'Why do people obey?' – or, for others like Durkheim, it was 'How will we know what to do?' – for Giddens the dilemma of the radical modern world is, 'Why and how do people trust?'.

Since for Giddens, the most fundamental fact of modern (especially late or radically modern) societies is that in them individuals are disembedded from primary relationships, the corresponding existential problem of the late modern age is 'trust versus risk', which is, it seems, the most urgent of the several uncertainties that come down from the basic fact of modern life: 'Modernity, as everyone living in the closing years of the twentieth century can see, is a double-edged phenomenon' (1990a: 7).[8] For Giddens, trust becomes the primary ethical question because radicalised modern societies are the social worlds in which individuals are, as he says, disembedded. Trust is not the same kind of ethical issue when persons live face-to-face and actions can be monitored directly. It makes less difference what others say about themselves upon presenting their credentials to strangers if, in the village or small city life of early modernity, one can observe, and hence control. But, in late modern societies everyone is a virtual stranger to every-one else because even those who have not left the village are perforce con-nected to others as much by virtual media of communication as by personal knowledge of that other. This fact even undercuts the power of personal knowledge of another. If I can call or fax in a matter of seconds another in some distant place to verify what a stranger *seems* to be and says she is, then a stranger's ability to pass in strange places on the strength of her personal word, or the visible qualities of actions, is always open for inspection. Faced with the prospect of an endless flow of information *about* an individual's character, complete confidence can never be sealed by a handshake. Thus trust becomes the major, critical issue in radically modern life because, literally, one never knows.[9]

This is the sense in which the practical ethic of daily life is just as cent-ral to Giddens' idea of sociology as it was to Weber's, or Habermas', and Durkheim's. But, for Giddens, much more explicitly than for Weber or Durkheim, the practical sociology of daily life is, at once, the resource and the rule of professional sociological knowledge. The sociologist – whether practical and discursive (that is, whether lay and professional) – is the uni-versal person of modern society. Sociology, in other words, is the competence whereby persons monitor their actions and the actions of others.

Sociology, therefore, is the *sine qua non* action in the recursive building up of structures and the maintenance of their virtual reality. Sociology, neces-sarily, is the means whereby those structures in all their virtuality recourse through the life of society. Yet, as Giddens recognises, sociological discourse cannot do its powerful work of carrying forth the structure of modern soci-eties without the unconscious, however minimally defined. Even though con-scious talk about its structures is the constitutive practice of modern societies, conscious talk, hence the virtual structures it composes, cannot go forth out of its symbiotic dependence on practical consciousness which is, as we have seen, effectively a practical unconsciousness.

In Giddens' scheme of structured social things, the unconscious serves two necessary purposes. (1) It accounts for the fact of practical action which would not take place at all if actors were obliged at *each and every moment* consciously to monitor, hence talk through, what they thought they were doing. (2) The unconscious, thereby, accounts for the virtual, recursive nature of social structures, which – because they are acknowledged to be virtual – would have no practical reality as rules and resources if, similarly, they were *nothing but* discursive facts. In the former respect, the unconscious allows actions their practical freedom; in the latter, it allows them their real weight – rules and resources available to structured action over time, across space.

But the key to Giddens' idea of the unconscious is the ever potential availability of that which is kept ready for discursive presentation outside, if not over-against, the conscious mind. Giddens' unconscious, therefore, is always in ready service. This is evident in Giddens' failed attempt to come

190

to terms with Freud.[10] Giddens' unconscious is a reservoir of memory, a resource. Freud's is the internal-Other, a force resistant to the conscious mind. Giddens cannot go so far as Freud for whom the unconscious was also the internal-Other of civilisation itself, because going this far would wreck the theory of modern structures. If virtual structures exhibit their properties only in instances of practices and 'memory traces' guiding an agent's conduct, then social memory must be 'for', not 'against' modern consciousness. In this delicate theoretical distinction, the fundamental fact of real and external social differences must be denied.

In the end, the final test of any social and political theory today is that of the prospect of a world of differences and the ability of a theory, in the shadow of such a possibility, to answer the question, *'What if it is so? How shall we know?'*. The question can also be put: *'If it turns out that there are real, incommensurable social differences among social groups, how shall we know what we know?'*.

One can begin to question Giddens on this point already, even within his earlier writings. That seemingly insignificant tick at the crucial moment in *Constitution of Society* when he admits he must have a theory of the unconscious, then refuses truly to have one, may well be the first sign of things to come. It makes an important ultimate difference whether the unconscious of social life is, simply, a resource for action in the world or, if it is, in the phrase of which much has been made, a dark continent within the self – that is, whether or not the individual bears within that which can never be utterly reconciled in conscious life. If so, it is much more than an argument by logical extension to state that, therefore, it must be so of life with others – that social differences may well be real.

The all-too-tidy modernist formula, to which Giddens clings, of agency as the source of actions is, to be honest, a conceit of the culture that believes there are no ultimate contradictions within, as there are no final social differences without and among the members of the social whole. This is the prospect that truly tests the *'What if it is so? How will we know?'* question. How, indeed, might we know that social differences are real, or not, if we begin and end with a language, however radical in its way, that seeks in the end to rescue the culture of modernity? To grant, as Giddens has done, that the structures of the world are virtual properties, and all that is thus entailed, is to go a long way towards beginning to answer the question. But it may not, and I think it does not, go far enough to answer the question of social differences. This becomes acutely important in Giddens' attempt, in *Beyond Left and Right*, to argue his social theory in precise political terms.

Beyond Left and Right begins, as Giddens usually does when tackling a problem, by granting the most difficult problems at hand, in this case: globalisation, the loss of tradition, and uncertainty. Though this list is more parsimonious than the one in *The Consequences of Modernity* (1990), his brief against post-modernity, it conveys the essential points of concern for those who take seriously post-modernity, with its supposition of social differences.

Though globalisation is often said, as Giddens does, to offer a new world of unifying possibility, it is also seen, by those Giddens would encourage, as a threat insofar as it rises on the collapse of an older, traditional, and certainty-producing colonial system. The prospect of a global world – as opposed to empires, or even economic world-systems – is the prospect that, out of the relative freedom of formerly colonised peoples, there will arise, not the short-run struggles over social differences, but a long-run of social harmony. Or, in Giddens' language, out of the short-run of disembedded-ness, there may arise a re-embedding of people that diminishes the power of their differences.

Not surprisingly, Giddens begins, thus, with reference to what may well be his most influential concept:

> Globalisation is really about the transformation of space and time. I define it as
> *action at a distance*, and relate its intensifying over recent years to the emergence of
> means of instantaneous global communication and mass transportation. (Giddens
> 1994a: 4)

In this brief definition one is reminded of the important third chapter of *Constitution* in which, immediately after (and as a consequence of) the chapter on the self and its consciousnesses, he systematically developed his ideas of time–space. What was at once exciting and disappointing in that chapter is that – even as it broke the classical barriers which for centuries had held time and space as original, thus separate, categories of understanding – it failed to account for the pre-condition of such a concept as time–space, namely: speed. Though he repeatedly pays lip-service to speed (as in 'instant-aneous' in the quote above), Giddens never develops the idea.

It is one thing to say that 'globalisation is action at a distance' – that is, movement in time over displaced (that is, virtual) space – but it is quite another to account for the central role of velocity in any theoretical abridge-ment of the supposed incongruity of time and space. As we know very well from even a passing acquaintance with the general theory of relativity, when time and space are joined in a virtual theoretical space (such as that of the far stellar regions), the speed with which objects move is never reliably a precisely measurable speed. When space is warped in relative times, velo-cities are so great as to be measurable only in virtual metaphors like light years. Though the magnitudes are different, this clearly is what is at issue in Giddens' discussion of structures as virtual properties no less than in his radically modern definition of globalisation.

To say that structures are virtual is to say that, by their very nature, they cannot be measured in real time against standard spatialised rulers. The very social arrangements Giddens grants in admitting to what he calls radicalised modernity are, thereby, the arrangements for which he has pre-pared his well-defined social theory of structuration. Structuration at some final metaphoric point is a concept that means to say that, for all practical purposes, social actions never end. If, then, they do not, then one must suppose that actions can never be said definitively to give rise to structures. In other words, at some point the recursivity of agents and structures cannot be spoken of without admitting what Giddens, without embarrassment, admits; namely: that structures are not real in the usual sense, they are virtual. What he does not admit, however, is that this must mean that, like all virtual properties, they are arrived at only by means of social velocities so great as to render statements such as 'action at a distance' nearly as metaphoric as is the measure 'light years'. They can be measured, to be sure, but only in units so grand as to be – here again, the phrase – beyond knowing.

Less abstractly, such a state raises important questions about any attempt to defend and revise such an ethical category as trust or, even, to describe such an ideal as the generative politics that are basic to Giddens' political theory. I take for my concluding point a text from the final chapter of *Beyond Left and Right*, in which Giddens defends one of the virtual concepts of his politics (what he calls an 'orienting ideal'), post-scarcity:

> The notion of the post-scarcity order, as an orienting ideal, and the critique of productivism, flow from these concerns. A post-scarcity system is not one in which economic development comes to a halt. It is, simply put, a system in which productivism no longer rules. I define productivism as an ethos where work is autonomous and where mechanisms of economic development substitute for personal growth, for the goal of living a happy life in harmony with others. This is the context in which a critical assessment of welfare institutions within Western societies can learn from the solidarities and life ethics of the informal sector. Such an approach does not in any way deny the hardships of the very poor, or the demoralisation which poverty can cause. Yet in overcoming productivism, the rich have much to learn from the poor and this situation is one factor raising the possibility of a lifestyle pact promoting generative equality. (1994a: 247)

There is much here to admire, most especially the critique of productivism made with reference to his ideal of life politics. But the vision of the form and content of universal harmony in radicalised modernity requires a generative politics that are difficult to imagine, much less act upon.

If, as the theory of structuration requires, this world is one in which action occurs at a distance, then we must ask what is the intended nature of the social contract Giddens envisages between, in the quote, the rich and poor? One hardly need doubt that now, any less than always, the rich have much to learn from the poor about how to live one's daily life. But, on the other side of the contractual table, if he really means that poverty is 'demoralising', then does not that mean that the poor do in fact suffer from a scarcity that may cripple, or cause them to withhold, their readiness to participate in a recursive compact with either the rich, or the now suddenly real (as opposed to virtual) 'welfare institution'? In the virtual aggregate of the current world economy, it may well be plausible to say that development is reaching its turn-over point into 'post-scarcity'. But, whether by the terms of mathematical modelling or by Giddens' own theory of virtually, such a virtual social condition may or may not encourage the reflexive capacities of the truly demoralised poor. On this, as on other of his political desiderata (violence, welfare, the environment), Giddens does not assume that the differences between those who are freed of the constraints of productivism and scarcity and those who continue to suffer them are real.

It is all too tempting, once one has made the commitment to the virtuality of structures, to assume by extension that their actual effects are also virtual. I doubt that they are for the real, as distinct from the virtual, poor, or for the most extreme victims of violence or environmental racism. Hence, the trouble with virtual spaces. They may be all that we have, but to learn to live with them, we must determine exactly what it means to act at a distance, and just at what velocity we must act in order to keep up with the rapid-fire of global processes. Like Giddens' prime minister, and the American president who is said to be the inspiration of New Labour, the dismantling of the old productivist welfare system, while excellent news for the economy as a virtual whole, is very bad family and personal news for the poor.

But, even these concerns are not the principal ones of the social theorist who must ever ask, *'What if it is so? How will we know?'*. What, indeed, if it is so that the poor are truly, not just virtually, different? How will we know according to Giddens' ideals? And what difference will it make? It's hard to say.

Notes

1. Parsons was clear about his method of analytic realism from the beginning in *Structure of Social Action*. For a discussion of the fate of this method in the work of Parsons's most astute critic and follower, see Alexander (1998).
2. I have discussed these troubles at length elsewhere. See Lemert (1997).
3. The present section is developed in greater detail as part of a comparison of Giddens to Bourdieu in Lemert (1995, Chapter 7).
4. This figure is used in both of his textbooks: Compare Giddens (1991b: 17) with Giddens (1987: 12), where the same figure is used. Why he resorts to so crude a figure in textbooks for young students is hard to say. By contrast, the formal presentation in reference to the duality of structures in the glossary in Giddens (1984: 374): 'Structure as the medium and outcome of the conduct it recursively organises; the structural properties of social systems do not exist outside of action but are chronically implicated in its production and reproduction.'
5. Giddens writes (1984: xxiii): 'What agents know about what they do, and why they do it – their knowledgeability *as* agents – is largely carried in practical consciousness. Practical consciousness consists of all the things which actors know tacitly about how to "go on" in the contexts of social life without being able to given them direct discursive expression'.
6. Giddens on discursive consciousness (1984: 374): 'What actors are able to say, or to give verbal expression to, about social conditions, including expecially

the conditions of their own action; awareness which has a discursive form.' On both practical and discursive consciousness, see 1984, Chapter 2.

7. See Chapter 2, 'The Unconscious, Time and Memory' in Giddens (1984).
8. See also Giddens (1991a) where he says (p. 3), with simple elegance, that 'trust in this sense is basic to a "protective cocoon" which stands guard over the self in its dealings with daily life'. Though trust is discussed in Giddens (1984), the earlier book on structures, it becomes an explicit theme in the later books (Giddens, 1990a, 1991a) which address directly the existential reality of modern life – in particular its disembedding nature. The disembedding theme is, in turn, dependent on his very influential theories of time–space in the chapter 'Time, Space and Regionalization', in Giddens (1984). See also Giddens (1992).
9. This paragraph is a free translation of Giddens (1991a) especially Chapter 2.
10. Giddens, at the crucial place, reads Freud through Erik Erikson from whom he derives the trust/risk dilemma. See 'Erikson: Anxiety and Trust', pp. 51–60 in Giddens (1984).

CHAPTER 10

An interview with Anthony Giddens

Editors: Perhaps we can begin by looking at the idea of nature. Historically and cross-culturally, different social relationships to nature and different cultural definitions of nature can be observed. Sociologists also have conceptualised nature–society relationships in different ways. In your own work, do you consider that there is really a nature 'out there', independent of our social conduct and social organisation which people struggle over, or has there never been a real nature, just different ways of relating to some features of experience that people call 'nature'?

AG: I would accept that nature exists! In this sense I could be considered a realist. However, what I have been interested in for some considerable time is analysing the contradictory relations that human beings have with nature. As corporeal beings we exist in material environments, yet human beings possess what I have described as a 'second nature' that can't be reduced to physical objects or events, and it is this second nature that marks the human distinctiveness from nature, maintains relationships with physical nature, and entails attempts to control it. These relationships between humans and nature are mediated through the institutions and practices that ensure the reproduction of the social. So whilst nature may exist 'out there', of greater significance is the paradoxical relation existing between humans and nature, between culture and nature, and this is best analysed, in my opinion, through understanding its internal incorporation, which means understanding that nature is not outside of categories of human thought and action, but an essential part of their organisation.

For example, if we examine the commodification of space in modern societies we see a changing relationship between city and country as capitalism developed. Before capitalism was established as a system of production the city, whilst maintaining a dependent relationship with the country, existed in distinct demarcation from it. As urbanism develops in capitalist organisation, the 'created environment' arrives, breaking down the separation of city and country. It is the way in which the physical world is appropriated and used in relation to other aspects of human social and cultural life that results in 'nature' taking on all these different meanings you mention. In my recent work, when I talk of the end of nature I'm interested in analysing the intrusion of human activity into every aspect of 'nature' and the environment, and the possibilities and risks attendant on the intrusion of technology and knowledge into the physical world.

To illustrate this we could consider how the meaning of the term 'natural foods' has a certain opposition to the way in which food is produced now. That sense of 'natural', as an opposition to 'industrial' food production, appears in everyday usage as a counter-reaction. There's not much that's 'natural' about this sense of nature. Another example would be 'natural water', available in plastic bottles in supermarkets, where 'natural' refers to healthy or pure in implied contrast to water that flows from the tap. These kinds of meanings are characteristic of everyday understandings of the terms 'nature' or 'natural', but distinctions of this kind are also a feature of the social sciences where there are distinctions made between nature and culture – for example, in the works of Lévi Strauss and many other writers. But I don't see myself as making any contribution to elucidating what nature 'really' or essentially means. I take it simply to mean those aspects of the physical world which are not directly influenced by human activity. As there are few such areas any longer, I use the term 'the end of nature'.

The end of nature, like the end of tradition, doesn't mean nature or tradition disappear, it simply means our relationship to the physical and social environment is substantially altered. Just as tradition today is not what tradition used to be, so 'the natural' is not what nature used to be. The meaning of 'natural foods', to return to my example, could only today make some sense against a background of the use of food additives, fertilisers and various other technologies in the processes that go into the production of food. The topic of food is a really interesting one and several sociological issues can be brought together through it, but what I'm trying to say here is that one wouldn't have these senses of 'nature' and 'natural' without all the rest – they don't make sense apart from that.

Editors: Can you say something about the idea of global futures? The question often raised by post-modernists is whether it is possible to imagine a global future as opposed to fragmented futures. Does your assessment of the end of nature point to any particular kinds of global future or do you see it as very open, full of very different kinds of potentialities?

AG: That seems to me several questions all wrapped into one but, yes, of course you can envisage global futures and that is part of what global futures have become: the fact that we do talk about them all the time. There is no logical sense in saying one can only talk about fragmentation; that's akin to the common refrain of 'an end to grand narratives' – but who is to say how 'grand' a narrative has to be before it is a 'grand narrative'? How can one have a notion of fragmentation without some notion of a whole to which it is being compared? I don't have any great problem with the concept of a whole, nor do I think anyone else should have. So, for example, you can certainly speak in general terms of the future of global financial systems, or the global economy, or global ecological issues. I am aware that there are people who disagree with that, and apparently someone has just written a book saying that I am a totalising thinker who refuses these ideas about fragmentation and therefore dangerous.

I prefer to understand contemporary social change through the concept of post-traditional, rather than post-modern, society. In a post-traditional context common frameworks of experience are organised by the institutional clusterings governing modern life, including the modern media and financial institutions – and their interconnections – which in many ways do create a unitary framework of experience and action. This unitary framework is constituted through the spread of universal symbolic tokens, the emergence of expert systems and the availability of mass cultural commodities through printed and electronic media. The separation of place from space is accompanied by the 'distanciation' of time and space from local contexts of action. Whereas in pre-modern societies the time of activity was intricately bound together with its spatial location, modernity standardises time across spatial contexts. This is reflected in the emergence of a distinctively modern form of temporality which creates a common history at the same time as accelerating the pace of social change. This is why I find the sole emphasis on fragmentation unsatisfactory, because it fails to appreciate new forms of common experience.

This doesn't mean that we all share a common future, nor that our idea of the future is clear. Since what is thought about the future influences it, that in a way destroys it. One could say, in a certain sense, that the future doesn't exist for us. We can think in terms of a diversity of future scenarios – and those scenarios themselves can influence what the future becomes. One of the most interesting areas in which this can be observed, where it is formalised, is in financial markets in the area of derivatives. Derivatives are basically complex ways of laying off risk. They are ways of constructing a range of possible futures. They actually define, however, a substantial part of what those futures become so they are not just statements about the future, they are part of the future.

Editors: Could you talk a little about the implications of all this for government? Is there a role for government when the future has become so problematic? Is the world simply spinning out of control?

AG: Well, of course these are some of the key questions of the age. Many see the impact of the global marketplace as making government largely obsolete. I don't believe this position is plausible however. We have to start thinking much more positively about the question of governance. We are moving into a global, cosmopolitan society driven by technological change and by markets over which we need to assert some degree of control. We can't have a Marxist scenario where we become total masters of our own history, but that doesn't mean that history escapes us completely.

Governance is needed to supply direction to people's lives and to reconcile competing interests. In contemporary societies, as well as on a global level, there are many different interest groups, voluntary groups, self-help groups, numerous pressure groups. Many of these groups, although by no means all, are organised towards political ends, ends which are often in conflict. There must be a means to decide which of those ends and interests are to be acted upon, and how they are to be balanced against others. Rather than focusing solely on 'the state', we need to promote the development of new forms of governance. The influence of national government has been affected by processes of globalisation but that doesn't mean government is no longer relevant, or that governance is unimportant: quite the contrary, in fact.

I prefer 'governance' to 'government' because there is no consolidated transnational government emerging comparable to the nation state, or even the European Community, but what can be seen everywhere are mechanisms of governance emerging. This is plain in the growth of global organisations. Looking at statistics one can observe a tremendous development of non-governmental organisations, many of which are routinely involved with global goods and services, such as, for example, telecommunications industries. On the level of industry and finance, the interesting area is the impact of global financial markets. I don't really think it's possible to allow global financial markets such free reign as they have at the moment. We need a debate about how they might be regulated, how the main agencies might be made more transparent and what some of the G7 countries could do if they decided to take some kind of action. Bound up with these issues are questions about the future of the International Monetary Fund and the World Bank, which are of course already, in significant ways, instruments of global governance. It is difficult to envisage the world economy without these institutions. Some people argue that we should get rid of them precisely because they are, as it were, instruments of governance. But those organisations should become more developed. For example, they could be endowed – maybe even the OECD – with more relevant powers, which could include keeping a more thorough-going index of democracy and transparency in rule-following in the international economic domain. George Soros has suggested there should be an international insurance corporation which would back up loans to a certain level. Also, governments at some point have to think of recovering tax revenue. In Western countries populations often won't pay very high tax revenues in the income tax system – governments have borrowed to fulfil their obligations by issuing bonds. Those bonds are a major element of global financial markets. I don't see why there shouldn't

be an attempt to recover some of that income by having a tax on transactions, such as the famous Tobin tax. The Tobin tax is not completely
unrealistic. There is also the possibility of the United Nations becoming a
more effective instrument of world governance; there are many possibilities
there for the future.

Other suggestions concern more democratic forms of governance. David
Held's version of a cosmopolitan democracy, for example, which I have
some sympathy with, proposes democracy going right up from local to
global level. This model takes the principle of autonomy as central to a
participative democratic structure aimed at empowering citizens. It requires
that various asymmetries of power which erode democratic autonomy are
tackled – autonomy itself is seen as a precondition of a fully democratic society that can balance freedom and justice. I see demands for autonomy and
self-determination as a result of the reflexive character of post-traditional
societies, and autonomy – providing it through policy frameworks and
creating the conditions for it to develop – is an important element in the
generative politics that I propose. Some of the contributors to this volume
mis-read, or misunderstand, my arguments in this area. It is quite wrong to
say that I do not address power relations.

Editors: A number of post-modern writers would ask whether it is possible
to generate or create the conditions for freedom for all or whether freedom
for some is bought at the expense of a lack of freedom for others?

AG: I don't regard this question as much to do with post-modernism. This
is the classical issue of liberal political theory: the limits of freedom and
where those limits should be. Ever since John Stuart Mill, liberalism has
developed a far more sophisticated approach than that available in post-
modernist theory, particularly in relation to questions of what the conditions and what the limits of individual freedom are.

I have no great interest in post-modernism. I see the world as still driven
by the forces of modernity. These are: the forces of science and technology
which are more powerful now than they ever were before; the spread of
capitalism, now becoming much more global than it ever was before; the
spread of the ideas of mass democracy whose time has come; massive
changes on the level of every day life, especially the changing relationship
between the sexes, which I take to be a global revolution in the making. All
these things are essentially forces of modernity. We face the need to deal
with them when they become global, when they penetrate everyday life
more deeply, and where their limitations, problems and paradoxes have
become more open. Reflexive modernisation means being aware of these
problems. Even though I use my share of them, I feel many of the 'post' and
'ending' words – post-modernism, post-industrialism, post-Fordism, post-
feminism and so forth – are likely themselves to end somewhere around the

new century. It's possible that there might then be a change in the *Zeitgeist* towards a more active, engaged and global outlook.

Editors: You wouldn't agree that it is possible to see in post-modern political theory an encounter with the limits of liberalism?

AG: Well, that depends on what is meant by liberalism. I was taking it in its classic sense, as liberal political theory – not simply market liberalism, or liberalism in the American sense, which is something different again. There are so many strands of liberalism, and so many diverse writings that come under the category of 'post-modernism'. In the work of people like Anna Yeatman, or Ernesto Laclau and Chantal Mouffe, there are concerns that overlap with liberalism. If one is talking about liberal democracy and its difficulties, or the impact of Western culture and its dominance over large parts of the rest of the world, then certainly there are areas in which at least some authors associated with post-modernism specialise. I'd find it hard to see what contributions post-modernists have made in the areas of social and political change I have been talking about, unless the category is used very widely, to include thinkers like Richard Rorty. But as I said, the vastly different writings that are referred to as post-modernist, let alone the great differences in liberalism, mean that this is a very difficult question to do justice to here.

Editors: Perhaps we can move away from post-modernism and return to something you were just talking about: the large scale forces of modernisation. Two forces in particular that have featured in your work are forces of rationalisation – of institutions, for example, – and forces of social reflexivity. Do these forces exist in contradiction or in tension or are they are part and parcel of the same modernising processes?

AG: The term 'rationalisation' is a Weberian term that I haven't used very often. What I have always said, and always thought, is that modern societies depend upon the collection of information. That goes back at least to the era of printing, which is crucial to the formation of the modern state, followed by a second phase, around the late eighteenth century. In this latter phase, the collection of official statistics and other forms of information-keeping, some of which were taken up by private bureaucracies as well as by Government agencies, were bound up with the concentration of power found in the modern state. This was followed by the emergence of electronic communication, led first of all by the invention of the Morse code and telegraph in the mid-nineteenth century.

However, information has various dimensions, like surveillance in general. It is a means of consolidating power, but it is also a means of contesting that power. These two dimensions can be seen in every organisation. A good example is the welfare state, which is a way of helping people, but a means of controlling them too. I see these two things as two sides of a coin but with considerable historical change built in. Today, there is a new development in communications structures, the global electronic order, involving satellite communication. We have to account for the shift from a situation where bureaucratic power seemed fairly stable and almost quasi-eternal to one now where there is a much more inchoate system of information and power – where bureaucracy seems a dinosaur.

In any situation where one is dealing with information there are various angles and possibilities with regard to power. If one looks at Foucault's writings, particularly in the recent collection of four volumes, it is clear that he was always of this. As a thought experiment, he wrote out the factor of the active use of information just to see where it would get him if he treated people as 'docile bodies'. It seems to have been a methodological decision, a conscious one to see what kind of analysis would result. The end result is a history that has no active subject at all, one devoid of agency. Foucault came to be locked into a position that was originally just a device.

Editors: Has the concept of reflexivity a place for the emotions?

AG: Certainly it has. I have written extensively about emotions and I've tried to point to the emotional undertones of everyday life, social change, leadership and identification with leadership figures. I argue that we only have emotional stability in our lives insofar as there is some overall regularity of social activity. If you don't have that then you are in trouble, which is why I write about trust. Trust, in its broadest sense – 'basic trust' – is part of the emotional apparatus of the healthy person. There must be some kind of emotional security that underlies all that, so I don't accept criticisms that I talk about reflexivity in too cognitive a way.

I have been interested in examining these questions in relation to self-identity and the body. In detraditionalised contexts, there are two distinct possibilities in terms of responses to opportunities and anxieties: one is a move towards greater autonomy on the part of the individual, and the other a relapse into some form of compulsive behaviour. If I could return to the example of food for a moment, eating disorders interest me because they are a down-to-earth example of what I'm describing: in this case the way in which information and knowledge about food and the body become part of what the body is. Anxieties concentrate directly on the body, and compulsion becomes an attempt to control – it may be possible to say that the body becomes a metaphor for social change, where broader fears are displaced on to a physical 'space' over which control may be exerted. My main argument though has been that the growth in addictive and compulsive behaviours can be understood as a reflection of the globalisation of food production and the detraditionalisation of diet that accompanies it.

Editors: How does this idea of reflexivity relate to the large scale forces of modernisation you were describing earlier?

AG: I separate out two senses of reflexivity. The most basic one is associated with action. To be an agent means understanding oneself as an agent, and others have to accept these actions and understandings. The other meaning of reflexivity is social reflexivity, which is about living in a society where large amounts of information come to us, which we have to make sense of. This is not merely background information, but constitutive of what we do and why we do it. Social reflexivity refers to a condition of social life in modern societies. One of the best examples I can give to illustrate this point is that of financial markets. Finance markets are institutionalised risk environments, where borrowers, savers and speculators are engaged in sophisticated exercises in reflexivity. Investors are choosing among an array of risks and methods of protecting against them, whilst borrowers try to adjust the terms of their capital received against the risks of the business enterprises for which it is utilised. Here, as in all institutionalised risk environments, risk is used actively, to create the 'future', which is then colonised. The astonishing scope of the futures markets is a case in point; investments, risks, are structured around a 'virtual' future, and in the process actually create future worlds. I recently had a dialogue with George Soros, who uses the same term (reflexivity) in roughly the same way as I do. His idea – on which he seems to have made his fortune – is interesting. He views financial markets as inherently unstable precisely because of their reflexive component. They are defined by how people understand the information they have and how they slot it back into the system. Everyone is trying to outguess everyone else, knowing that situation to be the case. These reactions constitute what financial markets actually are.

Editors: What is sociology's role in the changes you describe? Is there a tension between the position of the sociologist and the position of the engaged intellectual in relation to these changes?

AG: I would like to see sociology recover its central role in relation to current debates about where the world is moving. To some extent it has abandoned that role, partly because of the impact of neoliberalism, which suggests everything can be left to markets, and partly because of the influence of post-modernism which is politically and sociologically paralysing. We are in a world that seems to be changing as much as the world of the late eighteenth century. The forces that are changing it are fairly well-understood, but the consequences of those changes are extremely problematic. Sociologists should be at the centre of discussions about social change and its possible directions, opportunities and problems, helping to establish what consequences might ensue. More social scientists and sociologists should become engaged as public intellectuals, trying to shape debates about social and political policy.

Editors: There is a sense in which sociology's origins are bound up with the development of European nation states and with the process of state formation. Sociological knowledges were often related to the problems and potentials of state-formation in Europe. Given the globalising nature of the social changes you describe, does this mean that the sociologist becomes uncoupled from those kinds of questions of state?

AG: I don't think it was ever quite as clear as you are saying, if you mean that sociology had a direct connection to nation states and the formation of nation states. Some types of investigation of social life, such as the collection of official statistics that I mentioned before, had a connection with the emergence of state power. But from the very earliest days there was also an internationalism to sociology, as there was to economics and philosophy, and this was a feature of the Enlightenment. Consider, for instance, Kant's essay on perpetual peace. There we have a philosopher linked to the German state, but locating his reflections in a much wider international arena. This doesn't mean, of course, that we are stuck in the past with Kant or with nineteenth century sociologies: we are a long way beyond them. What I mean is that the question of the nation-state was never as dominant as you seem to be implying, and that internationalism has long been an important part of the origins of sociology, the other social sciences and philosophy

Editors: In your recent work you've talked about the need to constitute a radical political centre, and to think radically about political institutions like the welfare state. Do you see social reflexivity and globalisation creating such social changes that policy frameworks require a fundamental rethinking? Do you see yourself becoming more involved in issues of policy, as well as politics?

AG: Globalisation and social reflexivity have created enormous changes. On the economic front is a technological revolution that is transforming economic life; on the political front are numerous changes; socially we are seeing a transformation in the organisation of family structures and the way people choose to live their lives. As I said before, these changes are of the same magnitude as those brought during capitalist industrialism. It's hard to overestimate the degree of upheaval during this period, and we can compare the effects of social change then with those in the present. In the earlier period, as well as the decline of established economic activities and the growth of new industries, demanding new skills and attitudes and orientations to work, there were political upheavals as political structures changed and people fought against the established authority of Church and state and for the right to vote, participate in political life and form trade unions. Industrialisation was an uneven process, affecting different countries at different times and in different ways, but all experienced immense social upheavals as a result of the transition to industrial capitalism.

These upheavals generated a search for new systems of governance, new ways of regulating society and of providing for the population's welfare. The provision of large scale, state administered social insurance for the workforce was significant because it represented a changing view of poverty and social need. The Poor Laws encompassed a view of poverty as a responsibility of the individual, and often as a moral failing on the part of the individual. Social insurance, on the other hand, embodied a recognition that structural factors were a significant cause of poverty, such as unemployment caused by slumps in capitalist economic activity, or ill-health caused by working conditions. These different views of poverty, and of the state's responsibility for social welfare, structured the development of social protection systems in Europe, although countries organised their systems differently depending on their cultural, religious and political norms and ideologies.

It was only following the Second World War that the term 'welfare state' was coined. It has become so familiar that it is hard to remember that it came into wide usage only in the 1960s. This period saw a tremendous expansion of the state's involvement in welfare provision. Keynesian Welfare States differed in the way they organised these programmes but they shared three important characteristics. The first was the assumption that government could maintain life-long full employment, understood as male employment. The second was that the traditional nuclear family would be the norm, with women providing the bulk of primary care and married women receiving benefits tied to their husband's contribution record. The third was that the universality of many programmes symbolised a collective responsibility for, and sharing of, risk.

In this guise, the welfare state has come under strain over the last twenty years, for the reasons I've mentioned. The search is on for new policy frameworks and methods of provision – which require paying attention to the new structures and risks that we have to deal with now. We have to look for a different balance of risk and security in welfare systems. Despite their differences, welfare states have been based on a fairly passive notion of risk, with security seen mainly as the handing out of benefits. We have to find a new balance between individual and collective responsibility. The more open and reflexive the world becomes, the more we need to encourage people to take an active attitude towards their futures. At the same time, government has responsibilities towards its citizenry. Can we create a society that combines initiative and security – which encourages the go-getter but protects the vulnerable? No-one knows, but these should be the aims of welfare reform and more generally of revitalised social democracy. I've recently completed a short book about political issues, particularly the possibilities for a renewal of social democracy and, with Will Hutton, I'm editing a book on global capitalism.

Editors' note

This interview has been only lightly edited in order to preserve its informal and discursive style.

References

Afshar, H. (1994) 'Women and the Politics of Fundamentalism in Iran'. *WAF Journal*, 5: 15–20.

Ahmed, S. (1999) ' "She'll Wake up One of These Days and Find She's Turned into a Nigger": Hybridity, Identification and Passing'. *Theory, Culture & Society* (Forthcoming).

Alexander, J. (1982) *Theoretical Logic in Sociology*, Vol. I. Berkeley: University of California Press.

Alexander, J. (1996) 'Critical Reflections on "Reflexive Modernization"', *Theory, Culture and Society*, 13(4): 133–38.

Alexander, J. (1998) *Neofunctionalism and After*. Oxford: Blackwell.

Anderson, B. (1983) *Imagined Communities: Reflections on the Origins and Spread of Nationalism*. London: Verso.

Anderson, B. (1995) 'Ice Empire and Ice Hockey: two fin de siècle dreams'. *New Left Review*, 2(14): 146–50.

Anthias, F. (1982) *Ethnicity and Class among Greek Cypriot migrants – a Study in the Conceptualisation of Ethnicity*. Ph.D. Thesis, University of London.

Anthias, F. (1990) 'Race and Class Revisited: Conceptualising Race and Racisms'. *Sociological Review*, 38(1): 19–42.

Anthias, F. (1993) 'Gender, Ethnicity and Racialisation in the British Labour Market', in Ludwig, H. and Morokvasic, M. (eds) *Bridging States and Market*. Berlin: Sigma.

Anthias, F. (1994) 'Rethinking Race Conscious Policies in Britain'. *Innovation*, 7(3): 249–58.

Anthias, F. (1996) '*Rethinking Social Divisions*', Inaugural lecture series. London: Greenwich University Press.

Anthias, F. (1998a) 'Rethinking Social Divisions: Some Notes Towards a Theoretical Framework'. *Sociological Review* (forthcoming).

Anthias, F. (1998b) 'Evaluating Diaspora: Beyond Ethnicity?'. *Sociology* (forthcoming).

Anthias, F. (n.d.) *New British Cypriot Identities*. Unpublished paper, University of Greenwich.

Anthias, F. and Yuval Davis, N. (1992) *Racialised Boundaries: Racism and the Community*. London: Routledge.

Appadurai, A. (1990) 'Disjuncture and Difference in the Global Cultural Economy', in Featherstone, M. (ed.) *Global Culture*. London: Sage, pp. 295–310.

Archer, M. (1995) *Realist Social Theory: The Morphogenetic Approach*. Cambridge: Cambridge University Press.

Arditti, R., Klein, R. and Minden, S. (eds) (1984) *Test-tube Women. What Future for Motherhood?* London: Pandora.

Arnold, J. and Jordan, B. (1996) 'Poverty', in Drakeford, M. and Vanstone, M. (eds) *Beyond Offending Behaviour*. Aldershot: Arena.

Aye Maung, N. and Mirlees-Black, C. (1994) *Racially Motivated Crime: A British Crime Survey Analysis*. London: Home Office.

Back, L. (1996) *New Ethnicities and Urban Culture*. London: UCL Press.

Bailey, R. and Brake, M. (eds) (1975) *Radical Social Work*. London: Edward Arnold.

Banuri, T. (1990) 'Modernisation and its Discontents: A Cultural Perspective on Theories of Development', in Appfel Marglin, F. and Marglin, S.A. (eds) *Dominating Knowledge*. Oxford: Clarendon Press, pp. 73–101.

Barker, C. (1999) 'Empowerment and Resistance: "Collective effervescence" and other accounts', in Bagguley, P. and Hearn, J. (eds) *Transforming Politics: Power and Resistance*. London: Macmillan (in press).

Bateson, W. (1894) *Materials for the Study of Variation*. Cambridge: University Press. (Reprinted by John Hopkins University Press, 1992).

Bauman, Z. (1989) 'Hermeneutics and Modern Social Theory', in Held, D. and Thompson, J.B. *Social Theory of Modern Societies*. Cambridge: Cambridge University Press, pp. 34–55.

Baynton, D.C. (1997) *Forbidden Signs: American Culture and the Campaign Against Sign Language*. Chicago: University of Chicago Press.

BDA (British Deaf Association) (1987) *BSL – Britain's Fourth Language*. Carlisle: British Deaf Association.

Beck, U. (1992) *Risk Society*. London: Sage.

Beck, U. (1996) *The Reinvention of Politics*. Cambridge: Polity Press.

Beck, U. and Beck–Gernsheim, E. (1996) 'Individualization and "Precarious Freedoms": Perspectives and Controversies of a Subject–Object Oriented Sociology', in Heelas, P., Lash, S. and Morris, P. (eds) *Detraditionalization*. Oxford: Blackwell.

Beck, U., Lash, S. and Giddens, A. (1994) 'Preface', in Beck, U., Giddens, A. and Lash, S. *Reflexive Modernization: Politics, Tradition and Aesthetics in the Modern Social Order*. Cambridge: Polity Press, pp. vi–viii.

Becker, H.S. (1963) *Outsiders: Studies in the Sociology of Deviance*. New York: Free Press.

Beirne, P. and Sumner, C. (1997) 'Editorial Statement'. *Theoretical Criminology*, 1(1): 5–11.

Benton, T. (1991) 'Biology and Social Science: Why the Return of the Repressed Should be Given a (Cautious) Welcome'. *Sociology*, 25(1): 1–29.

Benton, T. (1993) *Natural Relations: Ecology, Animal Rights and Social Justice*. London: Verso.

Benton, T. (1994) 'Biology and Social Theory in the Environmental Debate', in Redclift, M. and Benton, T. (eds) *Social Theory and the Global Environment*. London: Routledge.

Benton, T. (1997) 'Imagine the Alternatives'. *Red Pepper*, 34: 22–3.

Benton, T. and Redfearn, S. (1996) 'The Politics of Animal Rights – Where is the Left?'. *New Left Review*, 215, Jan/Feb: 43–58.

Berman, M. (1982) *All That Is Solid Melts Into Air: The Experience of Modernity*. New York: Simon and Schuster.

Berry, P. and Wernick, A. (eds) (1992) *Shadow of Spirit: Post-modernism and Religion*. London: Routledge.

Bhabha, H. (ed.) (1990) *Nation and Narration*. London: Routledge.

Bhabha, H. (1994) *The Location of Culture*. London: Routledge.

Bhaskar, R. (1978) *A Realist Theory of Science* (2nd edn). Brighton: Harvester.

Bhaskar, R. (1989) *The Possibility of Naturalism* (2nd edn). Hemel Hempstead: Harvester.

Birke, L. and Hubbard, R. (1995) *Reinventing Biology. Respect for Life and the Creation of Knowledge*. Bloomington: Indiana University Press.

Blagg, H., Pearson, G., Sampson, A., Smith, D. and Stubbs, P. (1988) 'Inter-agency Co-ordination: Rhetoric and Reality', in Hope, T. and Shaw, M. (eds) *Communities and Crime Reduction*. London: HMSO.

Blaxter, M. (1990) *Health and Lifestyle*. London: Routledge.

Bologh, R.W. (1992) 'The Promise and Failure of Ethnomethodology from a Feminist Perspective: Comment on Rogers'. *Gender & Society*, 6(2): 199–206.

Bottoms, A.E. (1994) 'Environmental Criminology', in Maguire, M., Morgan, R. and Reiner, R. (eds) *The Oxford Handbook of Criminology*. Oxford: Oxford University Press.

Bottoms, A.E., Mawby, R.I. and Xanthos, P. (1989) 'A tale of two estates', in Downes, D. (ed.) *Crime and the City*. London: Macmillan.

Bourdieu, P. (1990) *The Logic of Practice*. Oxford: Polity.

Bowling, B. (1998) *Violent Racism: Victimisation, Policing and Social Context*. Oxford: Oxford University Press.

Boyne, R. and Rattansi, A. (eds) (1990) *Post-modernism and Society*. London: Macmillan.

Brah, A. (1991) 'Difference, Diversity, Differentiation'. *International Review of Sociology, special issue on Diversity and Commonality*, Series 2, No. 2, December, 53–73.

Brah, A. (1996) *Cartographies of the Diaspora*. London: Routledge.

Braithwaite, J. (1989) *Crime, Shame and Reintegration*. Cambridge: Cambridge University Press.

Braithwaite, J. (1993) 'Shame and Modernity'. *British Journal of Criminology*, 33(1): 1–18.

Braithwaite, J. (1995) 'Reintegrative Shaming, Republicanism and Policy', in Barlow, H.D. (ed.) *Crime and Public Policy*. Oxford: Westview Press.

Braithwaite, J. and Mugford, S. (1994) 'Conditions of Successful Reintegration Ceremonies: Dealing with Juvenile Offenders'. *British Journal of Criminology*, 34(2): 139–71.

Braithwaite, J. and Pettit, P. (1990) *Not Just Deserts*. Oxford: Oxford University Press.

Bryant, C.G.A. and Jary, D. (1990) *Giddens' Theory of Structuration: A Critical Appraisal*. London: Routledge.

Buber, M. (1937) *I and Thou*. Edinburgh: T.T. and T. Clark.

Buber, M. (1947) *Between Man and Man* (trans. R.G. Smith). London: Routledge and Kegan Paul.

Buber, M. (1952) *Eclipse of God: Studies in the Relation between Religion and Philosophy* (trans. R. Friedman *et al.*). New York: Harper.

Budick, S. and Iser, W. (eds) (1989) *Languages of the Unsayable: The Play of Negativity in Literature and Literary Theory*. New York: Columbia University Press.

Bunders, J., Haverkort, B. and Hiemstra, W. (eds) (1996) *Biotechnology: Building on Farmers' Knowledge*. London: Macmillan.

Burnside, J. and Baker, N. (eds) (1994) *Relational Justice: Repairing the Breach*. Winchester: Waterside Press.

209

Butler, J. (1993) *Bodies that Matter: On the Discursive Limits of Sex.* London: Routledge.

Calhoun, C. (1995) '"New Social Movements" of the Early Nineteenth Century', in Traugott, M. (ed.) *Repertoires and Cycles of Collective Action.* London: Duke University Press.

Campbell, B. (1993) *Goliath: Britain's Dangerous Places.* London: Methuen.

Campbell, C. (1996) 'Detraditionalisation, Character and the Limits to Agency', in Heelas, P., Lash, S. and Morris, P. (eds) *Detraditionalisation.* Oxford: Blackwell.

Carlen, P. (1996) *Jigsaw: A Political Criminology of Youth Homelessness.* Buckingham: Open University Press.

Castells, M. (1975) 'Immigrant Workers and Class Struggle in Advanced Capitalism'. *Politics and Society*, 5(1): 33–66.

Castles, S. and Kosack, G. (1973) *Immigrant Workers in the Class Structure in Western Europe.* Oxford: Oxford University Press.

Christie, N. (1977) 'Conflicts as Property'. *British Journal of Criminology*, 17(1): 1–15.

Christie, N. (1993) *Crime Control as Industry: Towards Gulags, Western Style?.* London: Routledge.

Christie, N. (1997) 'Four Blocks Against Insight: Notes on the Oversocialization of Criminologists'. *Theoretical Criminology*, 1(1): 13–23.

Clifford, J. (1994) 'Diasporas'. *Cultural Anthropology*, 9(30): 302–38.

Cohen, A. (ed.) (1974) *Urban Ethnicity.* London: Tavistock.

Cohen, L.E. and Felson, M. (1979) 'Social Change and Crime Rate Trends: A Routine Activities Approach'. *American Sociological Review*, 44: 588–608.

Cohen, P. (1972) 'Working Class Youth Cultures in East London', in *Working Papers in Cultural Studies 2.* Birmingham, Birmingham University Centre for Contemporary Cultural Studies.

Cohen, P. (1988) 'The Perversions of Inheritance: Studies in the Making of Multi-racist Britain', in Cohen, P. and Bains, H. (eds) *Multi-Racist Britain.* London: Macmillan.

Cohen, R. (1997) *Global Diasporas: An Introduction.* London: UCL Press.

Cohen, S. (1985) *Visions of Social Control.* Cambridge: Polity Press.

Collier, A. (1994) *Critical Realism. An Introduction to Roy Bhaskar's Philosophy.* London: Verso.

Collier, A. (1997) 'Critical Realism and Lay Knowledge'. Mimeo, Copy from the author, Southampton: University of Southampton.

Corea, G. (1985) *The Mother Machine. Reproductive Technologies from Artificial Insemination to Artificial Wombs.* London: Women's Press.

Corea, G. (1989) 'Junk Liberty', in Hynes, P. (ed.) *Reconstructing Babylon. Women and Technology.* London: Earthscan.

Corker, M. (1993) 'Integration and Deaf People: The Policy and Power of Enabling Environments', in Swain, J., Finkelstein, V., French, S. and Oliver, M. (eds) *Disabling Barriers–Enabling Environments.* London: Sage, pp. 145–54.

Corker, M. (1996) 'A Hearing Difficulty and Impairment', in Hales, G. (ed.) *Beyond Disability: Towards an Enabling Society.* London: Sage, pp. 45–56.

Cox, L. (1997) 'Reflexivity, Social Transformation and Counter Culture', in Barker, C. and Tyldesley, M. (eds) *Third International Conference on Alternative Futures and Popular Protest: Conference Papers Volume I.* Manchester: Manchester Metropolitan University.

Craib, I. (1992) *Anthony Giddens.* London: Routledge.

Currie, E. (1988) 'Two Visions of Community Crime Prevention', in Hope, T. and Shaw, M. (eds) *Communities and Crime Reduction.* London: HMSO.

Currie, E. (1996) *Is America Really Winning the War against Crime and Should Britain Follow its Example?* London: NACRO.

Currie, E. (1997) 'Market, Crime and Community: Towards a Mid-range Theory of Post-industrial Violence'. *Theoretical Criminology*, 1(2): 147–72.

Davies, M. (1969) *Probationers in their Social Environment* (Home Office Research Study 2). London: HMSO.

Dawe, A. (1970) 'The Two Sociologies', *British Journal of Sociology*, 21: 207–18.

Denzin, N. (1990) 'Harold and Agnes: A Feminist Narrative Undoing'. *Sociological Theory*, 8: 198–216.

Denzin, N. (1991) 'Back to Harold and Agnes'. *Sociological Theory*, 9: 264–68.

Derrida, J. (1989) 'How to Avoid Speaking: Denials', in Budick, S. and Iser, W. (eds) *Languages of the Unsayable: The Play of Negativity in Literature and Literary Theory*. New York: Columbia University Press.

Dickens, P. (1992) *Society and Nature. Towards a Green Social Theory.* Hemel Hempstead, Harvester Wheatsheaf.

Dickens, P. (1996) *Reconstructing Nature. Alienation, Emancipation and the Division of Labour.* London: Routledge.

Dodd, T. and Hunter, P. (1992) *The National Prison Survey 1991.* London: HMSO.

Dupré, L. and Saliers, D.F. (1990) *Christian Spirituality: Post-Reformation and Modern.* New York: SCM Press.

Durkheim, E. and Mauss, M. (1963) *Primitive Classification.* Chicago: University of Chicago Press.

Eagleton, T. (1997) 'Spaced Out'. *London Review of Books*, 24 April, 22–23.

Echols, A. (1989) *Daring to Be Bad: Radical Feminism in America, 1967–1975.* Minneapolis: University of Minnesota Press.

Elias, N. (1978) *The Civilising Process.* Oxford: Blackwell.

Ellison, N. (1997) 'Towards a New Social Politics: Citizenship and Reflexivity in Late Modernity'. *Sociology*, 31(4): 697–719.

Elster, J. (1983) *Sour Grapes: Studies in the Subversion of Rationality.* Cambridge: Cambridge University Press.

Erting, C. (1987) 'Cultural Conflict in a School for Deaf Children', in Higgins, P. and Nash, J. (eds) *Understanding Deafness Socially.* Springfield, Illinois: Charles C. Thomas.

Etzioni, A. (1993) *The Spirit of Community: Rights, Responsibilities and the Communitarian Agenda.* New York: Crown.

Fanon, F. (1986) *Black Skin, White Masks.* London: Pluto.

Farrington, D.P. (1996) *Understanding and Preventing Youth Crime.* York: Joseph Rowntree Foundation.

Featherstone, M. (ed.) (1990) *Global Culture.* London: Sage.

Featherstone, M., Lash, S. and Robertson, R. (eds) (1995) *Global Modernities.* London: Sage.

Felson, M. (1986) 'Linking Criminal Choices, Routine Activities, Informal Control and Criminal Outcomes', in Cornish, D.B. and Clarke, R.V.G. (eds) *The Reasoning Criminal.* New York: Springer-Verlag.

Fitzgerald, M. and Hale, C. (1996) *Ethnic Minorities, Victimisation and Racial Harassment: Findings from the 1988 and 1992 British Crime Surveys* (Home Office Research Study 154). London: Home Office.

Foshay, T. (1992) 'Resentment and Apophasis: The Trace of the Other in Levinas, Derrida, and Gans', in Berry, P. and Wernick, A. (eds) *Shadow of Spirit: Postmodernism and Religion.* London: Routledge.

Foster, J. and Hope, T. with Dowds, L. and Sutton, M. (1993) *Housing, Community and Crime: The Impact of the Priority Estates Project* (Home Office Research Study 131). London: HMSO.

Foucault, M. (1977) *Discipline and Punish*. London: Allen Lane.

Foucault, M. (1986) *The Care of the Self: History of Sexuality*. New York: Pantheon.

Friedman, J. (1997) 'Global Crises, the Struggle for Cultural Identity and Intellectual Porkbarrelling: Cosmopolitans versus Locals, Ethnics and Nationals in an Era of De-Hegemonisation', in Werbner, P. and Modood, T. (eds) *Debating Cultural Hybridity*. London: Pluto, pp. 70–90.

Galbraith, J.K. (1992) *The Culture of Contentment*. London: Sinclair-Stevenson.

Gallie, D., Marsh, C. and Vogler, C. (eds) (1994) *Social Change and the Experience of Unemployment*. Oxford: Oxford University Press.

Garfinkel, H. (1967) *Studies in Ethnomethodology*. Cambridge: Polity.

Giddens, A. (1971) *Capitalism and Modern Social Theory: An Analysis of the Writings of Marx, Weber and Durkheim*. Cambridge: Cambridge University Press.

Giddens, A. (1976) *New Rules of Sociological Method: A Positive Critique of Interpretive Sociologies*. London: Hutchinson.

Giddens, A. (1977) *Studies in Social and Political Theory*. London: Hutchinson.

Giddens, A. (1979) *Central Problems in Social Theory: Action, Structure and Contradiction in Social Analysis*. Basingstoke: Macmillan.

Giddens, A. (1982) *Profiles and Critiques in Social Theory*. London: Macmillan.

Giddens, A. (1984) *The Constitution of Society: Outline of the Theory of Structuration*. Cambridge: Polity Press.

Giddens, A. (1985) *The Nation State and Violence*. Cambridge: Polity Press.

Giddens, A. (1987) *Sociology: A Brief but Critical Introduction*. Fort Worth, Texas: Harcourt Brace Jovanovich.

Giddens, A. (1989) 'Reply to my Critics', in Held, D. and Thompson, J.B. *Social Theory of Modern Societies*. Cambridge: Cambridge University Press, pp. 249–301.

Giddens, A. (1990a) *The Consequences of Modernity*. Cambridge: Polity Press.

Giddens, A. (1990b) 'Structuration Theory: Past, Present and Future', in Bryant, G.A. and Jary, D. (eds) *Giddens Theory of Structuration: A Critical Appreciation*. London: Routledge, pp. 201–21.

Giddens, A. (1991a) *Modernity and Self-Identity: Self and Society in the late Modern Age*. Cambridge: Polity.

Giddens, A. (1991b) *Introduction to Sociology*. New York: W.W. Norton.

Giddens, A. (1992) *The Transformation of Intimacy*. Cambridge: Polity.

Giddens, A. (1994a) *Beyond Left and Right: The Future of Radical Politics*. Cambridge: Polity.

Giddens, A. (1994b) 'Living in a Post-traditional Society', in Beck, U., Giddens, A. and Lash, S. (eds) *Reflexive Modernization: Politics, Tradition and Aesthetics in the Modern Social Order*, Cambridge: Polity Press.

Giddens, A. (1995) *A Contemporary Critique of Historical Materialism*. Basingstoke: MacMillan. (2nd edn. First published 1981.)

Giddens, A. (1996) *In Defence of Sociology: Essays, Interpretations and Rejoinders*. Cambridge: Polity Press.

Gilligan, C. (1982) *In a Different Voice: Psychological Theory and Women's Development*. Cambridge, Mass: Harvard University Press.

Gilroy, P. (1987) *There Ain't no Black in the Union Jack*. London: Hutchinson.

Gilroy, P. (1993) *The Black Atlantic*. London: Verso.

Gilroy, P. (1997) 'Diaspora and the detours of identity', in Woodward, K. (ed.) *Identity and Difference*, London: Sage.

Goldberg, D. (1993) *Racist Culture*. Oxford: Blackwell.

Goldblatt, D. (1996) *Social Theory and the Environment*. Oxford: Polity.

Goodman, D. and Redclift, M. (1991) *Refashioning Nature*. London: Routledge.

Goodwin, B. (1994) *How the Leopard Changed its Spots*. London: Weidenfeld.

Graham, J. and Bowling, B. (1995) *Young People and Crime* (Home Office Research Study 145). London: Home Office.

Gregory, D. (1984) 'Space, Time and Politics in Social Theory. An Interview with Anthony Giddens'. *Environment and Planning D: Society and Space*, 2: 124–32.

Habermas, J. (1989) *The Theory of Communicative Action*, Volume 2. Cambridge: Polity Press.

Hall, S. (1990) 'Cultural Identity and Diaspora', in Rutherford, J. (ed.) *Identity: Community, Culture, Difference*. London: Lawrence and Wishart.

Hall, S. (1992) 'New Ethnicities', in Donald, J. and Rattansi, A. (eds) *'Race', Culture, Difference*. London: Sage.

Hannerz, U. (1992) *Cultural Complexity: Studies in the Social Organisation of Meaning*. New York: Columbia University Press.

Harris, J. (1995a) *The Cultural Meaning of Deafness: Language, Identity and Power*. Aldershot: Avebury Publications.

Harris, J. (1995b) 'Boiled Eggs & Baked Beans; a Personal Account of a Hearing Researcher's Journey through Deaf Culture'. *Disability & Society*, 10(3): 295–308.

Harris, J. (1996) 'Participant Observation of Deaf People in a Rehabilitation Unit – A Hearing Researcher's Account'. *Deaf Worlds*, 12(1): 12–17.

Hay, C., O'Brien, M. and Penna, S. (1994) 'Giddens, Modernity and Self Identity: The "Hollowing Out" of Social Theory'. *Arena Journal*, new series no 2: 45–76.

Heath, A. (1992) 'The Attitudes of the Underclass', in Smith, D.J. (ed.) *Understanding the Underclass*. London: Policy Studies Institute.

Hechter, M. (1987) 'Nationalism as group solidarity'. *Ethnic and Racial Studies*, 10(4): 415–26.

Heidensohn, F. (1986) 'Models of justice: Portia or Persephone? Some thoughts on Equality, Justice, Fairness and Gender in the Field of Criminal Justice'. *International Journal of the Sociology of Law*, 14: 187–98.

Heidensohn, F. (1988) *Crime and Society*. Basingstoke: Macmillan.

Held, D. and Thompson, J.B. (1989) *Social Theory of Modern Societies: Anthony Giddens and his Critics*. Cambridge: Cambridge University Press.

Helmreich, S. (1992) 'Kinship, Nation and Paul Gilroy's Concept of Diaspora'. *Diaspora* 2(2): 243–49.

Henry, S. and Milovanovic, D. (1996) *Constitutive Criminology: Beyond Post-modernism*. London: Sage.

Heritage, J. (1987) 'Ethnomethodology', in Giddens, A. and Turner, J. (eds) *Social Theory Today*. Cambridge: Polity.

Hewitt, R. (1986) *White Talk, Black Talk: Inter-racial Friendship and Communication amongst Adolescents*. Cambridge: Cambridge University Press.

Hirschi, T. (1969) *Causes of Delinquency*. Berkeley: University of California Press.

Hirst, P.Q. (1994) *Associative Democracy*. Cambridge: Polity Press.

Hirst, P.Q. and Thompson, G. (1996) *Globalisation in Question*. Cambridge: Polity.

Hochschild, A. (1983) *The Managed Heart: Commercialisation of Human Feeling*. Berkeley: University of California Press.

213

Holrege, C. (1996) *A Question of Genes: Understanding Life in Context*. Edinburgh: Floris.

Hope, T. and Hough, M. (1988) 'Area, Crime and Incivility: A Profile from the British Crime Survey', in Hope, T. and Shaw, M. (eds) *Communities and Crime Reduction*. London: HMSO.

Hynes, P. (1989) 'Biotechnology in Agriculture and Reproduction: the Parallels in Public Policy', in Hynes, P. (ed.) *Reconstructing Babylon: Women and Technology*. London: Earthscan.

Irwin, A. (1995) *Citizen Science. A Study of People, Expertise and Sustainable Development*. London: Routledge.

Joas, H. (1996) *The Creativity of Action*. Cambridge: Polity Press.

Jones, C., Wainwright, G. and Yarnold, E. (eds) (1986) *The Study of Spirituality*. London: SPCK.

Jones, J. (1991) 'Songs in the Key of Life' (Review of three books). *Nature* 354.

Jones, L. (1967) *Black Music*. Santa Barbara, California: Quill.

Jowell, R. (ed.) (1997) *British Social Attitudes: The 14th. Report: The End of Conservative Values*. Aldershot: Ashgate.

Kauffman, S. (1993) *The Origins of Order. Self Organization and Selection in Evolution*. Oxford: Oxford University Press.

Kilminster, R. (1991) 'Structuration Theory as a World View', in Bryant, C.G.A. and Jary, D. (eds) *Giddens Theory of Structuration: A Critical Appreciation*. London: Routledge.

Krishnamurti, J. (1954) *The First and Last Freedom*. London: Gollancz.

Krishnamurti, J. (1956) *Commentaries on Living*, 1st series. London: Gollancz.

Krishnamurti, J. (1975) *Beginnings of Learning*. London: Gollancz.

Krishnamurti, J. (1978) *The Wholeness of Life*. London: Gollancz.

Krishnamurti, J. (1985) *The Ending of Time*. London: Gollancz.

Kyle, J.G. (1991) 'Deaf People and Minority Groups in the UK', in Gregory, S. and Hartley, G. (eds) *Constructing Deafness*. Milton Keynes: Open University Press, pp. 272–77.

Lander, E. and Schork, N. (1994) 'Genetic Dissection of Complex Traits'. *Science*, 265: 2037–48.

Lane, H. (1991) 'The Medicalization of Cultural Deafness in Historical Perspective'. Paper Presented to the World Federation of Deaf Conference, Montreal, Canada.

Lane, T. and Roberts, K. (1971) *Strike at Pilkingtons*. London: Fontana.

Lash, S. (1994) *Reflexivity and its Doubles: Structure, Aesthetics, Community?*, in Beck, U., Giddens, A. and Lash, S. (1994) *Reflexive Modernization*. Cambridge: Polity Press.

Latouche, S. (1991) *La Planète des Naufragés*. Paris: Editions de la Découverte.

Layder, D. (1996) *Modern Social Theory*. London: UCL Press.

Lee, D.J. and Turner, B.S. (eds) (1996) *Conflicts about Class*. London: Longman.

Lee, R. (ed.) (1992) *Writings from Deaf Liberation: A Selection of NUD Papers, 1976–86*. Feltham: National Union of the Deaf.

Leibrich, J. (1993) *Straight to the Point: Angles on Giving up Crime*. Dunedin: University of Otago Press.

Lemert, C. (1995) *Sociology After The Crisis*. Oxford: Westview Press.

Lemert, C. (1997) *Post-modernism is Not What You Think*. Oxford: Blackwell.

Lessing, D. (1981) *Shikasta*. St Albans: Granada.

Levi-Strauss, C. (1969) *The Elementary Structures of Kinship*. Oxford: Eyre and Spottiswoode. (First published 1949.)

Levinas, E. (1967) 'Martin Buber and the Theory of Knowledge', in Schilpp, P.A. and Friedman, M. (eds) *The Philosophy of Martin Buber*. Illinois: La Salle.

Levins, R. and Lewontin, R. (1985) *The Dialectical Biologist*. Cambridge, Mass: Harvard University Press.

Lutyens, M. (1988) *Krishnamurti: The Open Door*. London: Murray.

Magri, L. (1995) 'The Resistible Rise of the Italian Right'. *New Left Review*, 214 Nov/Dec: 125–133.

Maguire, M. and Bennett, T. (1982) *Burglary in a Dwelling*. London: Heinemann.

Maguire, M., Morgan, R. and Reiner, R. (eds) (1994) *The Oxford Handbook of Criminology*. Oxford: Oxford University Press.

Mannheim, K. (1972) *Ideology and Utopia*. Routledge and Kegan Paul. (First published 1937.)

Mason, D. (1994) 'On the Dangers of Disconnecting Race and Racism'. *Sociology*, 28(4): 845–59.

Masters, G. and Smith, D. (1997) 'Portia and Persephone revisited'. Paper to Conference On Restorative Justice for Juveniles. Katholieke Universiteit Leuven, 12–14 May.

Matza, D. (1969) *Becoming Deviant*. Englewood Cliffs, NJ, Prentice-Hall.

May, C. and Cooper, A. (1995) 'Personal Identity and Social Change'. *Acta Sociologica*, 38: 75–85.

McAdam, D. (1988) *Freedom Summer*. Oxford: Oxford University Press.

McKibben, B. (1990) *The End of Nature*. London: Penguin.

McLuhan, M. (1964) *Understanding Media*. London: Routledge.

McNeish, W. (1997) 'The Anti-Roads Movement in the UK: a Sociological and Political Analysis', in Barker, C. and Tyldesley, M. (eds) *Third International Conference on Alternative Futures and Popular Protest: Conference Papers Volume I*. Manchester: Manchester Metropolitan University.

Meat Hygiene Service (1996) *1995–96 Annual Report and Accounts*. York: MHS.

Melucci, A. (1988) *Nomads of the Present*. London: Radius.

Mendes-Flohr, P. (1989) *From Mysticism to Dialogue*. Detroit: Wayne State University Press.

Meyendorff, J. (1974) *St Gregory Palamas and Orthodox Spirituality*. Crestwood, New York: St Vladimir's Seminary Press.

Miles, R. (1982) *Racism and Migrant Labour*. London: Routledge and Kegan Paul.

Miles, R. (1989) *Racism*. London: Routledge.

Miliband, D. (1994) 'Introduction', in Miliband, D. (ed.) *Reinventing The Left*. Cambridge: Polity.

Mills, C.W. (1943) 'The Professional Ideology of Social Pathologists'. *American Journal of Sociology*, 46: 165–80.

Mirrlees-Black, C., Mayhew, P. and Percy, A. (1996) *The 1996 British Crime Survey: England and Wales* (Home Office Statistical Bulletin 19/96). London: Home Office.

Morris, L. (1997) 'Globalization, Migration and the Nation-state'. *British Journal of Sociology*, 48(2): 192–209.

Mouzelis, N. (1989) 'Restructuring Structuration Theory'. *Sociological Review*, 37(4): 613–615.

Mouzelis, N. (1991) *Back to Sociological Theory*. London: Macmillan.

Mouzelis, N. (1995) *Sociological Theory: What went wrong?* London: Routledge.

Murray, C. (1990) *The Emerging British Underclass*. London: Institute of Economic Affairs.

Nasr, S.H. (1996) *Religion and the Order of Nature*. Oxford: Oxford University Press.

Nellis, M. (1995) 'Towards a New View of Probation Values', in Hugman, R. and Smith, D. (eds) *Ethical Issues in Social Work*. London: Routledge.

Newburn, T. and Stanko, E.A. (eds) (1994) *Just Boys Doing Business? Men, Masculinities and Crime*. London: Routledge.

O'Brien, M. and Penna, S. (1997) 'European Policy and the Politics of Environmental Governance'. *Policy and Politics*, 25(2): 185–200.

O'Brien, M. and Penna, S. (1998) *Theorising Welfare: Enlightenment and Modern Society*. London: Sage.

Oliver, M. (1995) *The Politics of Disability*. London: Macmillan.

Omi, M. and Winant, H. (1986) *Racial Formation in the United States*. London: Routledge.

O'Neill, J. (1998) *The Market, Ethics, Knowledge and Politics*. London: Routledge.

OPCS (1996) *Living in Britain: Results from the 1994 General Household Survey*. London: HMSO.

Pearson, G. (1975) *The Deviant Imagination*. London: Macmillan.

Pease, K. (1993) 'Individual and Community Influences on Victimisation and their Implications for Crime Prevention', in Farrington, D.P., Sampson, R.J. and Wikström, P-O.H. (eds) *Integrating Individual and Ecological Aspects of Crime*. Stockholm: National Council for Crime Prevention.

Peelo, M., Stewart, J., Stewart, G. and Prior, A. (1992) *A Sense of Justice: Offenders as Victims of Crime*. Wakefield: Association of Chief Officers of Probation.

Pepinsky, H.E. (1991) 'Peacemaking in Criminology and Criminal Justice', in Pepinsky, H.E. and Quinney, R. (eds) *Criminology as Peacemaking*. Bloomington and Indianapolis: Indiana University Press.

Pepinsky, H.E. (1995) *A Peacemaking Primer*. (http://www.soci.niu.edu~critcrim/pepinsky/hal.primer).

Pepinsky, H.E. and Quinney, R. (eds) (1991) *Criminology as Peacemaking*. Bloomington and Indianapolis: Indiana University Press.

Phillips, M. (1997) 'Who would deny this woman?' *The Observer*, 18 May.

Pieterse, J.-N. (1995) 'Globalisation as Hybridisation', in Featherstone, M., Lash, S. and Robertson, R. (eds) *Global Modernities*. London: Sage.

Pisapia, G. and Antonucci, D. (eds) (1997) *La Sfida della Mediazione*, Padua: CEDAM.

Rattansi, A. and Westwood, M. (1994) 'Modern Racisms, Racialised Identities', in Rattansi, A. and Westwood, S. (eds) *Racism, Modernity and Identity*. Cambridge: Polity.

Red–Green Study Group (1995) *What on Earth is to be Done?* Red-Green Study Group: 2, Hamilton Road, Manchester.

Robertson, R. (1992) *Globalisation*. London: Sage.

Robertson, R. (1995) 'Globalisation: Time-Space and Homogeneity-Heterogeneity', in Featherstone, M., Lash, S. and Robertson, R. (eds) *Global Modernities*. London: Sage.

Robins, D. (1992) *Tarnished Vision*. Oxford: Oxford University Press.

Robinson, J.A. (1963) *Honest to God*. London: SCM.

Rock, P. (1988) 'The Present State of British Criminology'. *British Journal of Criminology*, 28(2): 188–99.

Rock, P. (1994) 'British Criminology: Social Organization', in Maguire, M., Morgan, R. and Reiner, R. (eds) *The Oxford Handbook of Criminology*. Oxford: Oxford University Press.

Rogers, M.F. (1992a) 'They All Were Passing: Agnes, Garfinkel, and Company'. *Gender & Society*, 6(2): 169–91.

Rogers, M.F. (1992b) 'Resisting the Enormous Either/Or: A Response to Bologh and Zimmerman'. *Gender & Society*, 6(2): 207–14.

Rose, H. (1987) 'Victorian Values in the Test-Tube: the Politics of Reproductive Science and Technology', in Stanworth, M. (ed.) *Reproductive Technologies*. Cambridge: Polity.

Rose, N. (1996) 'Authority and the genealogy of subjectivity', in Heelas, P., Lash, S. and Morris, P. (eds) *Detraditionalization*. Oxford: Blackwell.

Rose, S. (1997) *Lifelines: Biology, Freedom and Determinism*. London: Allen Lane.

Roseneil, S. (1995) *Disarming Patriarchy: Feminism and Political Action at Greenham*. Buckingham: Open University Press.

Rothman, B. (1984) 'The Meanings of Choice in Reproductive Technology', in Arditti, R., Klein, R. and Minden, S. (eds) *Test-tube Women*. London: Pandora.

Rowe, W. and Schelling, V. (1991) *Memory and Modernity: Popular Culture in Latin America*. London: Verso.

Rowland, R. (1992) *Living Laboratories. Women and Reproductive Technology*. London: Lime Tree.

Rustin, M. (1995) 'The Future of Post-socialism'. *Radical Philosophy*, 74, Nov/Dec: 17–27.

Said, E. (1979) *Orientalism*. London: Routledge.

Saunders, B. (1982) 'Help for Problem Drinkers', in Plant, M.A. (ed.) *Drinking and Problem Drinking*. London: Junction Books.

Scott, J. (1995) *Sociological Theory: Contemporary Debates*. Cheltenham: Edward Elgar.

Scutt, J. (ed.) (1990) *The Baby Machine. Reproductive Technology and the Commercialisation of Motherhood*. London: Merlin.

Segal, R. (1995) *The Black Diaspora*. London: Faber and Faber.

Seidman, S. (1994) Introduction, in Seidman, S. (ed.) *The Post-modern Turn. New Perspectives on Social Theory*. Cambridge: Cambridge University Press.

Shaoul, J. (1997) 'Mad Cow Disease; The Meat Industry is out of Control'. *The Ecologist*, 27(5): 182–7.

Shove, E. (1995) 'Constructing Regulations and Regulating Construction', in Gray, T.S. (ed.) *UK Environmental Policy in the 1990s*. Basingstoke and London: Macmillan.

Silbernstein, L. (1989) *Martin Buber's Social and Religious Thought*. New York: New York University Press.

Skogan, W.G. (1990) *Disorder and Decline: Crime and the Spiral of Decay in American Neighborhoods*. New York: Free Press.

Smart, C. (1990) 'Feminist Approaches to Criminology, or Post-modern Woman meets Atavistic Man', in Gelsthorpe, L. and Morris, A. (eds) *Feminist Perspectives in Criminology*. Buckingham, Open University Press.

Smith, D. and Stewart, J. (1997) 'Probation and Social Exclusion'. *Social Policy and Administration* (Special Issue on social exclusion), 31(5): 96–115.

Sohn-Rethel, A.(1975) 'Science as Alienated Consciousness'. *Radical Science*, 2/3: 65–101.

Sohn-Rethel, A.(1978) *Intellectual and Manual Labour*. London: Macmillan.

Soper, K. (1995) *What is Nature?* Oxford: Blackwell.

Spivak, G. (1987) *In Other Worlds*. London: Methuen.

Stanworth, M. (ed.) (1987) *Reproductive Technologies. Gender, Motherhood and Medicine*. Cambridge: Polity.

Stewart, G. and Stewart, J. (1993) *Social Circumstances of Younger Offenders under Probation Supervision*. Wakefield: Association of Chief Officers of Probation.

Tarrow, S. (1995) 'Cycles of Collective Action: Between Moments of Madness and the Repertoire of Contention', in Traugott, M. (ed.) *Repertoires and Cycles of Collective Action*. Durham, North Carolina: Duke University Press.

Taylor, I., Walton, P. and Young, J. (1973) *The New Criminology*. London: Routledge and Kegan Paul.

Taylor, L. (1985) *Human Agency and Language*. Cambridge: Cambridge University Press.

Taylor, V. and Whittier, N. (1995) 'Analytical Approaches to Social Movement Culture: The Culture of the Women's Movement', in Johnston, H. and Klandermans, B. (eds) *Social Movements and Culture*. London: UCL Press.

Thompson, J.B. (1989) 'The Theory of Structuration', in Held, D. and Thompson, J.B. (eds) *Social Theory of Modern Societies*. Cambridge: Cambridge University Press, pp. 56–76.

Thompson, W-D'Arcy (1962) *On Growth and Form*. Cambridge: University Press.

Tilly, C. (1996) 'Contentious Repertoires in Great Britain, 1758–1834', in Traugott, M. (ed.) *Repertoires and Cycles of Collective Action*. Durham, North Carolina: Duke University Press.

Tomlinson, J. (1991) *Cultural Imperialism*. Baltimore: John Hopkins Press.

Touraine, A. (1981) *The Voice and the Eye*. Cambridge: Cambridge Univeristy Press.

Townsend, P. (1995) 'Persuasion and Conformity'. *New Left Review*, 213 Sept/Oct: 137–50.

Tucker, K.H. (1991) 'How New are the New Social Movements?'. *Theory, Culture and Society*, 8: 75–98.

Tyler, C.A. (1994) 'Passing: Narcissism, Identity and Difference'. *Differences*, 6: 212–48.

Umbreit, M. (1994) *Victim Meets Offender: The Impact of Restorative Justice and Mediation*. Monsey, NY: Willow Tree Press.

Van Dijk, J.J.M., Mayhew, P. and Killias, J.J. (1990) *Experiences of Crime across the World*. Boston: Kluwer.

Vertovec, S. (1996) 'Comparative issues in, and multiple meanings of, the South Asian religious diaspora'. Paper given to *Conference On The Comparative Study of the South Asian Diaspora Religious Experience in Britain, Canada and USA*, 4–6 November, School of Oriental and African Studies, London.

Waerness, K. (1984) 'Caring as Women's Work in the Welfare State', in Holter, H. (ed.) *Patriarchy in a Welfare Society*. Oslo: Universitetsforlaget.

Wainwright, H. (1994) *Arguments for a New Left*. Oxford: Blackwell.

Wallerstein, I. (1980) *The Modern World System II: Mercantilism and the Consolidation of the World Economy 1650–1750*. New York: Academic Press.

Wallerstein, I. (1990) 'Culture as the Ideological Battleground of the Modern World System', in Featherstone, M. (ed.) *Global Culture*. London: Sage, 31–56.

Ware, K. (1986) 'The Hesychasts: Gregory of Sinai, Gregory Palamas, Nicolas Cabasilas', in Jones, C., Wainwright, G. and Yarnold, E. (eds) (1986) *The Study of Spirituality*. London: SPCK.

Waters, M. (1995) *Globalisation*. London: Routledge.

Webster, A. (1991) *Science, Technology and Society*. Basingstoke and London: Macmillan.

Webster, C. (1997) 'Inverting racism: an empirical study of perpetrators of racial violence'. Paper presented to the British Criminology Conference, Belfast.

West, C. (1992) 'The New Cultural Politics of Difference', in Ferguson, R., Gever, M., Minh-ha., T. and West, C. (eds) *Out There: Marginalisation and Contemporary Cultures.* Cambridge, Mass: MIT Press.

West, C. and Zimmerman, D.H. (1987) 'Doing Gender'. *Gender and Society,* 1: 125–51.

Wilson, J.Q. and Kelling, G.L. (1982) 'Broken Windows: The Police and Neighborhood Safety'. *The Atlantic Monthly,* March: 29–38.

Woll, B. (1990) 'The Cultural Signs of a Misunderstood Minority'. *SEE4 News from Channel Four,* 25: 28–29.

Woodiwiss, T. (1997) 'Against Modernity'. *Economy and Society,* 26(1): 1–21.

Woodward, K. (ed.) *Identity and Difference.* London: Sage.

Young, A. (1996) *Imagining Crime.* London: Sage.

Young, R. (1990) *White Mythologies.* London: Routledge.

Zehr, H. (1980) *Mediating the Victim–Offender Conflict.* Akron, Pa: Mennonite Central Committee.

Zimmerman, D.H. (1992) 'They Were All Doing Gender, But They Weren't All Passing: Comment on Rogers'. *Gender & Society,* 6(2): 192–98.

Zizioulas, J. (1993) *Being as Communion.* Crestwood, N.Y.: St Vladimir's Seminary Press.

Index of citations to the work of Anthony Giddens

Bibliographical Note

The following index of citations covers the principle discussions of, and references to, each of Giddens' major works. The index is not exhaustive since, as might be expected, aspects of Giddens' work are discussed on almost every page. For guidance on specific topics, refer to the Subject Index (p. 224).

Author index

Afshar, H., 171
Ahmed, S., 154
Alexander, J., 70, 73, 84
Anderson, B., 130, 194
Anderson, B., 130, 172
Anthias, F., 165, 166, 168, 173, 175
Appadurai, A., 173
Archer, M., 73
Arditti, R., 107
Arnold, J., 135
Aye Maung, N., 131

Back, L., 130, 171
Bailey, R., 126
Banuri, T., 170
Barker, C., 80
Bateson, W., 105
Bauman, Z., 139
Baynton, D.C., 148
BDA, 148
Beck, U., 29, 50, 66, 84
Becker, H.S., 122
Beirne, P., 123
Benton, T., 49, 57, 58, 62, 100
Berman, M., 2
Berry, P., 96
Bhabha, H., 169, 171, 173
Bhaskar, R., 99
Birke, L., 110
Blagg, H., 135
Blaxter, M., 126
Bologh, R.W., 151

Bottoms, A.E., 123, 127
Bourdieu, P., 164
Bowling, B., 130
Boyne, R., 161
Brah, A., 159, 169, 172, 173
Braithwaite, J., 131, 132, 134, 135
Bryant, C.G.A., 17
Buber, M., 90, 91
Bunders, J., 111
Burnside, J., 133
Butler, J.,153

Calhoun, C., 74, 81
Campbell, B., 128, 131, 134
Campbell, C., 72, 90
Carlen, P., 128
Castells, M., 166
Castles, S., 166
Christie, N., 130, 132, 133
Clifford, J., 169, 173
Cohen, A., 168
Cohen, L.E., 123
Cohen, P., 130
Cohen, R., 168, 173
Cohen, S., 135
Collier, A., 120
Corea, G., 107, 110
Corker, M., 140
Cox, L., 165
Craib, I., 17
Currie, E., 129, 135

Subject index